Taming the Vernacular

TAMING THE VERNACULAR
From Dialect to Written Standard Language

edited by
JENNY CHESHIRE AND DIETER STEIN

LONGMAN
London and New York

Addison Wesley Longman Limited
Edinburgh Gate
Harlow, Essex CM20 2JE
England

and Associated Companies throughout the world

*Published in the United States of America
by Addison Wesley Longman Inc., New York*

© Addison Wesley Longman Limited 1997

All rights reserved; no part of this publication may be reproduced, stored in a retrieval system, or transmitted in any form or by any means, electronic, mechanical, photocopying, recording, or otherwise without the prior written permission of the Publishers or a licence permitting restricted copying in the United Kingdom issued by the Copyright Licensing Agency Ltd., 90 Tottenham Court Road, London W1P 9HE

First published 1997

British Library Cataloguing-in-Publication Data
A catalogue record for this book is
available from the British Library

Library of Congress Cataloging-in-Publication Data
Taming the vernacular : from dialect to written standard language /
  edited by Jenny Cheshire and Dieter Stein.
    p. cm.
  Includes bibliographical references and index.
  ISBN 0-582-29809-1 (pbk.). — ISBN 0-582-29808-3
  1. Standard language. 2. Language and languages—Variation.
 3. Dialectology. I. Cheshire, Jenny, 1946– . II. Stein, Dieter,
 1946– .
 P368.T36 1997
 418–dc21   97–8801
                                                                    CIP

Set by 35 in 9/11 pt Palatino
Produced by Longman Singapore Publishers (Pte) Ltd.
Printed in Singapore

Contents

List of Contributors   vii

1. The syntax of spoken language   1
   Jenny Cheshire and Dieter Stein

2. Dialect versus standard language: nature versus culture   13
   Jaap van Marle

3. Syntax and varieties   35
   Dieter Stein

4. Into and out of the standard language:
   the particle *ni* in Finnish   51
   Maria Vilkuna

5. Involvement in 'standard' and 'nonstandard' English   68
   Jenny Cheshire

6. *This, that, yon*: on 'three-dimensional' deictic systems   83
   Gunnel Melchers

7. Grammatical variation and the avoidance of stress
   clashes in Northern Low German   93
   Günter Rohdenburg

8. Norms made easy: case marking with modal verbs
   in Finnish   110
   Lea Laitinen

9. Articles and number in oral or close-to-oral varieties   125
   Brigitte Schlieben-Lange

10. Proscribed collocations with *shall* and *will*: the eighteenth
    century (non-)standard reassessed   135
    Leslie K. Arnovick

CONTENTS

11. The genitives of the relative pronouns in present-day English 152
    Aimo Seppänen

12. 'Ah'm going for to give youse a story today': remarks on second person plural pronouns in Englishes 170
    Susan Wright

13. Strengthening identity: differentiation and change in contemporary Galician 185
    Johannes Kabatek

14. Left dislocation in French: varieties, norm and usage 200
    Alain Berrendonner and Marie-José Reichler-Béguelin

15. Dialect variation as a consequence of standardization 218
    Dieter Wanner

16. The patternings of nonstandard syntax in German 232
    Beate Henn-Memmesheimer

Index 250

Contributors

Professor Leslie K. Arnovick, Department of English, University of British Columbia, Canada
Professor Alain Berrendonner, Department of French Linguistics, University of Fribourg, Switzerland
Professor Beate Henn-Memmesheimer, Department of German Linguistics, University of Mannheim, Germany
Dr Johannes Kabatek, Department of Romance Languages, University of Paderborn, Germany
Dr Lea Laitinen, Department of Finnish, University of Helsinki, Finland
Professor Jaap van Marle, P.J. Mertens Institute, Amsterdam
Dr Gunnel Melchers, Department of English, University of Stockholm, Sweden
Professor Marie-José Reichler-Béguelin, Department of French Linguistics, Universities of Fribourg and Neuchâtel, Switzerland
Professor Günter Rohdenburg, Department of English and American Studies, University of Paderborn, Germany
Professor Brigitte Schlieben-Lange, Department of Romance Languages, University of Tubingen
Professor Aimo Seppänen, English Department, University of Gothenburg, Sweden
Dr Maria Vilkuna, Research Institute for the languages of Finland, Helsinki
Professor Dieter Wanner, Department of Spanish and Portuguese, The Ohio State University, USA
Professor Susan Wright, Department of English, Northern Arizona University, USA

CHAPTER 1

The syntax of spoken language

Jenny Cheshire and Dieter Stein

1.1 Introduction

The chapters in this volume deal with the syntax of some present-day spoken varieties of language. Some of the best-known languages of Europe are represented here, as well as some that have been less well researched: between them the papers deal with Dutch, English, French, Finnish, Galician, German and Spanish. For these languages – and many others – it is the standardized varieties on which the most extensive syntactic research has been carried out, with the result that we know far less about the syntax of the other varieties of these languages. The cross-linguistic perspective that we adopt in this volume allows us to redress the balance and identify some common characteristics of the syntax of spoken language; we intend it also to help us understand the nature of the processes that are responsible for many of the differences between spoken colloquial varieties of language and the standardized varieties.

It is helpful for the languages represented in this volume to think of each of them as a continuum, with the syntactic forms that occur in formal written prose at one end of the continuum and the forms that we can recognize as occurring only in vernacular speech at the other end. In between these two poles is a range of syntactic forms and structures which occur in speech, some of which are conventionally considered as 'colloquial' by commentators on language while others tend to be labelled as 'dialect' or 'nonstandard'. Linguists often try to give these terms more precision. Thus they may label as 'dialect' features those that have a distinctive social or regional distribution (or both); and 'colloquial' features may be defined as those that occur in the informal speech styles of all speakers of the language, irrespective of their social or regional background. It is more difficult to precisely define 'nonstandard' features. To categorise a feature as 'nonstandard' is to treat it as if it has a 'standard' equivalent, but whilst we may know what the standard equivalent is for some morphological features (such as English *was* in *we was going out* or *hisself* in *he hurt hisself*), the general concept

1

TAMING THE VERNACULAR

of a 'standard' in language has never been clearly and satisfactorily defined, and it is very difficult to do so. It is probably more realistic to think in terms of the process of standardisation rather than of a standard language (see Milroy and Milroy 1985) and, as the last three chapters in this volume argue, it may well be more revealing to simply analyse the syntactic variation that exists in a language without imposing labels such as 'nonstandard', 'dialect' or 'colloquial' on the variant forms and structures. Nevertheless these labels continue to be widely used in linguistic description.

Despite their widespread use, and despite attempts to give precise definitions for them, the borderline between colloquial, dialect and nonstandard often remains fuzzy. This can be seen from the ways in which some of the contributors to this volume refer to their spoken data. Some use the term 'nonstandard' syntax, while others prefer 'dialect syntax'; still others simply refer to spoken syntax. The situation is made more complex still by the fact that once a written syntactic form of a language has been established, some speakers use the standardized syntactic forms in their speech, so that it becomes possible to talk of a 'spoken standard'. This point is made quite explicitly by van Marle in Chapter 2, where he describes how the standard may originate as a written variety and then come to serve as a norm for spoken language as well, at least for some speakers of the language. We have not attempted to impose a uniform terminology on the authors, as the kind of data that they are discussing is clear in their chapters: furthermore, since we are dealing with a continuum there is little point in attempting to impose divisions that would inevitably be arbitrary. The third chapter in the volume, by Stein, discusses further the idea of a continuum and the notion of a standard variety. In the remainder of this introductory chapter we will mainly use the term 'vernacular' syntax to refer to those features that are uncontroversially not part of the established standard: in other words, if we think in terms of a continuum, as mentioned earlier, we mean by 'vernacular' those features that are situated at some distance from the formal written pole, and more towards the vernacular spoken pole. We will also use the terms 'nonstandardized syntax' and 'spoken syntax' without attempting to distinguish between them. Our different terms reflect the arbitrariness of attempting to categorise fuzzy phenomena; but they refer, in all cases, to linguistic features that are not used in formal written prose.

1.2 Data on spoken syntax

The chapters in this volume are all written by researchers who have worked extensively on spoken language. In general, however, there is a sorry lack of empirical data on the syntax of speech. One of the aims of

THE SYNTAX OF SPOKEN LANGUAGE

this volume is to redress the balance, but it is nevertheless worth discussing in some detail the reasons for our lack of knowledge, since, if we are to increase our understanding of this topic, future researchers obviously need to overcome any problems there might be in the collection and analysis of this type of data.

To begin with, it is clear that the study of vernacular syntax suffers from the same methodological problems as the study of any kind of syntax: the relatively infrequent occurrences of the specific syntactic features that are being investigated. To some extent this problem is already being overcome by the availability of large-scale corpora of spoken language, which can yield large numbers of tokens of specific syntactic forms; but so far these corpora consist mainly of the speech of people who might be expected to use forms close to the written standard end of the continuum, and corpus linguistics has not yet produced much information about vernacular syntax.

A further reason for the lack of information on vernacular syntax is that most studies that have focused specifically on nonstandardized forms of language – in dialectology, for example – have analysed phonology rather than syntax. This is partly because the dialects are spoken varieties and obviously call for an analysis of their sound structure. It is also, however, because of the special attention that prescriptive grammarians have paid to syntax during the process of standardization. Syntax is the first aspect of language to be commented upon in terms of correctness and the first whose forms are subjected to evaluative categorisations into 'goodies' and 'baddies' – even before the onset of standardization proper (Stein 1994). Standardization has always gone hand in hand with an increasing use of written language; and written language is accompanied by a tendency for uniformity in language. For readers syntax cannot fail to register as a massive signal that hits the eye directly. The standard syntactic forms are constantly in the limelight, because of the attention that is given to 'correct' grammar in writing and then, by extension, in speech. For all these reasons the syntax of a language comes to be identified with the syntax of the standard variety by laypeople and sometimes even by linguists too. Thus, whereas for dialects it was the phonology that was self-evidently of interest, for standard varieties it is the syntax that has been more extensively studied – despite the importance of the nonstandardized varieties for our understanding of language structure, as van Marle argues.

An additional reason for the lack of attention to vernacular syntax lies in the theoretical conceptions of language that have held sway during the late nineteenth and twentieth centuries. When dialectology was paramount in linguistics, during the nineteenth century, the study of syntax was under-developed and the necessary analytical tools were not yet ready. During the structuralist period, in roughly the first half of the twentieth century, mainstream linguists operated with an intrinsically unitary concept of language rather than a variety-based concept. During the second half of the twentieth century generative linguists have pursued this view with a vengeance, with researchers analysing their intuitions about their own idiolect, implying, therefore, that syntax is homogeneous. Furthermore, since linguists are inevitably highly-educated academics their idiolects are probably more influenced by the norms of written language than those of any other speakers. Sociolinguists too have done relatively little to advance the study of syntax. They have, it is true, succeeded in putting the analysis of variation in language onto a proper scientific footing, but they began with the analysis of phonological variation and then became bogged down in wrangles about whether or not it is possible to use the same methods of analysis for syntactic variation (see, for example, Lavandera 1978, Labov 1978, Romaine 1980, Cheshire 1987). The result is that there is still no linguistic theory that explicitly addresses the theoretical status of non-standard versus standard varieties, nor that considers the extent to which the standard and nonstandard varieties should be considered to be part of a single linguistic system.

Yet another explanation for the lack of research on vernacular syntax is the emphasis in applied linguistic research on the standard language, which of course has always been the target variety in language learning and teaching. This emphasis is beginning to change a little as language learners and teachers become more interested in social and regional varieties of the target language (see, for example, Hughes and Trudgill 1987, a book designed to provide for learners of English as a foreign language some phonological and grammatical descriptions of several social and regional varieties of English). There is an awareness among schoolteachers – if not always among policy makers – of the educational implications of social and regional variation for the teaching of the native language (see, for example, the papers in Cheshire *et al.* 1989; see also, for English, Cheshire and Edwards 1993). On the whole, however, the descriptions of language that have been produced as reference grammars, pedagogic grammars and teaching manuals have been heavily biased towards the written standard, and this has contributed not only to the development of teaching models that are oriented towards the written language but also to the kind of images of language that dominate within society.

In historical linguistics, also, the syntax of the vernacular has been neglected, at least from the point in time when a standard can be said to have come into existence (thus, for English, this means between 1600 and 1800). From that point on, studying the 'history' of a language has usually meant dealing only with the standard variety, and historical research has traditionally paid little or no further attention to the dialects of the language. This has been termed the 'single-minded march' towards the standard (Lass 1994, Stein 1994). For example, Baugh and

THE SYNTAX OF SPOKEN LANGUAGE

Cable's much-used *A History of the English Language* states that the English pronoun forms *thou* and *thee* are in ordinary use today only among the Quakers (1978: 242), overlooking their survival in the everyday use of speakers of conservative regional varieties of English (for discussion, see Leith and Graddol 1996). Only very recently have dialects been put on the agenda once more for historical linguistics. By leaving out nonstandardized syntax from the study of the history of a language we make it impossible to relate present-day dialect forms to past dialect forms, and to establish historical continuities within the language as a whole. The dominant perspectives in historical linguistics, then, like the dominant perspectives in theoretical linguistics and applied linguistics, have tended to prevent us from seeing the structural make-up and structural possibilities of the whole spectrum of variation that makes up a language, and have led us instead to think in terms only of the standard.

1.3 Recurrent themes in this volume

For all these reasons it is impossible to consider nonstandardized syntax other than in relation to standardized syntax – as the term suggests – and it is not surprising, therefore, that the dialectic between 'standard' and 'nonstandard' comes into play in all the chapters in this volume.

Chapters 2 and 3 make similar points, albeit in different ways and with different illustrative examples. Both van Marle and Stein set out general principles that can explain the absence of dialect or extreme colloquial forms from the written standard, and vice-versa. The examples in these two chapters are taken from Dutch, German and English: other chapters in the volume show that many of these points apply equally to other languages. It is striking that the same kinds of filtering processes that Stein describes, which prevent certain syntactic forms from becoming part of the standard, operate on languages that are very different typologically and that have very different histories of standardization. For example, German is an inflectional language and Finnish even more so, whereas English is more analytic; yet similar filtering processes are at work in all three. Again, English has had a standard elaborated variety for about three centuries, Finnish for a single century at most, and Galician is still acquiring a standard: yet here too we can observe similarities in the construction of the standardized syntax of each language.

One of the principles discussed by Stein concerns the selection of syntactic forms as suitable for the written standard on the basis of their being audibly and visibly distinct from spoken language. We can see the operation of this principle very clearly in Vilkuna's contribution (Chapter 4), which shows that a clause-combining particle that is perfectly normal in spoken Finnish has now disappeared from the written standard, in which it had once been accepted. Vilkuna explains this as having nothing to do with the intrinsic syntactic structure of the language: it is simply that the particle has its origins in spoken language, where it fulfils several important functions appropriate for the spontaneity of face-to-face communication. These functions meant that the particle was not selected as part of standard Finnish, and they are ignored by present-day Finnish linguists. The chapter by Cheshire shows that the same kind of selection process has been at work during the standardization of English.

A second principle discussed in Stein's chapter is the stripping off of emotive meanings from forms that become associated with the written standard. These meanings are unnecessary and deemed inappropriate in formal essayist writing. This is well illustrated in Chapter 6, in which Melchers describes a more elaborated three-part system of deixis that existed in Middle English and continues to exist in some English dialects. The nonstandardized system has much greater potential for expressing affective meaning and this, together with its association with the types of meanings typically expressed by speakers rather than by writers, seems to account for the system not having become part of the written standard. In Chapter 5, Cheshire also illustrates this principle, showing how for two separate features of English syntax the affective meanings that serve to create involvement in face-to-face communication have been banned from the standard, even though this means forgoing a richer potential for expressing interpersonal meaning. Several other authors in the volume also mention interpersonal involvement or the expression of affective meaning as a factor evident in nonstandardized syntax, including Schlieben-Lange (Chapter 9) for German, Kabatek (Chapter 13) for Galician, and Laitinen (Chapter 8) for Finnish.

The syntax of the standard variety often seems to result from an explicit attempt by grammarians to tidy up the inherent fuzziness and indeterminacy of spoken syntax. This sometimes makes a structure more amenable to systematic description, but at the same time it becomes impossible to describe and explain the precise nature of that structure. Rohdenburg (Chapter 7) shows how the syntax of a spoken variety can be heavily influenced by the phonology, giving examples from a North German dialect. The result is that the syntax cannot be described in its own terms, and anyone who attempts to do so will have to give a 'messy' description, incompatible with the aims of linguists attempting to write descriptive grammars of the language. Laitinen's chapter makes a similar point, discussing the relation between syntax and pragmatics for case-marking on verbs of 'necessity' in Finnish. As Laitinen points out, case-marking was originally determined by pragmatic factors governing the use of these verbs in speech, but these pragmatic factors were too complex to be identified by the grammarians who tried to fix a single variety of standard Finnish. The result is that case-marking on these verbs in standard Finnish has been determined in a 'rational' way, based on a mixture of semantic criteria that is difficult to make explicit; and linguists who have attempted to analyse the syntax of Finnish in terms of a coherent theory have found it difficult to account for this aspect of Finnish syntax. Often, then, the result of standardization is that linguists who work on standardized syntax – and the majority do, as we saw earlier – are unable to unravel the complexities of a specific structural system, partly because they have been unwittingly influenced by the norms of the standard and partly because the standard variety has been made unwieldy and irregular.

In a striking demonstration from, among other examples, inflected conjunctions in Dutch, van Marle demonstrates how we can observe natural processes of linguistic change in dialects, though not in the standardized varieties; we can also observe the developmental processes inherent to a specific language. In the standardized varieties the normative pressures associated with codification tend towards a 'logical' elimination of variation, which prevents these natural developments from surfacing. In a similar vein, using examples from a number of languages ranging from Bavarian, German, French, Spanish and Portuguese, Schlieben-Lange demonstrates that in those areas of syntax that frequently preoccupy prescriptive grammarians (such as the distinctions between proper nouns and common nouns, or mass nouns versus count nouns) there is far more dialectal richness and variability than in the corresponding standardized varieties. Speakers tend to develop different meanings for the competing forms that exist in the dialects, whereas the ideology of the standard forces us to choose just one of the possible forms as 'standard' and to eliminate variation. The standardized variety therefore forgoes a significant potential for creating expressive meaning in favour of a unitary and purportedly more 'logical' solution.

The written standards, as 'unnatural systems', may adopt more 'logical' structures from prestige languages, such as the distinction in Dutch between indirect and direct object pronouns (*hun* and *hen*, respectively). However, speakers do not readily accept these structures in the spoken standard, let alone in the nonstandardized varieties. Nonstandardized syntax also prevails in the case of English *will*, as described by Arnovick in Chapter 10. Here, too, the grammarians' attempts to impose a pseudo-logical structure on the syntax of the standard have not been successful. Arnovick describes in detail the efforts of grammarians to set up explicit, logical rules for the use of *will* and *shall*. She demonstrates that the rules set out by eighteenth-century grammarians for using *will* and *shall* according to person of the verb have always had an uphill struggle against the preference of speakers to generalize the use of *will* to all persons of the verb. Debates about good style and handbooks of good usage in English would lack a paradigm issue if grammarians had not attempted to impose a norm from above in this way; but present-day usage suggests that their efforts have been in vain.

TAMING THE VERNACULAR

Several other chapters show how vernacular syntax preserves factors that are important to speakers in preference to the 'logical' factors that may be more important for grammarians and commentators on language. A further example is the persistence in nonstandardized syntax of the marking of animacy by syntactic means. Thus Laitinen mentions that case-marking on verbs of necessity in nonstandard Finnish continues to indicate animacy, and Seppänen (Chapter 11) shows that present-day colloquial British English reinforces a tendency to mark a distinction between animate and inanimate relatives, though the forms that mark the distinctions in the present-day nonstandardized varieties are not the same as those that occurred in the older ones. The new relative pronoun forms that Seppänen discusses also preserve a general tendency to create a genitive structure with two separate coreferential noun phrases: a tendency disliked by commentators, but one that survives in spoken English nonetheless. Creating interpersonal involvement is also important to speakers: this is mentioned by several of the contributors to this volume, as we have seen. Yet another factor that speakers seem to find important is the marking of a distinction between singular and plural second person pronoun forms. Standard English is unusual among the languages of Europe in having a single second person pronoun, making it impossible both to indicate the relative intimacy of the relationship between the speaker and the addressee and to indicate whether the pronoun refers to one person or to more than one person. Speakers use a range of strategies to enable them to make a distinction between singular and plural second person reference, including plural expressions such as *you two* or *all of you* (see Pawley and Syder 1983). Wright, in Chapter 12, demonstrates the widespread genesis and spread outside England of a distinctive pronoun to refer to plural second persons, a development that clearly reveals the preferred tendency of speakers of English. It is the marking of the distinction that is important to speakers, rather than the form that the distinction takes: this can be seen from the fact that the particular pronoun that develops in a new variety of English is not necessarily dependent on there being distinct singular and plural second person forms in the older varieties from which they have developed.

Kabatek's chapter on Galician deals very explicitly with the creation of norms and the conscious construction of a standard variety, examining the microstructure of the birth of standard Galician. Here we can witness the elevation to the status of standard of a number of structures from several different input varieties. The selectional processes reflect a range of different factors and show how, in some cases, external factors can over-ride the favourite principles of speakers. Thus some structures have been selected to be part of the standard because of a conscious desire to mark out standard Galician as different from Spanish: we can see this in the selection of inflected infinitives as standard forms, despite their origins in spoken language. These choices, then, reflect the particular socio-political context in which the standardization of Galician is taking place.

Standardization, however, is inevitably embedded in a socio-political context; we should therefore expect standard varieties to have been influenced, to a greater or lesser extent, by external factors. Laitinen discusses the construction of standard Finnish as part of the creation of a national Finnish identity: it was important for the standard to bridge the cultural gap between the Swedish-speaking upper class and the Finnish-speaking lower classes, and the solution was for the written standard to be based in part on sixteenth-century old written Finnish, while taking account of both European civilization and Finnish peasant culture. In other situations the selection of the structures to be considered as standard may have been motivated at least in part by the desire of upper-class speakers to mark themselves out as different from the lower classes (as discussed in Cheshire's chapter).

Several chapters in this volume discuss theoretical and methodological issues relating to 'standard' and 'nonstandard' syntax. In Chapter 14, Berrendonner and Reichler-Béguelin claim for French that it is more revealing to analyse different occurrences of a specific feature without trying to categorize them as characteristic of a discrete variety of the language, such as a colloquial style, or a social or geographical dialect. By freeing themselves from conventional methods of analysis and using an analytical procedure that is more appropriate for spoken discourse they demonstrate that the different tokens of left dislocation in their data can all be seen as different realizations of options that form part of a single system. Wanner (Chapter 15) deals with the question of how syntactic variation in the Romance languages can be accounted for in theoretical terms, this time on the basis of a syntactic analysis in terms of parameters. These two chapters demonstrate how the notions of 'relatedness' or 'same system' depend on the type of analysis that is brought to bear on the data – a point reminiscent of some of the papers in Abraham (1993). Henn-Memmesheimer adopts a similar perspective in Chapter 16, arguing that we should consider nonstandard varieties of German not as separate systems but as part of the same system, seeing variant forms as different realizations of the same basic choices. Seppänen's analysis demonstrates the fundamental identity of the mode of relativization that occurs in the many different varieties of English that he surveys; and Cheshire also argues that 'standard' and 'nonstandard' uses of the features that she discusses are essentially the same. These chapters, then, stress the coherence rather than the separateness of the syntactic variants that occur within a language (or within what some might want to consider the diasystems of a language). The conclusion seems to be that if we conceptualize syntactic variation *a priori* in terms of discrete social, geographical or stylistic varieties (or indeed according to any kind of dimension) we risk obscuring the nature of the syntactic relationships that exist within a language. This is perhaps especially obvious when analysing features that appear to lie on the fuzzy borderlines between 'standard', 'colloquial', 'dialect' or 'nonstandard', but the principle is one that we should assume to apply generally. Once the syntactic variation within a language system has been described we can attempt to identify regional or social correlations at that later stage; preliminary indications, however, are that these types of correlation are different where syntactic variation is concerned from those that have been so well documented for phonological variation (see, for discussion, Cheshire 1996).

1.4 Conclusion

Between them, then, the chapters in this volume single out a range of selection processes that work to designate certain syntactic structures and forms as 'standard'. These processes are directly related to the different functions of 'nonstandard' and 'standard' language: nonstandardized language has its origins in speech – in face-to-face communication – whereas the standardized variety usually originates in formal written communication. Some aspects of standardized syntax may then spread to the speech of certain individuals or social groups. The ideology of the standard values detachment and logical order – though the logic of standardized syntax is usually an illusion – and it marks out one social group relative to other groups in society, or to an external group (or, of course, to both). These factors, and others, are all discussed in more detail in Stein's contribution to this volume. Factors such as these seem to be independent of the structure of the languages themselves, though clearly the actual syntactic features that eventually come to distinguish 'standard' and 'nonstandard' syntax depend on the type of language concerned: it is hardly surprising, for example, that Rohdenburg and Laitinen, writing about inflected languages (German and Finnish respectively) both discuss verbal inflections. The grammatical features analysed in this volume are wide-ranging, including inflections and prefixes (Laitinen, Kabatek, Rohdenburg), intensifiers (Cheshire, Rohdenburg), determiners (Schlieben-Lange) and the noun phrase (Henn-Memmesheimer), modal verbs (Arnovick), verbal complements (Henn-Memmesheimer), pronouns (Kabatek, Wright, van Marle), relatives (Seppänen), clause combining particles (Vilkuna), conjunctions (van Marle), null subjects (Wanner), preposition copying (Rohdenburg), adverbials (Henn-Memmesheimer), left dislocation (Berrendonner and Reichler-Béguelin), deictic systems (Melchers) and negation (Cheshire).

As for the effect of grammarians on the selection processes outlined above, we are inclined to believe that this is less important than the

THE SYNTAX OF SPOKEN LANGUAGE

functions inherent in a standardized variety and the ideology that grows up around a standard once it has been established. Grammarians certainly play a role in reinforcing the use of forms that have been designated as 'standard', by codifying them in descriptive or pedagogic grammars; but it is speakers themselves and, above all, writers who have to use the forms consistently if they are to become accepted as standard, and it is the speakers of a language who have to accept, whether consciously or unconsciously, normative judgements about those forms that are to be deemed 'standard' and those that are not. In our view a more negative role played by prescriptive grammarians has been to obscure structural regularities in a language by trying to impose illusory systematic patterns on syntactic structure. Linguists, too, may unwittingly be guilty of this, and need to take on board the fact that there is more to be gained from seeing a language as the sum total of its varieties – or, better, as the sum total of its variant forms and structures – than from analysing the syntax of a single variety that has been artificially circumscribed. We hope that this volume will demonstrate the insights that can be gained from analysing nonstandardized syntax, and that it will inspire further research on syntax which will give prominence to the syntax of nonstandardized spoken language.

Note

We would like to thank Euan Reid for his helpful comments on this chapter; and Jennifer Coates for the title of this book.

References

Abraham, W. (ed.) 1993. *Dialektsyntax*. Opladen: Westdeutscher Verlag (Linguistische Berichte, Sonderheft: 5).
Baugh, A.C. and Cable, T. 1978. *A History of the English Language*, 3rd edition. London: Routledge.
Cheshire, J. 1987. Syntactic variation, the linguistic variable and sociolinguistic theory. *Linguistics* 25: 257–82.
Cheshire, J. 1996. Syntactic variation and the concept of prominence. In: J. Klemola, M. Kyto and M. Rissanen (eds), *Speech Past and Present: Studies in English Dialectology in Memory of Ossi Ihalainen*. Frankfurt: Peter Lang, pp. 1–17.
Cheshire, J. and Edwards, V. 1993. Sociolinguistics in the classroom: exploring linguistic diversity. In: J. Milroy and L. Milroy (eds), *Real English: the grammar of English Dialects in the British Isles*. London: Longman, pp. 34–52.

Cheshire, J., Edwards, V., Munstermann, H. and Weltens, B. (eds) 1989. *Dialect and Education: Some European Perspectives.* Clevedon: Multilingual Matters.

Hughes, G.A. and Trudgill, P. 1987. *English Accents and Dialects: an Introduction to Social and Regional Varieties of English.* London: Arnold.

Labov, W. 1978. Where does the linguistic variable stop? A reply to Beatriz Lavandera. *Working Papers in Sociolinguistics.* Austin, Texas: Southwest Educational Development Laboratory.

Lass, R. 1994. *Old English: A Historical Linguistic Comparison.* Cambridge: Cambridge University Press.

Lavandera, B. 1978. Where does the sociolinguistic variable stop? *Language in Society* 7: 171–83.

Leith, D. and Graddol, D. 1996. Modernity and English as a national language. In: D. Graddol, D. Leith and J. Swann (eds) *English: history, diversity and change.* London: Routledge.

Milroy, J. and Milroy, L. 1985. *Authority in Language.* London: Routledge.

Pawley, A. and Syder, F. 1983. Natural selection in syntax: notes on adaptive variation and change in vernacular and literary grammar. *Journal of Pragmatics* 7: 551–79.

Romaine, S. 1980. On the problem of syntactic variation: a reply to Beatriz Lavandera and William Labov. *Working Papers in Sociolinguistics.* Austin, Texas: Southwest Educational Development Laboratory.

Stein, D. 1994. Sorting out the variants: standardization and social factors in the English language 1600–1800. In: D. Stein and I. Tieken-Boon van Ostade (eds) *Towards a Standard English 1600–1800.* Berlin: Mouton de Gruyter, pp. 1–17.

CHAPTER 2

Dialect versus standard language: nature versus culture

Jaap van Marle

2.0 Introduction*

A time-honoured truth in linguistics is that the difference between standard languages on the one hand and dialects on the other primarily relates to differences in their socio-cultural functions. However correct this view may be, it should not be taken to imply that there are no systematic differences between standard languages and dialects on a structural level. Crucial to a correct understanding of the relationship between dialects and standard languages is that differences in socio-cultural function may have repercussions on their respective linguistic systems. In the following it is the systematic differences between standard languages and dialects that I will focus on. The discussion of these differences will be largely based on Dutch, although I assume that many of the observations dealt with below hold for other languages as well. Note that this discussion will be tentative in several respects, due to the fact that very few detailed investigations exist which aim at uncovering the systematic similarities and differences between dialects and standard languages.

This chapter is organized as follows. In section 2.1 a general sketch is presented of the relationship between a standard language and its dialects. In that section it is also stressed that there is a fundamental difference between standard languages that are exclusively written, and standard languages which, alongside their written form, can be said to have a spoken variety as well. In section 2.2 a survey is presented of the systematic differences between standard languages and dialects. However, before presenting this overview, it is pointed out that there is a class of differences between standard languages and dialects which are not rooted in a difference in status and/or function characteristic of the two types of language varieties in question. This is the case with the so-called archaic dialect features. From a systematic point of view, the latter kind of differences between dialects and standard languages are completely accidental. The main body of section 2.2, however, is devoted to a discussion of three 'spheres of difference' which do lead to systematic differences between standard languages and their related dialects. In section 2.3, finally, the conclusions of the preceding discussion are summarized.

2.1 Written standard, spoken standard, dialect

Well into the nineteenth century, the linguistic situation in the Netherlands – and, I presume, in many other European countries as well – can be characterized as in (1). The standard language functioned primarily as a written code, which meant that for centuries it was only a relatively small part of the population which was actively engaged in using it. Consider (1):

(1) level 1   written standard
     level 2   dialects

Typical of this situation is that there is hardly any interaction between the written standard and its related dialects, meaning that the two levels are largely independent of each other. That is, from the moment that the formation of the written standard was a fact, dialect features hardly penetrated into this largely written variety. The influence of the written standard on the dialects was highly limited as well.

In the Netherlands, the written standard developed in the latter half of the sixteenth century and in the beginning of the seventeenth century, i.e. in a period in which Latin had definitively fallen into disuse as the generally used – written – language of officialese. Characteristic of written standards is that they are prototypically used in formal situations. This lends written standards a solemn character. The linguistic echo of this solemn character is that written standards tend to display an *archaic* character in the sense that they exhibit characteristics no longer present in any kind of 'cultivated speech'. Not infrequently, written languages continue to encode grammatical distinctions that have disappeared from the spoken varieties completely. A classic example of the latter are the different endings of the modern French verb (e.g. *je/il parle, tu parles, ils/elles parlent*) which exclusively exist in writing, and which have no basis in the spoken language whatsoever. In addition, written standards often exhibit an artificial character due to the fact that they – at least in part – are the product of often naive 'language engineering'. To give an example, the written standard of Dutch represents a purposely elaborated language variety which had the urban dialects of central Holland as its starting point, but which at the same time was modelled after Latin and German, particularly in the realm of inflection (Roorda 1856, and cf. section 2.2.2).

Note, however, that written languages are artificial in another sense as well. Written languages represent language deprived of both its natural

DIALECT VERSUS STANDARD LANGUAGE

medium – its sounds and its intonation – and its natural context. In Kay (1977: 29) this is put into words as follows: 'Writing is language unsupported by all the vocal and visual signs and the process involving immediate feedback from the addressee.' Consequently, written languages are by definition poorer than spoken languages as far as their direct means of expression are concerned. Put differently, in comparison with their spoken counterparts written languages represent the unnatural option for several reasons. Most importantly, they lack what is generally considered one of the prime characteristics of natural language, namely a 'vocal dimension'. Not surprisingly, in the anthropologically oriented tradition that Kay (1977) belongs to, writing is considered 'culture as far as possible divorced from our primate nature' (*ibid.*: 29). However this may be, written languages may become systems in their own right. That is, precisely because of the fact that written languages are generally not spoken, they may develop properties which are not present in their natural counterpart, i.e. spoken language. Examples of such properties that are particularly characteristic of written languages are, for instance, the elaborate systems of sentence embedding that they may develop (Uhlenbeck 1979), or the complex – and often artificial – rules in the realm of pronominal deixis (cf. Verhoeven 1990 for Dutch). As a consequence of their relatively independent status, written languages may differ markedly from their spoken counterparts, which means that their systematic properties must be learned separately. This aspect of written languages was clearly observed by Koefoed when he charcterized a written standard as nobody's native language (Koefoed 1995).

Crucial to the situation in (1), then, is the fact that the language that was standardized and cultivated was by and large a written language. For centuries, to put it differently, standard Dutch was an 'unspoken language' (Wexler 1993). It was only in the course of the nineteenth century that a *spoken* standard gradually developed (Hagen 1990), meaning that (1) developed into (2):

(2)   level 1   written standard
        level 2   spoken standard
        level 3   dialects

Not surprisingly, the emerging spoken standard was rooted in the written standard or, more precisely, the written standard gradually came to be adopted as a norm for speaking.[1] Interestingly enough, the way this came about is rather unclear, but to my mind the following two elements should be distinguished: (i) The written standard became more and more a guideline for speaking, particularly among the well-educated urban elite. (ii) This process was primarily put into effect by the elite of the towns in the central Holland area, i.e. by speakers of dialects that were relatively close to the written standard (since, as was pointed out above, it was these dialects in which the written standard is rooted).

15

The fact that the written standard became a determining factor for speaking resulted in a language variety – the spoken standard – which is not as formal as the written standard, but which has as its defining characteristic the fact that *it is directed towards the written language*. That is, it is the written language which serves as a point of reference for the spoken standard; the more formal the situation is, the more evident the influence of the written language on cultivated speech. This implies that it is the written standard which influences its spoken counterpart.[2] In addition, it is my impression that it was in the course of the nineteenth century, too, that the dialects came under the influence of the standard language. Evidently, this is tantamount to claiming that it was at this time that the two levels distinguished in (1) started to lose their relative independence. It is tempting, of course, to associate the latter with the observation that it was precisely in this period that (1) developed into (2), i.e. with the fact that the written standard developed a spoken counterpart. That is, at that time there was question of a steadily growing number of bi-lectal speakers who, apparently, tended to consider the spoken standard as a point of reference for their dialects. Clearly, this implies that it is the spoken standard which influences the related dialects. This can be schematized as follows (but see below for a more precise statement):

(3) level 1   written standard
                    ↓
     level 2   spoken standard
                    ↓
     level 3   dialects

The picture emerging from (3) is that a standard language must be a spoken language itself in order to be able to affect – 'unsophisticated' – speaking (i.e. the dialects). The fact is that the dialects were hardly influenced by the standard language as long as it was predominantly written. As soon as the written standard developed a spoken variety, however, the dialects came under its influence.

In order to come to grips with the language variety characterized as spoken standard, it should be realized that spoken standards represent some sort of hybrid by definition. In consequence of the fact that a spoken standard is directed towards the written standard, the spoken standard, too, often exhibits a formal – and sometimes even archaic – character. Particularly in formal situations, the spoken standard tends to approximate to the written standard in many respects, meaning that in such situations the spoken standard can best be characterized as a 'vocalized written language'. However, for many speakers the spoken standard also represents the everyday language used to discuss everyday topics in everyday situations. In the latter case, obviously, the spoken standard functions in exactly the same way as the dialects. In my opinion it is this hybrid character of the spoken standard which underlies the fact that it is precisely this language variety which exhibits such marked differences between its H- and its L-registers (in other words, between its formal and informal styles). In its formal styles the spoken standard approaches the written standard and may even become more or less identical to it as far as grammar and lexis are concerned. In its informal styles, however, the spoken standard approaches the dialects, at least functionally. Both the informal styles of standard languages and the dialects represent informal, spoken language systems, and there may even be situations in which it is hard or even impossible to draw a clear dividing line between the informal registers or styles of the standard language on the one hand and the dialects on the other (Koelmans 1979).[3] Consequently, in the informal styles of standard languages the influence of the written standard is limited.

The outcome of the above is that spoken standards may rightly be characterized as language varieties that are 'richer' than other languages, in that they – unlike other language varieties – are hybrids as far as their function is concerned. This is directly reflected by the rich inventory of registers and styles usually at the disposal of spoken standards. The above findings are summarized in (4) (which replaces 2):

(4)   level 1   written standard

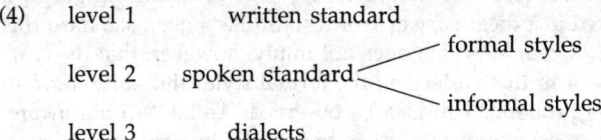

       level 2   spoken standard
       level 3   dialects

Although many details concerning the precise relationship between the informal registers/styles of the spoken standard on the one hand and the dialects on the other are unclear, it is tempting to start from the idea that there is an interaction between both levels. This would join in with the often observed gradual transition of the dialects into the spoken standard (e.g. Koelmans 1979). This potential interaction would imply that it is not only the case that the dialects are influenced by the spoken standard but that, conversely, the spoken standard is influenced by the dialects as well. Considering both aspects of the interaction between the spoken standard and the dialects, it seems natural to start from the idea that it is the informal styles of the spoken standard that play a crucial part. Specifically, because of the functional similarity between the informal layers of the spoken standard and the dialects, it is particularly the informal styles which may affect the dialects, and, similarly, it is the informal styles of the spoken standard which are open to dialect influence. Crucial to the interaction between the informal layers of the spoken standard and the dialects is that both processes may take place simultaneously. That is, we should reckon with the fact that the effects that the spoken standard has on the dialects and the penetration of the spoken standard by the dialects occur at the same time and in the same group of bi-lectal speakers.

Note that it is important to take this hybrid character of spoken standards into account since the systematics holding in the formal styles need not correspond at all to the systematics of the informal styles. To give an example taken from Dutch, in the formal styles of the spoken standard – parallel to the written standard – there is still a reflex of the three-gender system. This system, which as such was lost centuries ago, developed into a two-gender system, viz. a class of common nouns (comprising the former masculine and feminine nouns) associated with *de* as definite article and a class of neuter nouns associated with *het*. As far as pronominal deixis is concerned, however, many speakers of Dutch still feel uneasy about the overall use of *hij*/*hem* 'he/him' in relation to *de*-words, irrespective of the fact that the original feminine and masculine nouns have merged into one class of common nouns. In many cases – particularly in relation to abstract nouns – these speakers prefer the female pronouns *zij*/*haar* 'she/her', a phenomenon often ridiculed by calling it the *haar*-cultuur (lit. *her*-culture as well as *hair*-culture, a pun based on the homophonous character of the noun *haar* 'hair' and the oblique form of the female personal pronoun *haar* 'her') (Royen 1933). In the written standard this may even go so far that the gender of a noun is checked in a dictionary or wordlist. In the spoken standard this is impossible, of course, which does not imply, however, that the *haar*-culture is absent in this variety: in the formal styles the same trend to opt for female pronouns can also be observed. As far as I am aware, however, this trend is more or less absent in the informal styles.

Crucial to a correct understanding of the relationship between a written standard and the formal styles of its spoken counterpart is, however, the fact that these two varieties should not be equated either. Evidently, in this case, too, both varieties are not necessarily governed by identical sets of norms. Consider the following example taken from Dutch. In the written standard, there is a tendency to avoid the sequence 'Past Participle – Vf' in subordinate clauses as much as possible. Instead, in writing the order 'Vf – Past Participle' is clearly preferred by quite a number of standard Dutch speakers. Consequently, as far as writing is concerned, (5b) is preferred to (5a):

(5)   a. *ik geloof niet dat hij dat boek gelezen heeft*
        I believe not that he that book read has
        'I don't believe that he has read that book'
    b. *ik geloof niet dat hij dat boek heeft gelezen*
        I believe not that he that book has read
        'I don't believe that he has read that book'

As far as the spoken standard is concerned (both its formal and its informal styles), most speakers of Dutch are largely 'unaware' of this aspect of word order in subordinate clauses, meaning that they do not know which order they use themselves nor what order is used by other speakers. That is, in the spoken varieties of Dutch there is no question of a general avoidance of sentences of the (5a)-type. In all probability, the spoken Dutch sentences of the (5a)-type are much more popular than their (5b)-type counterparts, i.e. even for those who strongly prefer (5b)-type sentences in writing. The fact is that the (5a)-type sentences are generally considered to represent the unmarked option for the modern language (Haeseryn 1990).

To summarize, a distinction has been drawn above between standard languages that represent an exclusively written code, and standard languages which, alongside a written code, are also used in speaking. It may well be that spoken standards are atypical in several respects: on the one hand they are directed towards the written standard whereas on the other hand they are spoken languages, functionally similar to dialects. This dual character of spoken standards is reflected by the fact that in certain cases the formal styles resemble the written standard whereas the informal styles do not. In addition, it was pointed out that written standards should be assigned a status in their own right. Crucial to a correct understanding of written standards is that they do not necessarily exhibit the same systematic characteristics as their spoken counterparts. As we have seen, some phenomena occur only in the written standard; they even lack a parallel in the formal styles of the spoken standard.

Our above discussion of the relationship between a written standard, its spoken counterpart, and the related dialects can be schematized as follows:

(6) level 1   written standard

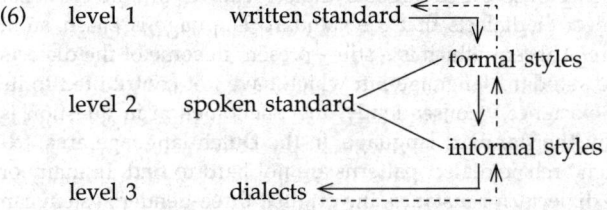

     level 2   spoken standard

     level 3   dialects

It may well be that (6) represents a somewhat over-schematized picture of the potential relationships between the various language varieties discussed so far. Hopefully, however, it helps us to come to grips with the intricate interplay of forces that a standard language and its related dialects may exhibit. As with (3), the non-dotted arrows in (6) indicate the basic patterns of influence. As we have seen, however, the situation may be considerably more complex than these basic patterns suggest. As discussed, it is not only often the case that the spoken standard influences the dialects, but the dialects may influence the informal layers of the spoken standard as well. This latter – secondary – pattern is indicated in (6) by means of a dotted arrow. In addition, the basic patterns in (6) do not express the fact that the written standard may be influenced by the spoken language as well. Features of the written standard which have no basis in 'cultivated speech' whatsoever run the risk of being abolished. In that case, the written standard is influenced by the spoken standard. As was pointed out above, the latter pattern seems to represent a considerably less steady force than the influence exercised by the written standard on this spoken counterpart. Hence the use of a dotted arrow in this case, too. Note, finally, that the relationship between the formal and the informal layers of the spoken standard has not been discussed. It is tempting to start from the idea that in this case there is also the possibility of two-way traffic between both levels. In conformity with the above I consider the influence exercised by the formal styles on their informal counterparts to represent the most constant force. However, in this case, too, a counter-movement which involves the penetration of the formal styles by their informal varieties should also be taken into account.

2.2 Systematic differences between dialects and standard languages

In discussing the systematic differences between dialects and standard languages, one should first of all set apart the differences which are *not* rooted in a difference in status and/or function between dialects and standard languages. Specifically, there is a class of differences between dialects and standard languages which are nothing but historical accidents. What I have in mind is the phenomenon that is generally known as the occurrence of so-called 'archaic' dialect features or patterns. That is, in the dialect or dialects that the standard language is based on, a certain feature is absent which is – still – present in some of the dialects related to the standard language but which have not contributed to its coming into existence.[4] Consequently, the phenomenon in question is also lacking in the standard language. In the Dutch language area, examples of such archaic dialect patterns are not hard to find. In many of the southern dialects, for instance, the original three-gender system can still be found. In addition, in the south-west, the gerund (the inflected infinitive) is still a living feature of the dialects in question; while in many eastern dialects, the first person singular of the indicative still has the -*e* ending.[5]

Evidently, the presence of such archaic features in the dialects and their absence in the standard language has nothing to do with a difference in function and/or status between the dialects on the one hand and the standard language on the other. At the time the written standard came into existence, these features simply no longer formed part of the dialects that the written standard was based on. Put differently, the

DIALECT VERSUS STANDARD LANGUAGE

differences in question are nothing but *differences between dialects*, really. That some of these dialects lie at the root of the standard language and others do not, is irrelevant to the status of these differences. Generally speaking, then, so-called archaic dialect features primarily bear upon differences between dialects, and they do not tell us anything about the systematic differences between dialects and standard languages.

2.2.1 *Dialect versus standard language: three spheres of difference*

In discussing the systematic differences between dialects and their related standard language, there appear to be three types of differences:

(a) Characteristics present in the standard language and absent in the dialects which should be attributed to the process of naive language engineering that standard languages are subject to.
(b) Characteristics absent in the standard language and present in the dialects, whose emergence should be attributed to the greater ease with which natural changes may take place (and particularly 'spread') in the dialects.
(c) Characteristics absent in the standard language and present in the dialects, whose emergence should be attributed to the fact that dialects are spoken languages *par excellence* in which strategies relating to the actual process of speech production are much more influential than in standard languages. Standard languages, in consequence of the fact that they are a vehicle for writing, do not give in to forces linked to speaking as readily as dialects which lack such a written counterpart.

In the remainder of this section the three 'spheres' which may give rise to systematic differences between standard languages and their related dialects will be further discussed. In 2.2.2 it is the effects of the process of naive language engineering that will be discussed. In 2.2.3 the focus will be on the ease with which language change may take place in the dialects, while in 2.2.4, finally, the fact that dialects are first and foremost spoken languages will be highlighted.

2.2.2 *Naive language engineering*

In discussing the relation between a standard language and its dialects, the time-honoured truth that standard languages may exhibit all kinds of phenomena that are lacking in the non-prestigious varieties (among which are the dialects) cannot be left out of consideration. Evidently, it is particularly the effects of the process of naive language engineering – the conscious elaboration and embellishment of, particularly, the written language – that one has in mind.[6] In relation to Dutch, for instance, it is common practice to stress that there was a time when the written

TAMING THE VERNACULAR

standard language was artificially provided with, among other things, a case system, a system of adjectival declension which distinguished between declensions in -*e* and in -*en*, a conjunctive, and an imperative plural (and see section 2.3 for additional examples illustrating the pursued embellishment). These phenomena are generally considered to be inspired by Latin and German. In written standards, which are unnatural systems for several reasons, there appears to be no strong limit on the introduction of such artificial innovations. Note that the influence of German was particularly strong. It has even been claimed that only those inflectional categories which have a parallel in German have been set up in Dutch. That is, according to this view inflectional patterns present in Latin but absent in German were never introduced in standard Dutch.

As is well-known and as has already been illustrated by examples taken from Dutch, features artificially introduced in standard languages are often borrowed from other – culturally prestigious – languages: Sanskrit in the case of many languages in Central and South-East Asia, and on the Indian sub-continent; Persian in Central Asia, the Indian sub-continent and Turkey; Arab in the Muslim world; Latin in Western Europa, etc. Of course, I am perfectly aware of the fact that borrowing from prestigious languages has often been questioned as a force which can change a language in general, i.e. as a force which may also affect the non-prestigious and primarily spoken varieties. This is particularly the case when the process of borrowing is considered to bear upon grammar. Consider, for instance, Gerritsen's contribution to the volume on *Internal and External Factors in Syntactic Change*. In relation to the stabilization of verb-last order in German and Dutch, Gerritsen notes the following:

> The stabilization of the verb-last order in German has been attributed to the imitation of Latin patterns (. . .). In principle this external factor could also have played a role in the rise of the same orders in Dutch. However, it is very unlikely that the rise of this order could be due to the influence of Latin. (. . .) Secondly, it is improbable that a nearly dead language like Latin could influence the syntactic development of a spoken language in a period like the Middle Ages when the majority of the people were illiterate.
> (Gerritsen 1992: 388–9)

It seems to me that this reasoning is incorrect. The issue is not to what extent a vernacular may be influenced by a dead language, but to what extent a dead language may influence a written language and to what extent these features borrowed by the written language may, in their turn, penetrate the spoken language. As was indicated above, written languages may be influenced by foreign languages very easily, particularly when the written language is used by a relatively well-educated elite (who, at least to a certain degree, know the donor language). Crucial in this connection, however, is the next stage, i.e. the question of whether the features borrowed into the written code may penetrate the spoken

DIALECT VERSUS STANDARD LANGUAGE

language. Clearly, in this connection we should differentiate between the language spoken by the elite – i.e. speakers who use the cultivated written code themselves – and the vernacular, i.e. the language spoken by people who are largely unacquainted both with the cultivated written code and with the donor language(s). In relation to this latter issue – the penetration of the vernacular by a cultivated written language – things are very unclear. The case of Ottoman Turkish suggests that the elite who *write* the cultivated variety may also adopt this variety as a spoken language. At the same time Ottoman Turkish illustrates that this cultivated variety of Turkish has never heavily influenced the everyday language of the majority of the population who in the eyes of the elite spoke only 'crude Turkish'. Consider Lewis's characterization of Ottoman Turkish:

> From the tenth century onward the Turks who had wandered into the Arab empire in western Asia became converted to Islam. They adopted the Arabic alphabet and a host of Arabic words, not only theological terms but the whole vocabulary of Arab thought and civilization. In the eleventh century the Turks under the Seljuk dynasty overran Persia, and Persian became the language of the Turkish administration and of literary culture. Thousands of Persian words thus joined the thousands of Arabic words that formed part of the educated Turk's vocabulary. The bulk of these Arabic and Persian borrowings were never assimilated to Turkish phonetic patterns. More, with the foreign words came foreign grammatical conventions. To offer an English analogy, it was as if we said not 'for obvious reasons' but 'for rationes obviae' or, 'what is the conditio of your progenitor reverendus?' instead of 'how's your father?' This hybrid language became the official language of the Ottoman dynasty, who at the end of the thirteenth century entered upon the inheritance of the Seljuks. It attained an extraordinary degree of flexibility, expressiveness, and grandeur, but it was caviar to the general; the speech of the majority of Turks was dismissed by the speakers of Ottoman as *kaba Türkçe*, 'crude Turkish'.
> (Lewis 1967: xx–xxi; orthography slightly adapted)

The above seems to imply that in the realm of grammar such foreign features adopted by the written standard do have the potential to penetrate the spoken language of those who used this cultivated variety in writing. What is unclear, however, is whether these features have the potential, too, to penetrate the spoken language of other groups as well, i.e. become an integral part of speaking in general. Evidently, this latter issue largely depends on the question of the extent to which speaking is directed towards the written standard or, phrased differently, whether the written standard has developed a generally used spoken counterpart. Viewed in this way, artificial innovations such as those discussed above in relation to Dutch and Turkish constitute an intriguing field of investigation. That is, artificially introduced innovations must not be ridiculed but they should be carefully studied since they throw an interesting light on the question of the extent to which features of the written standard may be adopted in speech or, phrased somewhat more precisely, in different speech styles and/or registers.

The following examples taken from Dutch seem to indicate that the spoken varieties of a language may indeed adopt such artificially introduced innovations, but note at the same time that the first example makes clear that all kinds of modifications may take place. Consider the history of the oblique form of the 3rd person plural personal pronoun. In the sixteenth and seventeenth centuries a distinction was introduced between *hun* ('indirect object') and *hen* ('direct object'). *Hen* in particular has often been criticized and ridiculed, since it is generally considered an artificial element which has no status in the 'living language' whatsoever. Consequently, many Dutch grammarians have suggested doing away with *hen* altogether (de Rooij 1990). However this may be, at present there are many speakers of the standard language who strongly prefer *hen* to *hun* as the oblique form of the personal pronoun (i.e. both as direct and as indirect object). For many of those speakers *hun* is quite unacceptable as a personal pronoun, *hun* being exclusively associated with the possessive pronoun. In the language of these speakers, to put it differently, *hen* is very common – even in informal styles – irrespective of its artificial roots (de Rooij 1990, van Marle 1992). Note, however, that in the grammar of those speakers who have incorporated *hen*, the distribution of *hen* (and, for that matter, *hun*) has nothing to do with the one suggested by the sixteenth-century grammarians.

Similarly, the 3rd person reflexive pronoun (singular and plural) *zich* (*hij wast zich* 'he washes himself'; *zij wassen zich* 'they wash themselves') has often been considered to represent an artificially introduced innovation from the seventeenth century that is inspired by German *sich* (van der Wal 1992). This reflexive pronoun has become an integral part of the spoken standard, even in its informal styles.

What the above two examples have in common is that they, at least in part, have a clear lexical dimension: both in the case of *hun/hen* and even more so in the case of *zich*, it is primarily the choice of lexical elements with which we are concerned. That is, up till now I have not seen a convincing example of an inflectional or a syntactic pattern which has penetrated the spoken standard, and which started as an artificially introduced innovation in the written language.[7] Unlike their written congeners, spoken standards, apparently, are not ready candidates for grammatical elaboration.

2.2.3 Resistance to change

The second sphere connects to the observation made time and again by dialectologists that dialects are much more prone to language change than standard languages, due to the fact that in the former the norms for correct usage are generally considered to be much more relaxed. This is particularly so in the case of so-called 'natural change', i.e. language change which acts upon imbalances in the language system. These changes somehow or other increase the transparency of the system, meaning that they optimize its learnability. In sum, in consequence of their norm sensitivity, standard languages are much more conservative than dialects as far as the effects of natural change are concerned.

Morphology, particularly, makes this point clear. In standard Dutch, some auxiliaries exhibit different vowels in the singular and in the plural: see, for instance, *ik mag* 'I may' vs *wij mogen* 'we may', *ik zal* 'I shall' vs *wij zullen* 'we shall', *ik kan* 'I can' vs *wij kunnen* 'we can'. In the dialects, this unsystematic vowel alternation has often been lost, resulting in regularized plural forms such as *wij magge, wij zalle* and *wij kanne*. In the standard language the difference in stem vowel has never been subject to analogical levelling.

As in most other Germanic languages, in the Dutch dialects verbs come in two types; regular ('weak') verbs and irregular ('strong') verbs. Throughout the history of Dutch, strong verbs shifted to the class of weak verbs. Interestingly, in some of the Dutch dialects this regularizing trend is much stronger than in the standard language. In the dialects spoken in the Province of Limburg, for instance, verbs such as *komen* and *zwemmen* have become regular, meaning that they form their preterites by means of the addition of the regular preterite ending -*de* to the verb stem and not by means of a change of the stem vowel as in standard Dutch.

Changes in the pronominal system illustrate the same point (van Marle 1992). In many of the Dutch dialects, the pronominal system is much more 'reduced' than in the standard language. Specifically, in the standard language personal pronouns generally distinguish between subject and oblique forms, see (7) where the focus is on the plural form (obviously, the 2nd person is exceptional):

(7) personal pronouns in standard Dutch (plural forms)

	subject forms	*oblique forms*
1st pers.	wij	ons
2nd pers.	jullie	jullie
3rd pers.	zij	hun, hen, ze

In the dialects this system has often been subject to change. Specifically, in a number of dialects (particularly those in the south-west) – and also in Afrikaans – there is a syncretism in form between the subject forms and the oblique forms, meaning that the above system has often developed into:

(8) personal pronouns in Dutch dialects (plural forms)

	subject forms	*oblique forms*
1st pers.	ons	ons
2nd pers.	jullie	jullie
3rd pers.	hun	hun

(For the sake of clarity I have used the forms of the standard language to characterize the system that can be found in the dialects in question and in Afrikaans.)

Specifically, in the dialects the tendency to reduce difference in form in the marked context (marked 'plural' in contrast to unmarked 'singular') has come into force, apparently hardly hindered by the conservative force of the norms.

As said, there can be no doubt that the ease with which natural change takes place in dialects, as opposed to standard languages, is a consequence of the fact that in the former the norms are much less elaborated than in the latter. Hence, in dialects all kinds of regularizing trends get a chance. Particularly the morphological examples make this clear, in that the new system is generally more transparent than the system before the change. Evidently, the preterites in *-de* are in line with the regular system whereas the strong preterites with stem vowel alternation are not, while the loss of the vowel alternation in the plural forms of auxiliaries such as *mogen*, etc, has a similar effect. That is, what seems to be happening here is that in dialects, exceptional forms do not have the strength to 'block' the emergence of their regular – rule-driven – counterparts. This indicates that the ease with which dialects give in to language change is primarily a matter of 'norms', since the phenomenon of blocking is nothing but the outcome of the efficacy of the lexical norms (cf. van Marle 1985: chs 5 and 6). In dialects, apparently, irregular forms may be neglected much more easily than in standard languages, due to the more relaxed attitude of their speakers towards norms. In my view, this more relaxed attitude is the direct result of the fact that dialects are not regularly used in formal situations: the norm awareness in standard languages is first of all the product of the formal situations in which standard languages are used, writing (in many cases, at least) being one of them.

The relative lack of overt norms in informal speech (including dialects) is also evidenced by another phenomenon: the ease with which morphological adaptation may occur. Morphological adaptation – particularly prominent in relation to loan words – involves the redundant addition of the formal characteristics of the morphological category that the loan word is semantically related with, but of which it is not a member as such (van Marle 1993). To take an example: in Dutch many personal names are formed by means of *-er*. Personal names borrowed from other languages, as a rule, do not contain this suffix. These loan words, however, may be adapted to this pattern by redundantly taking *-er*. An example is *Moslimm-er* for *Moslim*, which I recently recorded an 8-year-old boy saying. It is directly comparable with older examples such as *dragon-der*, *medicijn-er* (cf. French *dragon* and *médecin*), *Batakk-er* (cf. *Batak*), etc. (see van Marle 1993 for more examples, both inflectional and derivational). As I pointed out in van Marle (1993), in many cases the forms resulting from adaptation are not readily accepted in that they run against the norms of the prestigious – and often learned – part of the lexicon that loanwords frequently form part of. Hence, many instances of adaptation are 'colloquialisms' or belong to the language of children who have mastered the system of the language but who are still unaware of (parts of) its overt norms. Not surprisingly, in dialects morphological adaptation is much less impeded, too (see van Marle, in preparation).

In my opinion, it may well be that this difference in norm awareness represents one of the fundamental differences between dialects and standard languages. The strong norm awareness in the latter represents a powerful conservative force, meaning that in standard languages, the chances for natural change to operate are significantly less than in dialects. That is, in standard languages the purely systematic forces experience much more resistance from socio-cultural forces than in dialects where the systematic forces associated with natural change seem to have much more free play. The conclusion of the latter must be that linguists who are interested in the efficacy of the purely systematic forces in language – i.e. forces unhindered by the social norms – should not study standard languages in the first place *but dialects!* In standard languages, the efficacy of non-systematic – i.e. socially motivated – forces is strongest, meaning that it is here that the largest number of unnatural, marked solutions can be found. As such, this is interesting enough, but for students of language *structure* this may be a good reason to change their prime interest and pay more attention to the non-prestigious language varieties instead. Note, finally, that it is not always clear where these norms come from. The origin of the preference for the order 'Vf – Past Participle' in the written standard of Dutch (see the examples in (5)), for instance, cannot simply be traced down to the influence of Latin or German.

2.2.4 Dialects: exclusively spoken

It is my impression that the third sphere may give rise to the most salient differences between dialects and their related standard languages. A warning is in order here, however. Since systematic investigations are largely lacking, the following remarks are necessarily tentative, even more so than the remarks in the preceding sections. Being purely spoken language systems, dialects may give in to the effects of strategies relating to the actual process of speech production much more readily than standard languages. To put it differently, in the dialects the efficacy of performance mechanisms governing speech production may be more prominent than in standard languages. The fact is that in dialects the number of forces potentially counterbalancing these production mechanisms are much smaller. First, as we have seen, in dialects the overt norms are less elaborated and less prominent than in standard languages.

Second, in standard languages – in Western society so intimately related to writing – there is the question of a constant influence of the written language which directly counterbalances the effects of speaking. In dialects the influence of the elaborated written code is much more marginal, if present at all (see section 2.1).[8]

An intriguing example of the way dialects may give in to mechanisms relating to speech production, may be the emergence of so-called 'inflected conjunctions' in the Dutch dialects. This phenomenon has aroused the curiosity of linguists for decades (van Haeringen 1939, 1958; see Hoekstra and Smits, in preparation, for an overview), and see (9) for some examples:

(9) a. *iech deenk tot-s te leeg-s*
      I think that-2 sg you lie-2 sg
      gloss: I think that you lie
     b. *ik denk datt-e ze lieg-e*
      I think that-plur they lie-plur
      gloss: I think that they lie

Linguists differ considerably as to the interpretation they assign to both the origin and the synchronic status of the inflected conjunctions in the Dutch dialects. Without wishing to give the impression that other – purely grammatical – forces are irrelevant to the emergence of the inflected conjunctions, I am inclined to consider this phenomenon first of all as a manifestation of a process of 'phonology-driven' analogy. The basic facts seem to be as follows. The origin of the inflected conjunctions should be located in the inverted order, i.e. in the sequence 'inflected verb-personal pronoun' (van Haeringen 1958). That is, in terms of (9a)–(9b), it is the sequences *leeg-s te* (lit. 'lie you') and *lieg-e ze* (lit. 'lie they') which are crucial. The formal characteristics of these sequences, then, are extended ('generalized') to the other prototypical case where the personal pronoun occupies the second position, i.e. after a conjunction. That is, by analogy with *leegs te* and *liege ze*, *tot te* and *dat ze* developed into *tot-s te* and *datt-e ze*. Among the Dutch dialects there are considerable differences as to the extent to which this phenomenon is systematized. In addition, in many cases it is unclear to what degree the extension of the phonological characteristics of inverted *leegs te* and *liege ze* is accompanied by reinterpretation. That is, is *tot-s te leegs* the correct synchronic segmentation or should we start from *tot-ste leegs* in which the ending *-s* and the pronoun *te* have amalgamated into one clitic *ste*? However all this may be, I take the line that a process of phonology-driven analogy lies at the root of the inflected conjunctions in Dutch. Given this view it is anything but surprising that the occurrence of inflected conjunctions is limited to the Dutch dialects and that this phenomenon is unknown in the standard language, even in its most informal manifestation. Evidently, within this approach it is only natural to consider this distinction between the dialects on the one hand and the standard language on the other to be a manifestation of the fundamental difference between the two types of language varieties in question. Being exclusively spoken, dialects may incorporate the effects of the process of speech production much more readily and on a much larger scale than standard languages. One such effect, it seems to me, is the fact that dialects are more open to the efficacy of all kinds of phonologically oriented processes. In dialects, to put it differently, we should reckon with the fact that phonological forces are more prominent than in standard languages, in consequence of the fact that the exclusively spoken dialects may incorporate the effects of speech production much more readily than the standard which need not be a spoken language at all.

Interestingly, the same conclusion was arrived at by Rohdenburg (this volume). On the basis of different kinds of phenomena Rohdenburg took the stand that the trend to systematize in phonological (particularly, prosodic) terms is much more prominent in dialects than in standard languages (see, further, Chapter 7).

2.3 Conclusions

The basic idea of this chapter is that standard languages and dialects may differ more fundamentally from each other than is often assumed. As is generally agreed upon, the main difference between dialects and standard languages relates to differences in their socio-cultural status. However, many linguists seem to have overlooked the fact that this socio-cultural difference may have all kinds of repercussions, some of which directly bear upon the structural level.

Standard languages – and particularly written standards – are subject to conscious elaboration and embellishment. All kinds of artificial rules and distinctions have been introduced to deal, for instance, with the distribution of related forms such as *shall* and *will* in English (see Arnovick this volume) or *hun* and *hen* in Dutch (cf. section 2.2.2). In addition, standard languages are the product of scrutinizing by generations of grammarians with regard to the question of whether the constructions they contain are 'logical'; hence the general aversion to, for instance, double negation. Crucial to all instances of elaboration and embellishment is, however, that they do have the potential to become an integral part of the written language and that, subsequently, they may even penetrate the spoken standard (although some phenomena qualify for entering the spoken standard much more strongly than others).

A consequence of the fact that in standard languages – written or spoken – norm-awareness is much more conscious than in dialects, is that natural change may proceed more smoothly in dialects than in standard languages. The result is that all kinds of internally-driven change get more of a chance to take place in dialects than in standard languages.

Finally, since dialects are language systems that are exclusively spoken, they may reflect the effects of processes typical of speech production much more directly than standard languages. In the written variety of standard languages, the effects of these processes are counterbalanced by the many rules that determine writing, whereas spoken standards – particularly in their formal styles and registers – are influenced by writing to such an extent that they do not exhibit the full extent of the effects of speech production. This is directly evidenced by the fact that there are phenomena which are wide-spread in the dialects but which are unknown in the standard language, either written or spoken.

There can be no doubt that the exploration of the differences between dialects and standard languages that constituted the topic of the present paper is highly tentative. It can only be hoped that some of the views taken in this paper will stimulate further research.

Notes

* I am indebted to Caroline Smits who commented on several versions of this chapter. In addition, I am also grateful to Geert Koefoed for his critical comments on the pre-final version.
1 Note that the adoption of the written standard as a norm for speaking proceeded far from smoothly. The rise of a spoken standard has led to fierce discussions, which, in the end, resulted in an adaptation of the *written* standard. The fact is, that in the end many features characteristic of the early written standard – but which had no base in whatever form of cultivated speech – were abolished. Evidently, this cannot but lead to the conclusion that in this case it is the spoken standard which influences its written counterpart (see below).
2 As can be inferred from note 1, I do take into account the fact that, alongside the influence exercised by the written standard on its spoken counterpart, the spoken language, in its turn, may also influence its written congener. However, I am inclined to consider the influence of the written on the spoken language to be more constant and fundamental than the influence of the spoken standard on its written counterpart.
3 Evidently, this is particularly the case with the dialects that the standard language derives from. However, the same phenomenon may also occur in the case of regionally coloured varieties of the spoken standard and the dialects spoken in the same area.
4 In many cases the feature in question used to form part of the dialects underlying the standard language as well, meaning that it has disappeared in consequence of some process of language change. Hence

its characterization as 'archaic'. Note that this scenario, though common as such, does not represent the only possibility. A given dialect, or group of dialects, may have developed a certain characteristic, which the dialect(s) underlying the standard languages have not. In this case the dialect(s) in question are innovative, whereas the standard language is conservative. This situation is far from uncommon since dialects may be highly innovative, cf. sections 2.2.3 and 2.2.4. It is my impression, however, that the archaic dialect patterns have aroused more attention than their innovative counterparts.

5 Note that standard Dutch is based on the dialects spoken in the central Holland area. As far as morphology is concerned, these dialects are much more eroded than the dialects of the eastern and southern parts of the Dutch-speaking language area. Consequently, in these latter dialects many features can be found that are no longer present in the standard language and the dialects that standard Dutch is rooted in. Consequently, the fact that many (particularly eastern and southern) dialects are morphologically richer than the standard language is only a by-product of the fact that these dialects are morphologically richer than the western dialects that standard Dutch originates from.

6 The position of derivational morphology is highly remarkable. In the Dutch language area, there appears to be a fundamental difference between the dialects and the standard language. In comparison to standard Dutch, derivational morphology is marginal in the dialects. It is not absent, but it is underdeveloped. Consequently, in the standard language all kinds of derivational processes are present which are lacking in the dialects. Crucial in this connection is the question to what extent these derivational patterns are actively used in the spoken standard. (In van Marle 1996 it is suggested that the activity of quite a number of these patterns is limited to the written standard.) However this may be, it may well be that derivational morphology represents a field *par excellence* where elaboration can be taken in hand.

7 This implies that Latin influence in the case of the stabilization of the verb-last order in German and Dutch discussed by Gerritsen (cf. above), is not particularly obvious. That is, although I do not agree with Gerritsen's reasoning, her conclusion may be correct.

8 Within the context of this chapter, I have chosen to discuss the so-called avoidance strategies under the same heading, although they no doubt represent a phenomenon that is completely different from the one discussed above. The reason is that, at least in part, avoidance strategies may also relate to the actual process of speech production. A certain feature is considered difficult to handle in actual performance – even by speakers who know the language well – and a strategy is employed to circumvent this difficulty. Not infrequently, such avoidance strategies are associated with language learning or language unlearning – and not without reason – but I wonder whether this is

the whole story. Dialects suggest that avoidance strategies are not limited to those two situations, but that these strategies may also be used in situations in which casual speech is not counterbalanced by a more formal usage.

In many Dutch dialects, the phenomenon can be found that the inflection of main verbs is avoided. In the dialects there is a remarkably strong tendency to avoid tensed verb forms, by using a periphrastic construction consisting of the auxiliary *doen* 'to do' + infinitive. Judging from the materials presented in Nuytens (1962), in some dialects the use of periphrastic *doen* + infinitive is remarkably wide spread. Consider the examples in (10) and (11) that are taken from Nuytens (1962) and which stem from a dialect spoken in the north-east of the Netherlands. In (10) and (11) the (a) examples are dialectal and their counterparts in (b) represent the standard language:

(10)   a. *in school doe ik niet meer praten*
          lit.: in school do I no more talk (inf.)
       b. *in school praat ik niet meer*
          lit.: in school talk I no more
          gloss: 'in school I don't talk any more'

(11)   a. *als we weer verpleegstertje spelen deden*
          lit.: when we again nurse play (inf.) did
       b. *als we weer verpleegstertje speelden*
          lit.: when we again nurse played
          gloss: 'when we played for nurse again'

In relation to the rise of this pattern one may point to several factors. As to the present tense one may point to the fact that the class of so-called 'separable complex verbs' is rather complicated as far as actual production is concerned. According to Nuytens it is in relation to these verbs that periphrasis with *doen* is particularly prominent. However, as is stressed by Nuytens (1962), in the present tense the avoidance of inflection is not restricted to this class of verbs and the examples in (7) and (8) illustrate this. In the preterite, one may first of all stress the general fact that the simple past is remarkably infrequent in many dialects, the periphrastic perfect (which consists of the auxiliaries *hebben* 'to have' or *zijn* 'to be' in combination with a past participle) being much more prominent. Evidently, periphrasis with *doen* joins in with this construction, in that both constructions are of the periphrastic type. In addition, in relation to the preterite, one may also point to the fact that in Dutch there are regular and irregular verbs, with the distinction between them not transparent. By using periphrasis with *doen*, this problem is avoided at once: one only has to learn the forms of the verb *doen* – which, in consequence of their irregularity have to be learnt anyway – and combine these forms with the infinitive. However unclear the systematic basis of *doen*-periphrasis precisely may be, the marked difference between the dialects and the standard language is striking. In the former this trend is remarkably widespread, whereas in the latter – both in its written and spoken versions – this phenomenon is unknown. Again, this seems to indicate that the coming into existence of this phenomenon directly relates to the purely spoken character of the dialects and the lack of counterbalancing forces that have written languages as their base.

References

de Rooij, J. 1990. Over *hun* en *hen*, en *hun*. *Taal en Tongval* 42: 107–47.
Gerritsen, M. 1992. Internal and external factors in the stabilization of verb-last order in Dutch infinitive clauses. In: M. Gerritsen and D. Stein (eds), *Internal and External Factors in Syntactic Change*. Berlin/New York: Mouton de Gruyter, pp. 355–94.
Haeseryn, W. 1990. Syntactische normen in het Nederlands. Doctoral Dissertation, Katholieke Universiteit Nijmegen.
Hagen, A.M. 1990. Groepsportret van het Nederlands. *Onze Taal* 59: 32–9.
Hoekstra, E. and Smits, C. (in preparation). Vervoegde voegwoorden in de Nederlandse dialecten: een aantal generalisaties.
Kay, P. 1977. Language evolution and speech style. In: B.G. Blount and M. Sanches (eds), *Sociocultural Dimensions of Language Change*. New York: Academic Press, pp. 21–33.
Koefoed, G. 1995. Over de waardering en normering van twee Surinaamse talen: Surinaams en Sranan Tongo. Unpublished paper, Rijksuniversiteit Utrecht.
Koelmans, L. 1979. *Inleiding tot de historische taalkunde van het Nederlands*. Utrecht: Bohn.
Lewis, G.L. 1967. *Turkish Grammar*. Oxford: Oxford University Press.
Nuytens, E. 1962. *De tweetalige mens*. Assen: Van Gorcum.
Roorda, T. 1856. Over het onderscheid tusschen spreektaal en schrijftaal inzonderheid in onze moedertaal. Verslagen en Mededeelingen der Koninklijke Akademie van Wetenschappen, *Afdeeling Letterkunde* 1: 93–118.
Royen, P. Gerlach 1933. Haar-kultuur. *De Nieuwe Taalgids* 27: 289–301.
Uhlenbeck, E.M. 1979. Schriftelijk en mondeling taalgebruik. *Forum der Letteren* 20: 211–17.
van der Wal, M.J. 1992. Dialect and standard language in the past: the rise of Dutch standard language in the sixteenth and seventeenth centuries. In: J. van Leuvensteijn and J. Berns (eds), *Dialect and Standard Language in the English, Dutch, German, and Norwegian Language Areas*. Amsterdam: North-Holland, pp. 119–29.

van Haeringen, C.B. 1939. Congruerende voegwoorden. Reprinted in C.B. van Haeringen, *Neerlandica*. The Hague: Daamen, 1962, 246–59.

van Haeringen, C.B. 1958. Vervoegde voegwoorden in het Oosten. Reprinted in C.B. van Haeringen, *Gramarie*. Assen: Van Goor, 1962, pp. 309–18.

van Marle, J. 1985. *On the Paradigmatic Dimension of Morphological Creativity*. Dordrecht: Foris.

van Marle, J. 1992. Iets over het werk van Jaap de Rooij: een plaatsbepaling aan de hand van enkele proniminale kwesties. In: J.B. Berns and J. van Marle (eds), *Variatie in de Nederlandse standaardtaal*. Amsterdam: P.J. Meertens-Instituut (Cahiers, nr. 5), pp. 3–21.

van Marle, J. 1993. Morphological adaptation. In: G.E. Booij and J. van Marle (eds), *Yearbook of Morphology*. Dordrecht: Kluwer, pp. 255–65.

van Marle, J. 1996. On the interplay of inherited and non-inherited features in Afrikaans derivational morphology. In: H.F. Nielsen and L. Schøsler (eds), *The Origins and Development of Emigrant Languages*. Odense: University Press, pp. 103–15.

van Marle, J. (in preparation). De morfoloog en het dialectwoordenboek.

Verhoeven, P.R.F. 1990. Voornaamwoordelijke aanduiding in het hedendaagse Nederlands. *De Nieuwe Taalgids* 83: 494–513.

Wexler, P. 1993. Unspoken languages. Papers read at the XIth International Conference of Historical Linguistics. Los Angeles, August 1993.

CHAPTER 3

Syntax and varieties

Dieter Stein

Section 3.1

The study of dialect grammar can never be the study of dialect grammar alone, but always the study of dialect grammar in its dialectic with the study of standard grammar. On this basis, several types of questions can be asked:

Is there any systematic relationship between standards and dialects in the area of grammar? Are there processes or forms that are observed in only one of these two forms? Is there something like a 'dialect grammar' in general terms, or a 'standard grammar' in the sense that there are disjunctive sets of forms? This would then mean that the reasons for these differences would have to be seen as residing in the nature of these varieties themselves. The empirical precondition for this hypothesis would indeed imply that these different sets of forms would have to be observed in more than one language.

Before continuing the discussion proper it is as well to clarify some varietal notions. For our Western SAE (Standard Average European) language situation, which most of the chapters in this volume address, it seems useful to think of a continuum of varieties (Koch and Oesterreicher 1990) with the dialect at one end and written standard (henceforth WS) at the other, which would more or less coincide with orality vs literacy, and vernacular vs most formal styles. Thus, for most people the local dialect is also the vernacular and the most 'oral' variety possible. At the other end of the continuum, the written standard would be subject to what has been termed 'essayist literacy' (Besnier 1988), which would be part of the ideology of the standard as laid out in Milroy and Milroy (1985 and 1993). Pawley and Syder (1983) use another terminology, but refer to essentially the same phenomenon. For them, the vernacular and Literary English ('the formal written style', p. 553) are at opposite poles. There is a squishy borderline between the features to be counted as 'dialectal' and as 'colloquial'. In addition, certain colloquial structures thought of as 'dialectal', in the non-regional sense, and 'vulgar' complicate the picture further. The issue is, however, not of crucial importance for the following discussion.

It should be pointed out that since the following discussion is to some extent programmatic in character it seems in order to confine exemplification mainly to English, although the claim is made that the general point is in principle valid for other varietally comparable languages.

Section 3.2

What explains the absence of certain forms in the standard varieties of several languages? It has often been argued that dialects preserve residues of older historical stages. Put in these general terms, the question would make little sense, since all varieties of all languages preserve residues of older historical stages. What is the reason for and the nature of these 'residues'? The only way to establish the nature of these residues as varieties-determined is to show that they tend to be preserved in different dialects of different languages without the likelihood of a structural development determination.

A methodological note is in order in this place. It is clear that we are dealing here with tendencies, not with absolutes. In other words, we cannot expect ALL dialects of one language or indeed several languages to show the same development in the area under investigation. It is enough that some dialects of some languages should show the same development. For instance, it counts as an argument if several dialects from several languages have preserved double negation, but there are surely dialects that do not have double negation.

It is probably possible to distinguish several sets of forms that are preserved in dialects, but do not appear in the standard. A first set concerns forms like the English irregular verbs, where a large number of irregular past and past participle forms are preserved in the dialects (cf. Lass 1994 and Cheshire 1994). Obviously, what matters here is the very fact that only ONE form was nobilitated and accepted into the standard language – a fact typical of a principle that might be called 'no variation' (Milroy and Milroy 1993: 4), which is at the very heart of standardization. Beyond the very general operation of this principle, it is difficult to see why one form was selected and the respective others were not. There must be principles of selection at work which tell against one form and are in favour of another. The type of factor at work in this case was probably of a more linguistic nature, and less of an externally determined kind, as in the cases to be discussed in more detail below. For the sake of simplicity, let us call this type of factor an 'internal factor'.

When working on a comparison of DO and cognate Germanic forms like German TUN (Stein 1992), one of the striking features turned out to be the absence of aspectual forms in the standards, and their massive presence in the dialects. It is surely not possible to account for what must be called a systematic difference between the two varieties in several languages by any structural or 'internal' factors.

This example surely fulfils all methodological requirements that have to be stipulated for a case that would definitely point to a varieties-based explanation: the cases we have in mind to look at here are such that individual structural factors could be cited for each individual language, but the composite finding across languages makes it difficult to maintain that this was the decisive factor.

What is the reason for the absence of aspectual uses of DO and cognates? Why should aspectual uses be more undesirable in the WS? There is a connection between aspect and intensity which has been pointed out by Labov (1984); and the expressions of intensity, or subjective emotions, are banned from prototypical WS, a point that will have to be taken up in more detail later. In addition, it seems generally to be the case that the expression of aspect is evaluated as rather lowly, and tense a little higher. There may be a sense that from one of the functions of aspect – the expression of discourse grounding management, especially in narratives – the expression of aspect may be connotationally tied to orality in addition to being tied to mixed language varieties – all of which are not congenial to the decorum of essayist literacy (cf. below).

Milroy and Milroy (1985 and 1993) have made it clear that varieties have their ideologies, particularly in a situation like the one arising in the seventeenth and (particularly) eighteenth centuries, with a dichotomy arising between WS and dialect, part of which was the demotion of 'dialectal' from 'regional' to 'socially inferior'. For idealizational purposes, we will here behave as if there were only these two poles: spoken dialect and WS. Part of the ideology of WS was that it is the exponent of 'essayist literacy'. This is an ideal of a type of writing which aims to restrict writing to the expression of propositional meanings, at the expense of expressive-subjective elements. It is the type of writing that is taught in essay courses. The suppression of emotional meanings has effects also on the prescription of punctuation practices, such as the semicolon. Much of the prescriptive discussion of punctuation practices amounts to injunctions against oral or prosody-based punctuation, or rather overpunctuation.

It is clear that the rise of this stylistic ideal in the eighteenth century implied the evolution of linguistic means for expressing of propositional, and non-emotional types of meanings. It is largely coterminous with what the Prague school has termed 'intellectualization', and must have been an important force in fostering meaning changes in existing forms, as a typical case of change from above.

An important aspect of essayist literacy is that it is part of what might be called the self-consciousness of varieties: part of the decorum of that variety must have been that it should be different from the 'other', particularly the spoken language. This 'otherness', or intended distance from spoken language, is part of the self-awareness or ideology of the WS. It is the very same deliberate distance effect from the spoken or whatever is the 'normal' language that has been shown for the first major written 'high' English language in the sixteenth century. In Stein (1990) it was shown how the older *-eth* ending of the 3rd sing. present, which had more or less disappeared from the spoken language, was revivified to serve as a marker for high written style. This function of the old ending was only possible because it was audibly (or legibly, for that matter) different from the spoken ending *-s*.

Similarly, von Polenz (1993: 15) points to the restitution of a wordfinal *-e* as the mark of WS, as well as a marker of the distance from spoken language. What matters for WS is varietal distance. In any case, WS must be audibly and visibly different from the spoken language – it must be de-oralized: features that are reminiscent of or sound like oral, or are tied to functions that are performed in oral language, must go.

Section 3.3

It seems, then, that the reasons for the absence of dialectal and/or (very) colloquial forms from WS are of different types:

1. A general principle of standard languages: no variation. Within that principle, internal linguistic factors may be at work in determining choices, as in the case of English irregular verbs.
2. External principles determine the banning of types of forms NOT accepted into WS. These may be of two basic types:
    (a) An ideology of language based on presumed Latin models and its 'logic', as investigated in Leonard (1929/1962).
    (b) Factors derived from the ideology of essayist literacy, such as anti-orality.

If it seems possible to identify a finite number of principles that seem to account for more than one stigmatized structure, it is obviously also the case that some of these principles overlap, or are partially included in each other, or that the absence of a particular structure from the standard language can be accounted for by more than one factor.

A first group of examples may be used to identify the problem. Certain structures occurring in dialect and (very) colloquial language seem to have one characteristic in common:

> PRINCIPLE: *No double surface realization.*

The preferred structure is unique segmentalization (i.e. realization of content on the surface). This implies an injunction against 'doubling' structures, double marking or pleonastic structures. Doubling was considered an error, as in 'from whence', and 'from thence' (Leonard 1929/1962: 40). Pleonasm was discovered in plenty of places (Leonard 1929/1962: 190).

The unique segmentalization of propositional meanings lies at the heart of many injunctions against all kinds of expressions: propositional meaning elements must be expressed (cf. below, comment on zero-relatives), but must also not be expressed doubly, which would be 'illogical'. This is of course done in oral language, also for good 'functional' and emotional reasons.

The underlying reason for this principle was probably an undercurrent in eighteenth-century ideas about language (persisting in present-day folklore ideologies about language) that languages ought to be 'logical'. This takes many shapes, one of these being that there ought not to be double segmentalizations. Indeed, 'reason', 'analogy' and 'differentiation' were the ultimate court of appeal for deciding on the nobility or otherwise of forms (Leonard 1929/1962: ch. V, 59ff). Part of this was a 'one meaning–one word' ideology. This in turn is related to a *Verdinglichung* of words and meanings, such that one word is to represent one meaning only, and the other way round. In addition, the boundary between meanings and words must be clear and categorical. This aspect of the principle explains why punning falls from favour (De Grazia 1990).

This logical factor would account for the injunction against structures that seem to have the same referent, such as resumptive pronouns, pronominal copies such as 'why the disciplines being hungry pluck'd the Ears of Corn, it seems strange to us' (Thomas Browne) and the case of resumptive DO as in:

> These men, casting largess as they go of Definitions, Divisions, and Distinctions, with a scornful interrogative do soberly ask whether . . .
> (Sydney, 'Apology', line 378, taken from Stein 1990: 57)

Apart from the 'logic' reason not to have double segmentalization, resumptive structures are typical of oral language, which does not have the benefit of editability, or of preserving the sensory input, and which therefore is in need of more redundancy. In other words, the motivation could be called a

> PRINCIPLE: *Avoidance of perceived oral provenience.*

Other 'doubling' structures include: double relatives ('which that'), double negation and double modals ('she might could come').

Obviously, the two principles discussed up to now – no doubling as the 'logical' factor and the 'oral provenience' factor – would coalesce in banning these forms from WS.

TAMING THE VERNACULAR

Some of the doubling structures have subjective/emotional/expressive (henceforth simply 'emotional') meaning, a meaning element not congenial to 'essayist literacy':

PRINCIPLE: *Emotional meanings are dispreferred.*

Examples for expressions of this type of meaning would be found in such structures as:

for he had no liking not he to stage plays
I can't myself tell you
come you (imperative)

Reflexives generally have an element of intensity. In the case of the other doublings it can be pointed out that, generally, doubling is iconic of intensity. So it seems that for most of the structures more than one factor can be cited to account for the fact that the structure in question is not allowed in WS.

It is now possible to proceed in two possible orders: to list eligible structures one by one and give the type of factor that might be responsible for negatively connoting it for WS, or to give a – very finite – list of such factors and cite the structures to which it could apply. We will follow the first procedure, since explicit information on eighteenth-century prescriptive metacomment will be adduced for each structure.

Structures like the following present a specific challenge for the identification of exactly what causes them to be dispreferred in WS:

them books

Obviously, there are structures where it is difficult to figure out whether the dispreferred status is inherent in the very fact of non-concord (the Latin and logic factor Type 2a) and dialectality or to which extent the dative is a factor in its own right. A form like *her* as in *H'm! 'er's a bright spark* (D.H. Lawrence, *Sons and Lovers*, p. 126), besides showing 'wrong' congruence by having the dative form in subject position, is probably part of a wider dialectal tendency to use the dative in its case role as affected entity, and thereby in its subjective aspect. It would account for the frequent occurrence of datives in several shapes in dialects which are banned from WS, such as ethical datives. In other words, the common denominator would be, apart from the 'logic' factor, the emotionality aspect.

Certain kinds of segmentalizations seem dispreferred. Zero-relativization in subject position (as in *anyone doesn't turn in their paper in time gets failed*) is marginalized in English. In object position it is colloquial, certainly not WS. Ellipsis is dispreferred, since it is seen as a typical element of spoken language, also a sign of non-autonomy, and as such also reminiscent of oral language. Typically, spoken language is richer in non-verbalized context and thus needs less support from verbalized context. It is therefore less autonomous. Linguistic elements which are used in non-autonomous language therefore tend to be dispreferred.

Ellipsis is one of those elements where reference is secured by non-linguistic context, and therefore more prone to be used in non-autonomous language. All the structures in which meaning is not segmentalized could be subsumed under a

PRINCIPLE: *The unique segmentalization of propositional meanings.*

Discontinuous constituents – interrupted segmentalization – are dispreferred from a different point of view. Stranded prepositions (*a habit up with which I will not put*) and the split infinitive in English (*to thoroughly eat up*) are dispreferred for Type 2a reasons: they do not conform to the Latin-based idea of one uninterrupted word.

The brace construction seems universally dispreferred (German *ich habe ein Buch gekauft*; the formally identical English *I have a book bought* is causative, which the German structure is not). Internal and varietal reasons seem to conspire to make for its disappearance from English (Stockwell 1984). Gerritsen (1984) argues that it is dispreferred for varietal reasons, thereby pointing to a different type of reason for the dispreferred status of a number of structures:

PRINCIPLE: *Structures that are perceived as connected to language mixing tend to get stigmatised.*

This applies to both aspect and to analytical forms generally. It also applies to the so-called 'empty' uses of DO and Germanic cognates, since many of the uses do not carry propositional meaning, but intensity and discourse meaning. Generally, analytical forms are much more frequent in non-standard varieties ('the beauty of thee', D.H. Lawrence, *Sons and Lovers*). Apart from being different from the Latin synthetic model, analyticity is generally more strongly associated with contact – and therefore lowlier – varieties. The status of Yiddish as a non-standardized contact variety is a paradigm case, where many of the factors and linguistic phenomena discussed here flow together.

It is, however, not quite clear whether this factor – analyticity, contact variety and lowly status – is on a par with the other factors cited, since the effect of this factor sets in much earlier than the other factors. Still, it is a matter of external valuations that has an effect on whether variants are preferred or dispreferred in the standards.

Marked syntactic structures, such as preposings, inversions and dislocations are more associated with the vernacular, oral end of the varieties continuum. Historically, it makes sense to consider those structures as marked only once there is a grammaticalized XSVO word order. To a large extent, they receive their marked status and the additional meanings derived therefrom only through the character of these forms as marked.

dislocations: left/right:
this man he didn't have any money
ever on Saturday they come, the Jewish folk

preposings:
him John killed
to the man he gave the money

inversions:
through the roof fell a chair

All of these structures present topicalizations, and all of them – although to various degrees of intensity – have two additional meaning components, in addition to their propositional meanings: a discourse-structuring meaning and an emotional meaning (Dorgeloh 1997, Stein 1995). As a non-propositional, subjective, emotional meaning element it is uncongenial to the WS, and would be dispreferred under the heading of the principle of banning the expression of emotions. It is also dispreferred under another heading, related to orality (cf. below). Pawley and Syder point out that, in Italian, left dislocations are banned from WS to such a degree that they are totally ignored in grammatical description – a good case in point for the argument made in the introductory chapter to the present volume concerning the relationship between WS ideology and theoretical descriptions of 'the' language, and also a classical case in point for Ehlich's (1994: §4.8.) observation that the popular and folklore linguists' image of a particular language is invariably the written variety.

Raidt (1993: 291) calls locative structures in relatives and demonstratives 'a widespread phenomenon in non-standard patterns of several Germanic languages'. A system particularly rich in these directional and place deictic forms is Bavarian. They are often 'considered "colloquial" or even "vulgar"'.

which where
der wo
this here, that there (OED: dialectal and vulgar)
der da

Locatives are dispreferred because they evoke the concrete physical speech situation such as prevails in oral communication: they are perceived as non-autonomous language, i.e. of meaning saturation by non-verbal context.

> PRINCIPLE: *Non-autonomous elements are dispreferred.*

It may well be said that this principle is really a reflection of the 'orality' principle. This non-autonomy aspect of the 'oral provenance' factor is very intimately connected with, if not the same as, what has been termed the 'pragmatic mode' by Givón (1995), as opposed to the syntactic mode. WS would be the extreme version of the 'syntactic mode'.

Apart from the 'emotional' overtones of marked syntactic structures like dislocations, inversions and preposings, there is another aspect which would make for their dispreferred status in WS. Since they are part of 'natural sentencing' (Osgood and Bock 1977), they model the actual production of speech: what comes first to the mind comes first in the utterance, a natural production principle that applies to all topicalizations. To the extent that these marked syntactic structures are due to the operation of a principle of natural sentencing, they 'sound' or 'read' oral, and are dispreferred under this aspect too. Pawley and Syder (1983: 563f) point out further aspects that make the oral provenance of these structures visible: their function as floor-holding or seeking devices, or to buy encoding time.

For Pawley and Syder (1983, §1.3, 557ff), this aspect, following Kay (1977), of de-situatedness of WS is in fact the primary distinguishing parameter between dialect and vernacular on the one hand and WS on the other: the difference is between 'conversational language' and 'autonomous language' (557). Information that is non-verbally present must be segmentalized at the surface in more context-independent WS language. The effect of this is, among other things, the absence in WS of unspecific expressions. Combined with the tendency, noted earlier, of signifying only propositional meaning elements, it would account for the positive and negative constraints of segmentalization observed here.

Again, this factor probably coalesces with others in assigning dispreferred status. Thus, the double relativiser discussed above (*which that*) is dispreferred for a number of reasons, not only for its status as a 'doubling' structure, but also for its non-autonomous character.

Finally, tags express meanings that are associated with oral language. They invite or enlist the hearer's presence and participation in endorsing the propositional content expressed. Edwards and Weltens (1985) give a wide range of tags current in English dialects.

> PRINCIPLE: *Segmentalization of non-propositional meanings is dispreferred.*

These meanings are considered empty and useless. In fact, to the exclusion of aspectual – and grammaticalized – meanings they often do carry discourse-structuring meanings and act as ploys to move constituents into preferred information positions. To the latter extent they are indeed propositionally empty. In addition, like dislocations, they mirror the pragmatics of the production process and directly make reference to non-verbalized context. They thus directly address the pragmatics of oral communication. This oral provenance makes them additionally dispreferred.

The same applies, of course, to the particles in German and English, which have always been at the centre of legislation against oral elements in language.

Section 3.4

It would not be surprising if the linguistic debate in the eighteenth century took up the issues discussed here: Why are certain forms not good enough to be accepted into the WS? After all, it would be a reasonable assumption that the grammarians' comments would not be unrelated to the targeted characteristics of the WS, although their compass would be the much wider field of the standard language at large. The *loci classici* for this type of discourse is the *Dictionary of English Normative Grammar* (1991) (DENG) and Leonard (1929/1962).

Before looking at these, it is as well to point out that there is no necessary connection between explicit metacomment in the grammarians' writings and the operation of the factors discussed here. In other words, the fact that the grammarians do discuss a certain structure as 'inelegant' or similar can only be counted as supportive or ancillary evidence for the dispreferredness of a structure. Much less still can the predicates assigned to individual structures like 'inelegant' or 'improper' provide any clue to the factors effectively at work. On the other hand, the fact that a structure is NOT the subject of metacomment by the grammarians in no way implies that it is NOT dispreferred with respect to WS.

There are more cautions against overinterpreting the eighteenth-century grammarians' comments. The grammarians' activities as a metalinguistic, conscious, and in large part socially motivated folklore pursuit are very different in motivation and nature from the operation of the factors under discussion here, although their operation may to some extent be reflected in the grammarians' activities – hence the justification of including them here. But by and large it would probably have to be assumed that the selectional factors under discussion here, including those discussed by Pawley and Syder (1983), are unconscious in their operation and only indirectly reflected in overt normative discussion.

In addition, it is well known that the grammarians' metacomment is highly selective, as is the present-day normative discussion. For instance, one of the permanent foci of normative discussions are the modal auxiliaries, both in different modern languages and in the eighteenth century (Arnovick, Chapter 10 in this volume).

In DENG, the discussion of syntactic variants is predominantly represented in the chapter on 'Transposition' (414ff). However, while there is some comment on other structures, the main concern is adverb placement ('Adverbial positions are a major concern of the grammarians...', 416). As for the other structures discussed in this section, there is some comment, under the heading of 'deferment' (426ff), of discontinuous constituents as 'inelegant' or 'colloquial'. A preposed direct object is termed 'impro/inel', i.e. improper and inelegant (417). Left-dislocations are labelled 'brb/Fr/impro', i.e. barbarous, French, and improper (428). A preposed verb phrase (under the heading 'Reshuffle', 429) is labelled 'absd' (i.e. absurd). So there is some amount of indication that deviations from the canonical word order, especially to the extent that they are marked structures with 'emotional' effects, are indeed commented upon and classed as undesirable in view of WS.

Leonard's (1929/1962) work, the main exponent of work on Type 2a factors (the 'logical' type), also gives further indication that particles were considered 'vulgar'. Generally, he points to the neo-classical theories of style as inhibiting closeness to oral language (117), in particular the reflection of the production process and the pragmatics of it, and to the establishment of 'an elaborate critical apparatus for inhibiting expression' (117). The war on contractions (170ff) has to be seen as an exponent of the war against oral language, comparable to the war in Germany against the particles.

Section 3.5

While the earlier discussion was centred on how WS did not accept certain structures because of varietal conditions, it is worth considering the question of how the specific varietal conditions of the WS favoured the development of certain forms and meanings, which may or may not have arisen under the varietal conditions of a dialectal, non-written situation. The debate on whether literacy has in fact changed grammars (and minds) has a long-standing tradition (Olson 1994). Some of the adaptive developments in terms of more autonomous syntactic strategies have been elaborated by Pawley and Syder (1983). Here we will only point to a number of meaning developments that seem to be suggestive of a hypothesis to the effect that they may have been fostered by the conditions of WS.

Brinton (1994) points to the rise of a number of structures in the expression of perfectivity in English that arise between 1600 and 1800 and have in common the fact that they are all segmentalizations of propositional meanings. In addition, the development of DO in English, especially its grammaticalized meanings (question, negation, emphatic DO), represents a development that can be described in semantic terms as the marking of propositional/epistemic meanings.

For all of these developments it is possible to identify good syntactic reasons why and how they should have taken place. However, what they have in common cannot be overlooked: they all segmentalize propositional meanings, they all appear on the scene at a time when the effect and the functions of written language set in (between 1600 and 1800) and they are all developments that are part of, and are nobilitated as part of, the WS. Research in the effects of literacy on language (Olson 1994, Ong 1987) has long argued that written language is inclined to the

TAMING THE VERNACULAR

expression of epistemic meanings. These processes must be presumed to be independent of the uniformizational effect of writtenness, and also of socially motivated processes that took place in the eighteenth century.

The implication of the previous discussion was that most of the structures discussed above are part of 'the language', but not of the WS. The closer one gets to the more spoken, colloquial and, finally, dialectal end of the continuum, the more likely one is to encounter the forms discussed above. In terms of the discussion in the introductory chapter to this volume (Cheshire and Stein), the perceived discontinuity in the history was largely an artefact of linguistic historiography: the language that appeared in the written form (in WS!) and the language that was the subject of the description of the language, was closer to the WS end, and not to the dialectal end, of the continuum. In fact, the varietal suppression of the type of form described in section 3.3 was to a large extent also socially governed and included the branding of expressions as 'vulgar' and 'dialectal' (Berger 1978: 71ff). The label 'dialectal' eventually even came to acquire a non-local meaning, simply referring to forms that were not accepted into the higher status variety. The point to make here is that it is not possible to segregate the effects of written language decorum as described above from the effects of social valuations. The former were probably operative before the latter.

So there is an effect of 'suppression' of forms as 'dialectal', 'vulgar', or whatever the label may be – a process that took place in the seventeenth and eighteenth centuries. The interesting effect to observe is that a three-stage process has variously occurred: a primeval, pre-WS stage (stage 1), a stage of suppression (stage 2) and a later stage (stage 3) characterized by the re-emergence of certain forms suppressed in the second stage. Chafe (1984) describes three types of medial/varietal presence or absence of forms, which all have in common that seventeenth- and eighteenth-century prescriptivism has the effect of banning these structures from the written language, for reasons discussed in the previous sections.

As one type of example, Chafe (1984: 97) gives the absence of reference-constituting demonstratives in (oral) narrative in writing ('. . . and he saw these two foreigners', Chafe 1984: 97). During the prescriptive phase (stage 2) this use was banned from writing, whereas in present times it appears to be allowed back in the writing styles closer to colloquial spoken language. This feature is quite typical for a class of expressions that have been characterized as betraying their oral provenance since their semantics is tied to a non-autonomous use of language: this type of use of a demonstrative presupposes a visually present context in cognitive focus. Another example Chafe gives is the use of *will* for future reference, with *shall* as the 'correct' form, and with *will* now – in phase 3 – coming back full force after a period of varietal suppression. The suppression of the future use of *will* was probably due to a Type 2a factor. The injunctions against the split infinitive seem to be another case in point, also coming back in full force now in phase 3. The split infinitive would be dispreferred because of split constituency.

Another candidate for this type of pattern might well be so-called 'empty' uses of DO, which now seem to be getting back even into written language (*We do now land in San Francisco*). Further candidates for structures that seem to be increasingly gaining acceptance in WS are the following:

> zero subject relativiser: *anyone thinks he can do without linguistics will be hanged*, as part of a more general re-rise of zero relativization. (Bauer 1994: 73ff)
>
> the re-rise of *which* with human antecedents, as in *slapdash attitudes of some operators which break safety rules*. (Bauer 1994: 78ff)
>
> auxiliary inversion: *Thus does Mr. Karadzic provide* . . .

The point to notice here is that prescriptivism has the effect of banning forms from WS in an initial phase of its establishment. In phase 2, there is something like a 'liberalization' effect in that forms formerly banned are again allowed back into writing, much of which may well be the consequence of something like a re-oralization. It may well be the case that the relative re-oralization effect identified by Biber and Finegan (1989) is a reflection of the same phenomenon, i.e. the transition from stage 2 to stage 3.

So what could at first sight be interpreted as a case of a traditional linguistic change, i.e. the appearance of a new form in 'the language', is really a case of the varietal submergence of forms that are still in 'the language' – it is only that they do not appear in the variety that was taken to represent the language, the WS variety, in which all the written documents appear. So it should also be pointed out that the processes described here – varietally determined disappearance and re-emergence of forms – is a process distinctly different from the processes described in Brinton and Stein (1995), where genuine structural phenomena are described. They are also different in kind from the type of process described by Rickford (1992) like Black Vernacular English invariant *be*, where a process of convergence seems to be reversed in order to signal identity by means of a form that is visibly and audibly very different from the standard language, i.e. where this difference makes a difference in signalling social identity. In this type of case we have a reversal of a diachronic trend for purely social reasons, from which the varietally determined process described here is very different.

The question this chapter was trying to raise is just how much of what has formerly been described as syntactic development with individual or broader explanations may be due to external varietal factors. While it seems suggestive to identify a finite number of interrelated principles at work in causing the absence or presence of structures in

WS and dialects, much more work needs to be done to identify these structures in individual languages and to attribute to them the type of meaning or pragmatic function that would determine their positioning at one or other end of the contiuum. Obviously, the main operating area for these factors was the point at which WS arose and became established, i.e. the transition from stage 1 to stage 2. These forces are still operative in today's language, and especially in stylistic, educational and folklore ideals about language. But they are decreasing in force and effect as a result of processes of linguistic divergence, which in turn are the result of the linguistic marking of group or social identity.

References

Bauer, Laurie 1994. *Watching English Change*. London, New York: Longman.
Besnier, Niko 1988. The linguistic relationship of spoken and written Nukulaelae registers. *Language* 64: 707–36.
Berger, Dieter A. 1978. *Die Konversationskunst in England 1660–1740. Ein Sprechphänomen und seine literarische Gestaltung*. München: Fink.
Biber, Douglas and Finegan, Edward 1989. Drift and the evolution of English style: A history of three genres. *Language* 65: 487–517.
Brinton, Laurel J. 1994. The differentiation of statives and perfects in Early Modern English: The development of the conclusive perfect. In: Dieter Stein and Ingrid Tieken-Boom van Ostade (eds), pp. 135–70.
Brinton, Laurel J. and Stein, Dieter 1995. Functional renewal. In: Henning Andersen (ed.), *Historical Linguistics 1993. Selected Papers from the ICHL XI, Los Angeles, 16–20 August 1993*. Amsterdam: Benjamins, pp. 33–47.
Chafe, Wallace 1984. Speaking, writing and prescriptivism. In: Deborah Schiffrin (ed.), *Meaning, Form, and Use in Context: Linguistic Applications.* Washington: Georgetown University Press, pp. 95–104.
Cheshire, Jenny 1994. Standardization and the English irregular verbs. In: Dieter Stein and Ingrid Tieken-Boon van Ostade (eds), pp. 115–33.
Dorgeloh, Heidrun 1996. *Inversion in Modern English: Form and Function*. Amsterdam/Philadelphia: Benjamins.
Edwards, Viv and Weltens, Bert 1985. Research on non-standard dialects of British English: Progress and prospects. In: Wolfgang Viereck (ed.), *Focus on England and Wales*. Amsterdam: Benjamins, pp. 97–139.
Ehlich, Konrad 1994. Funktion und Struktur schriftlicher Kommunikation. In: Hartmut Günther and Otto Ludwig (eds), *Schrift und Schriftlichkeit. Writing and Its Use*. Berlin, New York: de Gruyter, pp. 18–41.
Gerritsen, Marinel 1984. Divergent word order developments in Germanic languages: A description and a tentative explanation. In: Jacek Fisiak (ed.), *Historical Syntax*. Berlin: Walter de Gruyter, pp. 107–37.

Gerritsen, Marinel and Stein, Dieter (eds) 1992. *Internal and External Factors in Syntactic Change.* Berlin: Mouton de Gruyter.

De Grazia, Margreta 1990. Homonyms before and after lexical standardization. *Deutsche Shakespeare Gesellschaft West. Jahrbuch.* Bochum, pp. 143–56.

Givón, Talmy 1995. *Functionalism and Grammar.* Amsterdam: Benjamins.

Kay, Paul 1977. Language evolution and speech style. In: Ben G. Blount and Mary Sanches (eds), *Sociocultural Dimensions of Language Use.* New York: Academic Press, pp. 21–33.

Koch, Peter and Oesterreicher, Wulf 1990. *Gesprochene Sprache in der Romania: Französisch, Italienisch, Spanisch.* Tübingen: Niemeyer.

Labov, William 1984. Intensity. In: Deborah Schiffrin (ed.), *Meaning, Form, and Use in Context: Linguistic Applications.* Washington: Georgetown University Press, pp. 43–71.

Lass, Roger 1994. Proliferation and option-cutting: The strong verb in the fifteenth to eighteenth centuries. In: Dieter Stein and Ingrid Tieken-Boon van Ostade (eds), pp. 81–113.

Leonard, Sterling A. 1929/1962. *The Doctrine of Correctness in English Usage, 1700–1800.* Madison: University of Wisconsin. Reissued 1962, New York: Russell & Russell.

Milroy, James 1992. A social model for the interpretation of language change. In: Matti Rissanen, Ossi Ihalainen, Terttu Nevalainen, and Irma Taaitsainen (eds), *History of Englishes. New methods and interpretations in historical linguistics.* Berlin, New York: Mouton de Gruyter.

Milroy, James and Milroy, Lesley 1985. *Authority in Language. Investigating language prescription and standardization.* London: Routledge.

Milroy, James and Milroy, Leslie (eds) 1993. *Real English: The grammar of English dialects on the British Isles.* London: Longman.

Nevalainen, Terttu and Raumolin-Brunberg, Helena 1994. Its strength and the beauty of it: The standardization of the third person neuter possessive in Early Modern English. In: Dieter Stein and Ingrid Tieken-Boon van Ostade (eds), pp. 171–216.

Olson, David R. 1994. *The World on Paper: The conceptual and cognitive implications of writing and reading.* Cambridge: Cambridge University Press.

Ong, Walter J. 1987. *Orality and Literacy: The Technologizing of the World.* London: Methuen.

Osgood, Charles E. and Bock, J. Kathryn 1977. Salience and sentencing: Some production principles. In: Sheldon Rosenberg (ed.), *Sentence Production. Developments in Research and Theory.* Hillsdale, N.J.: Erlbaum.

Pawley, Andrew and Syder, Frances H. 1983. Natural selection in syntax: Notes on adaptive variation and change in vernacular and literary grammar. *Journal of Pragmatics* 7: 551–79.

Polenz, Peter von 1993. Sprachsystemwandel und soziopragmatische

Sprachgeschichte in der Sprachkultivierungsepoche. In: Andreas Gardt, Klaus J. Mattheier and Oskar Reichmann (eds), *Sprachgeschichte des Neuhochdeutschen, Gegenstände, Methoden, Theorien*. Tübingen: Niemeyer, pp. 39–67.

Raidt, Edith H. 1993. Linguistic variants and language change: Deictic variants in some German and Dutch dialects *vis-à-vis* Afrikaans. In: Jaap van Marle (ed.), *Historical linguistics 1991: Papers from the 19th International Conference on Historical Linguistics, Amsterdam, 12–16 August 1991*. Amsterdam: Benjamins, pp. 281–93.

Rickford, John R. 1992. Grammatical variation and divergence in Vernacular Black English. In: Marinel Gerritsen and Dieter Stein (eds), pp. 175–200.

Stein, Dieter 1990. Functional differentiation in the emerging English Standard Language: The evolution of a morphological discourse and style marker. In: Henning Andersen and Konrad Koerner (eds), *Historical Linguistics 1987: Papers from the 8th International Conference on Historical Linguistics (Lille, 31 August–4 September 1987)*. Amsterdam: Benjamins, pp. 489–98.

Stein, Dieter 1992. *Do* and *tun*: A semantics and varieties based approach to syntactic change. In: Marinel Gerritsen and Dieter Stein (eds), *Internal and External Factors in Syntactic Change*. Berlin: Mouton de Gruyter, pp. 131–57.

Stein, Dieter 1994. Sorting out the variants: Standardization and social factors in the English language 1600–1800. In: Dieter Stein and Ingrid Tieken-Boon van Ostade (eds), pp. 1–17.

Stein, Dieter 1995. Subjective meanings and the history of inversions in English. In: Dieter Stein and Susan Wright, *Subjectivity and Subjectivisation. Linguistic Perspectives*. Cambridge: CUP, pp. 129–51.

Stein, Dieter and Tieken-Boon van Ostade, Ingrid (eds) 1994. *Towards a Standard English 1600–1800*. Berlin: Mouton de Gruyter.

Stockwell, Robert P. 1984. On the history of the verb-second rule in English. In: Jacek Fisiak (ed.), *Historical Syntax*. Berlin: Walter de Gruyter, pp. 575–92.

Sundby, Bertil, Bjorge, Anne Kari and Haugland, Kari E. 1991. *A Dictionary of English Normative Grammar 1700–1800* (Studies in the History of the Language Sciences, 63). Amsterdam: Benjamins.

CHAPTER 4

Into and out of the standard language: the particle *ni* in Finnish

Maria Vilkuna

4.1 Introduction

When a written standard is developed for a language, it is typical that some structures present in the pre-standard varieties are not taken over into the standard language and that their use eventually becomes stigmatized. The case described in this chapter shows a slightly different development. When the modern standard for written Finnish was being established (see Laitinen, this volume), the practice of using *niin*, 'so', in clause combination was taken over, but later the convention became perceived as unsuitable in written usage and was fairly effectively pruned. It is hard to say exactly how and why this was achieved, as explicit statements are not found in the literature in spite of a general consensus that the form is undesirable in writing. This chapter concentrates on the character of the phenomenon and its intrinsic connection to the unplanned spoken mode.

The particle *niin* is extremely frequent in Finnish and has several uses which are not relevant in the present context, often corresponding to the English word *so*. Example (1) illustrates both the construction to be discussed (in (1a), (1b)) and an irrelevant instance (in (1c)). In order to save space and to make the structure under discussion as transparent as possible, example translations appear in pseudo-English, rather than as morphological glosses plus idiomatic translation. *Ni* is glossed as boldfaced **ni**. The clause or other preceding sequence that *ni* relates to is italicized both in the example and its translation. The translations preserve original pauses: a comma for a short pause without final intonation and a period for a final pause.

(1) a. ja mun äitini sano sitt et nytt ei täst tuum mitään että, *kun nää kurssit mennee näim pikään* **niin**, mm, te saatte nyl lopettaa
'and my mother said then that this won't do anymore *because these classes take so long* **ni**, mm, you'll have to stop going now'
b. ja *sit ku tulee rauha* **niin** kyl te sitt opitte tanssimaa [nauraen] ilman kurssejaki,

and *when peace comes* **ni** sure you will then learn to dance [laughs] even without classes
c. ja **niinhäm** me sit opittiinki. (HKI)[1]
and so-clitic we then learnt-too
'and so we did then'

Niin in (1a) and (1b) combines a *kun*, 'when, because', clause and its governing clause. Several criteria can be used to distinguish between this type of *niin* and the other uses of the word: the latter are accentable and can be modified by words such as 'quite'; they can bear sentential clitics such as *-hAn* in (1c), and they occur after conjunctions such as *ja*, 'and'. The type of *niin* discussed in this chapter is destressed, non-modifiable, and does not host sentential clitics. Furthermore, it does not occur after coordinators because it seems to be a clause-combining element itself. *Niin* is also used in conversation as a minimal feedback item indicating agreement (Sorjonen 1996). Although some aspects of this use are clearly relevant for a full picture of the construction discussed here, the issue is beyond the scope of the present chapter.

Following Ekerot (1988), I will refer to the construction under discussion as the 'so' construction or, to use the Finnish word, the *ni* construction. *Ni* is an allusion to the frequent reduced form of the particle; other reduced variants are *nin* and *nii*. As Sirelius (1894: 132) observed, the particle is more readily reduced in the 'so' construction than in its other functions.

The clause-combining *ni* is, according to my experience, perfectly regular and grammaticalized in all varieties of spontaneous spoken Finnish, although *ni* may be omitted in formal situations such as public statements by politicians and officials who are used to a planned speech mode. Intonationally, *ni* in these cases tends to cliticize to the previous clause, but a pattern where *ni* occurs after a short pause together with the second clause is not uncommon. Repeated instances also occur, with the first *ni* cliticized to the subordinate clause, the second looking more like a hesitation marker.

The clauses followed by *ni* typically belong to the so-called adverbial clauses, as complement clauses are unlikely to appear in the relevant position (however, see example (8) below). In traditional terminology, the first of the clauses combined by *ni* is a subordinate clause modifying the second, its governing clause. In this chapter, the two clauses will be simply called Clause 1 and Clause 2, as I will not be interested in postponed subordinate clauses. It is enough to think of Clause 1 as containing a forward-looking marker of clause-combination (that is, a conjunction) that creates an expectation for another clause to which it bears the appropriate temporal, causal or conditional relation.

The *ni* construction is met in a much wider variety of contexts than clause combining, although treatments of standard Finnish generally mention only this use. This chapter starts with a survey of the use of clause-combining *ni* in written Finnish and briefly explores its treatment in prescriptive Finnish grammar. The second part of the paper presents a fuller picture of the *ni* construction and treats *ni* as a continuation marker used in contexts of a heavy planning load in spontaneous conversation.

4.2 Clause-combining *ni* in written Finnish

4.2.1 'So' in Germanic and Finnish

Så, 'so', abounds in present-day Swedish, especially in colloquial varieties, as discussed by Ekerot in a comprehensive study of the construction (1988). The clause-combining use illustrated in (2a) is fairly common in written language as well, but 'so' following an initial adverbial, as in (2b), is more frequent in speech.

(2) a. Om vädret tillåter **så** genomföres övningen.
If weather permits **so** is-carried-out training.
b. På måndag **så** reser vi till Köpenhamn.
On Monday **so** travel we to Copenhagen.

The 'so' construction occurs in all Scandinavian languages except Icelandic. It is also found in German, although a more common pattern uses *dann* 'then'; compare (3a) and (3b):

(3) a. Wenn du morgen Zeit hast, **so** können wir ins Theater gehen.
b. Wenn du morgen Zeit hast, **dann** können wir ins Theater gehen.
'If you have time tomorrow, so ~ then we can go to the Theatre.'

According to Ekerot, Swedish grammarians have had trouble keeping the 'so' construction separate from doubling, a dislocation construction where Clause 1 is detached from Clause 2 and represented by a pronominal copy inside the latter. An example of such a doubling pattern is (3b). Thus, Swedish grammarians have considered the equivalent of the 'so' construction in (3a) as identical to the equivalent of (3b), with Swedish *då* as the pronominal copy.

The 'so' and doubling constructions are obviously functionally intertwined. However, it is easy to show, for both Swedish and Finnish, that the two are different. First, the doubling pronominal can be placed in any position where such a pronominal can independently occur, while 'so' is confined to the initial position. Second, doubling and 'so' can co-occur. This can be seen in (1b), repeated below, where the doubling element *sit(t)*, 'then', occurs in a sentence-medial position.

(1) b. ja *sit ku tulee rauha* **niin** kyl te *sitt* opitte tanssimaa ilman kurssejaki
and *then when comes peace* **ni** sure you *then* learn to-dance without classes-even

Instances of doubling together with *ni* can be found in many of the examples below: (5)–(9) and (17). The doubling pronominal will be italicized.

Ekerot (1988) treats the 'so' construction as an order-related phenomenon which has its most important functional motivation in the obligatory inversion caused by the Germanic verb-second (henceforth, V2) word order of declarative main clauses. Due to this rule, the systematic relation of word order and sentence type – V2 declarative versus V1 yes/no question – is overruled in cases with preposed subordinate clauses. To use standard GB terminology, we might see 'so' as an expletive Spec-CP filler (see Holmberg 1986: 113–18 for a generative description). The functional motivation for 'so' is especially strong in the inverted conditionals analogous to the English *Had I seen it* . . . , and with loosely integrated elements such as speech act adverbials and many types of adverbial clauses, which *så* handily marks as belonging to the subsequent clause. Ekerot also emphasizes the role of the 'so' construction as a continuation signal in spoken language.

Ekerot (1988: 271) observes that an analogous construction exists in Finnish, but predicts that it must be a marginal phenomenon given that the functional motivation, the obligatory V2 pattern, is missing. But the construction is far from marginal, and although its use differs from its Swedish counterpart, especially with NPs and initial adverbials, the clause-combining use seems to follow similar lines. The question obviously arises whether *ni* should be treated as a straightforward instance of Swedish influence. I am not in a position to answer this question. However, it is clear that the influence would not be new or superficial; *ni* is not restricted to dialects in contact with Swedish-speaking areas, and samples of Eastern dialects (exemplified by (7) below) seem to show the same distribution of *ni*, as does present-day Helsinki speech.

4.2.2 Ni *in written Finnish*

Of the various uses of *ni* to be introduced in section 4.3, only the clause-combining use seems to occur in present-day public written Finnish with any frequency, and even this type of *ni* is strongly disfavoured. However, professional writers seem to be aware of *ni* as a spoken language phenomenon, and newspapers occasionally use *ni* in direct quotes. I surveyed the central clause combinations in some present-day text corpora[2]: the 1987 issues of the weekly political and cultural magazine *Suomen Kuvalehti* (abbreviated to SK87 below); a collection of short stories by Eila Pennanen; and a detective novel by Matti-Yrjänä Joensuu. The results are given in Table 4.1; in the Pennanen and Joensuu texts, only the two most frequent subordinators occurred often enough to be compared.

The total percentages of *ni* compared with its absence were 68 vs 32 per cent for Joensuu, 86 vs 14 per cent for Pennanen, and 91 vs 9 per cent

Table 4.1: The frequency of *ni* following a preposed subordinate clause in present-day written Finnish.

	Without *ni*		With *ni*		Total
jos 'if'					
Joensuu	21	52.5%	19	47.5%	40
Pennanen	45	72.6%	17	27.4%	62
SK87	1427	85.4%	244	14.6%	1671
Kun 'when, because'					
Joensuu	34	82.9%	7	17.1%	41
Pennanen	96	94.1%	6	5.9%	102
SK87	2030	94.6%	116	5.4%	2146
vaikka 'although'					
SK87	406	95.1%	21	4.9%	427
koska 'because'					
SK87	170	97.7%	4	2.3%	174

for SK87. The high percentage of *ni* use in the detective novel is probably due to the large proportion of dialogue it contains, but individual preferences may be involved as well. Some features of Clause 2 structure can be observed to act in favour of *ni*: ellipsis (minimally, absence of verb), imperative mood, interrogative form, and marked word order.

All through the data, only 'if' clauses can be said to favour *ni* to any degree. This may be due to partial lexicalization, as conditionals are typically characterized as 'if–so' relationships in Finnish. Moreover, conditionals also favour *så* in Swedish (Ekerot 1988: 44–5). With the exception of conditionals, *ni* is thus quite infrequent in written language, especially if compared to its practically obligatory presence in spoken language.

4.2.3 Authorities

The most influential Finnish grammar was written by E.N. Setälä in the late nineteenth century (see Laitinen, this volume). Revised editions of Setälä's grammar were used at Finnish universities as late as the 1970s. Setälä's first editions present clause-combining *ni* as a legitimate item (e.g. 1880: 51–2), and the same can be found in the most recent edition (1973: 133–6). Setälä's description was based on common usage, as can be concluded from the four syntactic surveys of regional varieties written shortly after the first editions of the standard grammar: Setälä (1883), Sirelius (1894), Latvala (1899), Kannisto (1901). These all mention the *ni* construction, Setälä and Kannisto pointing out that it is optional. It therefore appears that the use of *ni* was thriving at the end of the nineteenth century and was not due to superficial Swedish influence on the written form, unlike so many other phenomena at the time.

People involved in teaching or language guidance typically think of *ni* as belonging to spoken language, pruning occurrences deemed as 'excessive'. However, explicit statements of the norm obeyed here are not easy to find. This contrasts with the Swedish situation, where attempts to regulate the use of *så* go back at least to the early eighteenth century (Ekerot 1988: 35–6).

For example, the first and foremost authority on 'good' Finnish usage of the first half of the present century, Saarimaa, does not comment on *ni* in his first usage guide (1930). Later, Saarimaa (1941 and 1943) explicitly warns against *ni* in one special case, namely when the clause combination is embedded under a higher clause. This is repeated in the usage guide of 1947 (p. 188) but was omitted from its later editions, as it was shown by Ikola (1951) to have been based on a faulty syntactic analysis. Saarimaa's response to Ikola (1951) admits that his earlier claim was too strong, but warns against *ni* in the embedded construction in concise, compact, and especially elevated style, 'as it has a slackening effect'. His rejoinder contains no direct statement against the *ni* construction; it is common in spoken language but 'should not be condemned in higher styles either'. However, general opinion against the *ni* construction seems to have been up in the air at the time, judging from the fact that Kettunen, a famous advocate of 'free' usage in his time, considers it necessary to defend *ni* (1949: 173–4).

Another negative statement can be found in a later style guide (Rainio 1968: 97). When discussing the stylistic virtue of compactness, Rainio says in passing that *ni* between clauses 'appears clumsy'. Other similar works – grammar books for schools and composition guides – remain remarkably silent on the issue of *ni*. The authoritative Modern Finnish Dictionary from the 1960s presents clause-combining *ni* with several examples, characterizes one subtype as belonging to spoken language, and mentions that it can be omitted. The attitude of present-day prescriptivists will be discussed at the end of the next section.

4.2.4 Ni *and* V2

The situation is slightly different in older prose. Recall that four authors, Setälä, Sirelius, Latvala and Kannisto, published monographs on dialect syntax in the late nineteenth century, discussing *ni*. It is therefore of some interest to look at the usage of these scholars themselves. This appears to conform to the general picture of the time: clause combinations are, with few exceptions, rendered with either inversion (V2) in Clause 2 or *ni* without V2. That is, the structures opted for are those in

Table 4.2: Clauses following a preposed subordinate clause in Lizelius (1775–6).

	ni only	*ni*+V2	V2 only	Total
että 'because'	1	5	4	10
jos 'if'	16	15	4	35
koska 'when'	3	3	6	12
kuin 'when'	7	4	21	32
sittekuin 'after'	1	6	10	17

(4); the present-day Finnish variant without either *ni* or inversion seems to be absent.

(4) a. *Kun subjektina on yksiköllinen kollektiivisana, ( )* **seuraa** *sitä predikaatti joskus monikollisena.* (Sirelius 1894: 45)
 'When the subject is a singular collective word, ( ) follows it [object] the predicate sometimes in plural.'
 b. *Kun subjekti on sulkeutuneena predikaattiin,* **niin** *predikaatti yleisimmin on monikossa.* (Kannisto 1901: 9)
 'When the subject is incorporated into the predicate, **ni** the predicate mostly is in plural.'

Once again, conditionals seem to resort to *ni* as a norm; on the basis of a cursory examination, this practice is exclusive in Setälä (1883).

This picture is similar to that from a century earlier, with one difference. The first Finnish newspaper *Suomenkieliset Tieto-Sanomat*, published in 1775–6 by Antti Lizelius, shows the frequencies cited in Table 4.2.[3] (The conjunctions used by Lizelius differ in meaning from their present-day uses.)

Lizelius uses *ni* more than present-day authors, and appears to differ from his successors 100 years later in freely allowing the particle with inverted Clause 2 (*ni + V2*), i.e. using the normal Swedish pattern. Again, conditionals favour the particle.

In Finnish, a subject often occurs after the finite verb, e.g. in order to conform to the 'old before new' principle (see Vilkuna 1989). Germanic V2-type post-verbal subjects can be identified on the basis of the lack of such a pragmatic motivation. The *ni* construction seems to become complementary with V2 in the nineteenth century. Contrary to the authorities' attitude to *ni*, opposing V2 inversion has been one of the favourite topics of Finnish prescriptivists. Their attempts were successful: word orders that can be characterized as V2-modelled are infrequent in present-day writing, and in the second half of the present century, certain scholars have considered it necessary to warn against the other extreme. However, V2-type inversion is still occasionally found in Clause 2. It is natural to suggest that the avoidance of clause-combining *ni* might have something to do with the gradually diminishing role of V2 in written Finnish, but the exact connections need to be clarified.

In general, modern opinion considers *ni* and V2 inversion as complementary strategies of clause boundary marking. This generalization was to my knowledge first mentioned by Kettunen (1949: 173–4). Ikola (1977: 161–3) recommends moderate use of inversion in Clause 2, especially with the negative auxiliary and, judging from his examples, auxiliary verbs in general. *Ni*, he says (p. 161), 'makes the transition from the subordinate clause to the governing clause more natural, less clumsy'. Itkonen (1982: 91–2) offers similar recommendations of inversion: only a short destressed subject should precede the verb in Clause 2. As for *ni*, Itkonen (1982: 273) mentions its connection to spoken language and, again, recommends it in writing if Clause 2 does not begin with a verb and the clause boundary is unclear.

Present-day authorities thus seem to set great weight on clause-boundary disambiguation either by *ni* or by a ('light') finite verb. In addition, the use of a comma following Clause 2 is required, if not always obeyed. In an SVO language with flexible word order, such as Finnish, marking the transition between Clause 1 and Clause 2 is obviously important from the point of view of processing, as there may be a number of consecutive nominal phrases that must each be attached to its appropriate verb. In principle, either *ni* or initial placement of the finite verb could be made obligatory to achieve this goal. Spoken Finnish uses *ni*; the recommended moderate use of V2 described in the modern prescriptive treatments is clearly a written-language phenomenon.

On the other hand, the clauses are (ideally) separated by a comma, and context is a powerful disambiguator. *Ni* may therefore be considered redundant, a vice often condemned by prescriptivists. This is obvious in the Swedish tradition, which has long been committed to restricting the use of the 'so' construction to occasions in which it 'has a function' (Ekerot 1988: 35–6). For Finnish, Kettunen (1949: 173–4) points out two contrary pressures: the apparent redundancy of *ni* ('and we all know that redundancy should be avoided') and the 'stiffness of style' resulting from the absence of *ni*. The expressions 'slack' or 'clumsy' by Saarimaa and Rainio, mentioned in the previous section, may also refer to redundancy.

In written language, then, clause-boundary marking devices such as *ni* may be seen as simple disambiguators. Turning now to the use of *ni* in spoken language we shall see that *ni* has further functions.

4.3 The larger picture: *ni* as a continuation marker

It seems to me that investigating elements such as *ni* will shed some light on how performance forms grammar. In particular, spontaneous

THE PARTICLE *NI* IN FINNISH

conversation, which does not allow for post-editing in the sense that writing does, is likely to reveal something about online processing of linguistic structures. This section is an overview of the Finnish *ni* construction and its role as a continuation marker in spontaneous spoken language, typically utilized to mark smooth progress in contexts of complexity or 'syntactic weight' (Hawkins 1994; note that explicit clause boundary indication as discussed in 4.2.4 is in accordance with the view proposed by Hawkins). We will see that the clause-combining *ni* construction is a special case of this general picture.

4.3.1 Nominal phrases

Hawkins' Early Immediate Constituents Principle predicts that Finnish should postpone heavy phrases such as complex NPs. In written texts, quite extreme examples with complex subject phrases occur (Vilkuna 1991), but spoken language prefers clause extraposition as in (5a) and (5b):

(5)   a. **se** on kummallista että Mikko jäi kiinni
         it is odd that Mikko got caught
      b. **se** jäi kuka ensimmäiseks joutu kiinni
         it [= (s)he] stayed who first got caught

Another option is to use *ni*, as in (5c) and further in (6)–(8). The complex construction is left-detached, typically, but not necessarily with doubling, and *ni* appears at the boundary of the detached element.

(5)   c. se että Mikko jäi kiinni **ni** *se* on kummallista
         it that Mikko got caught **ni** *it* is odd

(6)   [Interviewer: How would you choose the seeker in a hide-and-seek game?]
      EK: nii siin oli, kaikki vapaaehtosest *kuka halus jäädän* **ni** *s(e) ne* jäi sitte, sit *se kuka ensimmäiseks joutu kiinni* **ni** *se* jäi. (HKI)
      'EK: yes everyone was there voluntarily *whoever wanted to stay* **ni** *(s)he* stayed then, then *the-one who was first caught* **ni** *(s)he* stayed.'

Example (7) illustrates two typical *ni* contexts. The first *ni* follows a complex NP with a relative clause, and the second is a clause-combining *ni* with doubling.

(7)   AR: [I have heard a bear can be aggressive towards people.]
      LN: em minä tiijäm mitä, eihän nuo sanonut, sehän tuo *se sohvi josta minä tuolla jo puhuj joka on kymmentä vuotta vanahempi joka on tuolla kunnalliskoessa* **nin** sehän tuo sano nij jotta, ei se muullo ihmisellet tahot tehäp pahhoo van *sillon kun sillä on syksyllä kiluaeka* **nin** *sillon* se eij oot tapataattu. (et)tä se tulloo ihmisem peälle.
      (Räisänen 1987: 10; accentuation marking omitted.)

'I don't know, they didn't say, but [it was] *she that Sohvi* [woman's name] *I already told you about who is ten years older who is in the nursing home* **ni** [it was] *she* [who] said that it does not tend to hurt people at other times but *when it has rutting time in the autumm* **ni** *then* it is not guaranteed to behave itself. that it will attack people.'

In (8) we first find a left detachment with a copy but without *ni*, showing that *ni* is not obligatory in these contexts. In the *ni* example, a complement clause headed by the pronoun *se* 'it' is detached and doubled:

(8)   Katri teki sen erinomasesti ja, mä uskosin että *toi laulukin, se* on melkeen ku osa Katria itseänsä, eli, siin istuu kaikki osat kohdalleen. *se että se nyt on vähän pilvissä liikkuva teksti, tavallaan,* **niin**, *se* taas ehkä johtuu siitä että mulle itselleni tekstittäjänä aina sillon tällön tulee tämmösiä, vapauden kaipuukohtauksia, –
(Pop-song lyrics writer interviewed in TV, 1993)

'Katri [singer] did it [song] excellently and, I believe that *the song too, it*'s almost like a part of Katri herself, that is, everything is in its place. [the fact] *that it is a text that is up in the clouds, sort of,* **ni** *that* is maybe because I myself as a writer now and then get these, attacks of longing for freedom, –'

A natural conclusion from the above patterns of heavy NP detachment is that their syntax is the same as that of the clause-combining *ni* constructions discussed in the previous section. In both patterns, the heavy constituent – adverbial clause, NP, or complement clause – is outside the governing clause, and *ni* signals that there is a connection between the two parts. It is natural that doubling pronouns are more frequent (although not strictly obligatory) with detached argument NPs than with adverbial clauses.

If only NPs with clausal modifiers were to undergo left detachment with *ni*, it would be easy to dismiss *ni* as a mere clause boundary marker. This is not the case, however; both argument and adjunct NPs and PPs occur with *ni* and doubling, although adjunct instances such as those in (9) are clearly more common.

(9)   ja lumlie-, -linnoja sitte kiireestir rakentamaaj ja, lumilyhtyjä mut *silloj jouluna* **ni** ei tulluk kysymykseenkää et tälläistä ois tehtyk kun, lunta oli satanuj jouluaaton, ja joulun-, *sinä yönä sitte, joulupäivää vastenn yöllä* **ni** ei *sillom* päässyk kirkkoonkaa sitten ku sai niin kahlata, – (HKI)

'and [all children went] quickly to build snowcastles and, snow lanterns but *then at Christmas* **ni** it was out of the question that such things should have been done when, the snow had been falling all through Christmas eve, and Christmas-, *that night then, the night before Christmas* **ni** *then* you couldn't even go to church [as there was so much snow].'

It remains to be found out whether instances like this are motivated by syntactic weight, as suggested for Finland Swedish by Ivars (1993). Saukkonen (1972: 21), in one of the earliest serious attempts to characterize syntactic differences between spoken and written Finnish, suggests that the 'filler word' *niin* may have a function in breaking up long syntactic sequences, especially when their referents are first mentioned. Saukkonen discusses a test where people had to tell the same story orally and in writing, and his subjects made frequent use of sentence-medial *ni*. As Saukkonen says, *ni* in (10a) (my numbering) may be considered to be isolating a heavy unit; (10b) demonstrates another mechanism for the same purpose. A written composition would obviously produce (10c).

(10) a. *Yksi 90-vuotias mies* **niin**, *ajoi parkkeerauspaikalle.*
 one 90-year-old man **ni** drove to the parking-lot.
 b. **Oli** *yksi 90-vuotias mies* **joka** *ajoi parkkeerauspaikalle.*
 was one 90-year-old man **who** drove to-the-parking-lot.
 c. *Eräs 90-vuotias mies ajoi parkkeerauspaikalle.*
 One 90-year-old man drove to-the-parking-lot.
 (Adapted from Saukkonen 1972)

A similar line of thinking is now familiar from studies on so-called 'preferred argument structure': lexical argument phrases only appear one per clause in spontaneous discourse (e.g. Du Bois 1987).

4.3.2 Textual satellites

Ni may also connect two main clauses in Finnish. Some of the relevant cases are unquestionably accepted as standard and are also familiar from Germanic languages:

(11) *Auta minua* **niin** *minä autan sinua.*
 help me so I help you.

Occurrences of *ni* such as (12) could be taken to represent the same relation:

(12) *mä, menin siit aidan yli sitte meijän, omaam pihaan* **ni**, *ne oli kaikki ovett oli auki, ja, ikkunatt oli, kappaleina, mutta ei ollu missää tulta eikä tulipaloo eikä ollu mitää, ja tuota, sit ku mä tulin, meil oli vaan kaks huonetta semme keittiö ja kamari nin ku sanottii mä tulin keittiöö* **ni**, *kaikki astiat oli lattialla huja hajaj ja, ja tot- st mä meni sinnek kammariin* **ni**, *isävai-* [naurahtaa] *isävainaa nukku siil lattialla –* (HKI)

'*I climbed over the fence to our, own yard* **ni**, all the doors were open, and, the windows were, in pieces, but there was no fire anywhere or anything, and well, then *when I came, we only had two rooms a kitchen and a chamber like we used to say I came into the kitchen* **ni**, all the crockery was on the floor all over the place and, and well- *then I went to the chamber* **ni** my late fath- [laughs] my late father was asleep on the floor –'

My conclusion, however, is that linking two clauses with *ni*, without an explicit subordinator, creates a textual relationship in which the first clause is subordinated in a pragmatic sense. The first clause acts as background material, and the second clause is part of the main storyline. To use Matthiessen and Thompson's (1988) terminology, this way of linking results in the interpretation of the first part as a satellite of the second. In other words, *ni* marks transitions from digressions to the main storyline. This conclusion is partly motivated by the fact that 'Clause 1' need not be one clause. As shown in (13), *ni* may relate to a longer segment of preceding discourse. The example illustrates a situation typical of narration: the speaker introduces the characters of the story before proceeding into the plot. The structure of the narration has been clarified here by indentation:

(13) – ja, sitte, mä muistan
    yks, (Ihol) Lasse hänki on kuollu jo oli Viipurim poikia asu siin naapuri, talossa sit joutui tuli tännen niin ku ku se, Viipuri luovutettiin, asu siim Pasilas kanssa **ni**,
mä tuli yks päivä skolasta **ni**
se sit tuli, tuli siihe sano et hei Pena että, et hänel o hyvä pisnes et, ratapihal on, on tota, ö tommone, koko, tavaravaunu, juna, täys lanttuja, et mennää illalla pöllimää. (HKI)

'– and, then, I remember
    one Lasse Iho he's dead already too was a guy from Viborg lived there next, door then ended up came here when, Viborg was given over, lived there in Pasila also **ni**
I came from school one day **ni**
he came, came there said that hey Pena, that he's got a good business that, there's, there's, well, a whole, wagon, train, full of turnips, that lets go lift them at night.'

In (13), the important memory that the speaker is about to reveal when he says 'I remember' is not the personal history of his friend Lasse but the raiding of the train wagon by him and Lasse. However, Lasse as the instigator of the raid has to be introduced, and this introduction is terminated by *ni*. Note also the second occurrence, which can be analysed as implicit temporal subordination of the type just discussed, but which belongs to the scene-setting part of the story as well.

Example (7) above can also be seen from this perspective. Although formally a detached complex NP, the section preceding the first *ni* instance is an introductory detour. The main storyline is the behaviour of bears, but the speaker chooses to specify the source information and identify this person with an earlier mention in the discourse. This kind of introductory segment is therefore a side sequence, and the return is marked by *ni* – irrespective of the syntax of the detour.

4.3.3 Interactive construction of ni

Continuation with *ni* may also be interactive. It is not uncommon in everyday discourse that a topic is introduced by one speaker using an adverbial clause or a complex NP and the expected *ni* is produced by the addressee as a signal of attention. The first speaker may then continue, possibly starting with a *ni* of her own. A recorded example that illustrates this comes from a telephone conversation:

(14) L: No kuule se asia j- jonka takia mä soitan oikeesti,
 T: **nii**.
 L: on Leenan syntymäpäivä. (Sorjonen 1996)

 'L: Well listen the reason I'm calling really,
 T: **Ni**.
 L: is Leena's birthday.'

Whether jointly negotiated or not, a turn-initial *ni* may connect the turn to its speaker's earlier contribution. As formulated by Marja-Leena Sorjonen (pers. comm.), *ni* indicates that the current turn is to be construed as a continuation of a line of argument, narration, etc., started earlier but possibly interrupted by some kind of side sequence. This happens in the following (from my personal notes):

(15) [MV arrives in the middle of a lively discussion.]
 JH to MV: 'Maybe you as an old linguist could help us.'
 [Several turns of general joking about the word 'old'.]
 MV: **Ni**?
 JH: [states the problem]

4.3.4 Clause combining and on-line speech production

We have now seen that the *ni* construction is meaningful and functionally motivated; it belongs to the resources for structuring and taking care of the flow of spontaneous discourse. Let us finish by returning to clause combining. Spontaneous speech provides some structural options not available in standard writing, and the *ni* construction has a role in their production and understanding. First, stacking of subordinate clauses in the manner shown by (16) is not uncommon in spoken Finnish:

(16) kyl mä muistan aina ku äiti sano mullek *ku mä menin kaupaskik käymää* **ni**, *ko mä hai, reikäleivä* **ni** *ko mä tulin kotii* **ni** mä olij järsinys sen ympäri iha, ympäri siit aina [ilmeisesti näyttää kuinka], siin tullessa ku se oli lämmin se leipä et. (HKI)

'I do remember always when mother said to me *when I went to the shops* **ni**, *when I brought a rye bread* **ni** *when I came home* **ni** I had been nibbling all around it always [presumably shows how], on my way home when it was warm, the bread.'

Here, from the point of view of the final product, an adverbial clause seems to modify a clause modified by another adverbial clause. Such an organization is quite exceptional in written texts. Without *ni*, stacking of preposed clauses gives a result that is complex and hard to process. This is not the case in spoken language, where *ni* helps the discourse participants to interpret each consecutive clause as a continuation of the previous one.

Second, again from the point of view of the final product, subordinate clauses often constitute 'double-binds' or 'overlap' structures (Franck 1985, Hakulinen 1987). Examples of this are (17) (two instances) and (18). In an overlap, the clause bears the appropriate relation to both the preceding and the following clause. The function of *ni* is to make the latter connection explicit.

(17) mut minusta niin, olis ollut viisasta *joss olis mailman kieleksi otettu tosiaan esperanto*, **niin**, *silloj* jokainen, ymmärtäisi toistaam *meni se mihinkä maaham vaan* **ni**, aina osais, sitä kiältä, – (HKI)

'but in my opinion ni, it would have been wise *if they had really taken Esperanto as the world language*, **ni**, *then* everyone, would understand each-other *which ever country he went to* **ni**, he would always know, that language, –'

(18) ne oli niin huvittavan näkösii ja sitte me mentii katsomann *ku ne anto semmosen näytöksen* **ni** me mentiin katsomaan niitä ja, – (HKI)

'they looked so funny and then we went to see *when they gave a kind of show* **ni** we went to see them and –'

A third type of complex construction involves a sentence-medial heavy constituent, such as a subordinate clause, or a complex NP. These are systematically avoided in written Finnish (Vilkuna 1991).

(19) mä voisin sit *ne kupit jotka ei mahu* **ni**, ottaa tähän kassiin (overheard)

'[client to salesperson who is packing cups] I could then *those cups that do not fit in* **ni**, take here in my bag'

(20) se oli menossa *ennen kun lukukausi alkaa* **nin** käymään siel
Arizonassa (overheard)
'she was going *before the term begins* **ni** to visit [that place in] Arizona.'

Stacked adverbial clauses, overlaps and medial subordinate clauses are an integral part of unplanned speech production. *Ni* provides a signal of continuation and facilitates interpretation. Nevertheless, a chunk of material as complex as an entire clause interrupting a smaller sequence probably creates an undesirable situation from the processing point of view. Thus, an explicit repair mechanism, repeating, is often resorted to. An example of this with an overlap is (18) above.

4.4 Conclusion

Although the clause-combining *ni* construction is regular and grammaticalized in spoken Finnish, it is resisted in present-day written Finnish to a degree that remains something of a mystery, as it does not seem to have been subject to an explicit prescriptive norm. If looked at from another perspective, as was done in the second part of the chapter, this resistance is much less mysterious. The extensive use of the construction in spontaneous speech reveals its character as a spoken-language phenomenon *par excellence*. *Ni* is used in contexts where it is important to signal that the turn is being continued, either following heavy phrases or when an earlier line of discourse is resumed after a side sequence. Traces of such processing and interactional work can easily be considered redundant in writing.

Acknowledgement

I would like to thank Marja-Leena Sorjonen for sharing her interest in *niin* with me.

Notes

1 The sources of the attested examples are given in parentheses. Most examples are marked 'HKI' and come from the *Helsinki Spoken Language Corpus*, a set of interviews originally made for sociolinguistic purposes in 1972–3 (Paunonen 1995 [1982]) and currently stored in the University of Helsinki Language Corpus Server (UHLCS) at the Department of General Linguistics. The transcription has been slightly simplified.
2 These are also stored in UHLCS.
3 The material is included in the corpora of the Research Institute for the Languages of Finland.

TAMING THE VERNACULAR

References

Du Bois, John W. 1987. The discourse basis of ergativity. *Language* 63: 805–55.

Ekerot, Lars-Johan 1988. *Så-konstruktionen i svenskan* [The *so* construction in Swedish]. Lundastudier i nordisk språkvetenskap A 42. Lund: Lund University Press.

Franck, Dorothea 1985. Sentences in conversational turns: a case of syntactic 'double-bind'. In: M. Dascal (ed.), *Dialogue. An Interdisciplinary Approach*, Amsterdam: John Benjamins, pp. 233–45.

Hakulinen, Auli 1987. Eiköhää siit tullu ekonoomi siit tuli nii. Eräiden lausesulaumien tarkastelua [On syntactic overlap in Finnish]. *Fennistica festiva in honorem Göran Karlsson septuagenarii*, 11–20. Åbo: Åbo Akademi.

Hawkins, John A. 1994. *A Performance Theory of Order and Constituency*. Cambridge: Cambridge University Press.

Holmberg, Anders 1986. *Word Order and Syntactic Features in the Scandinavian Languages and English*. Stockholm.

Ikola, Osmo 1951. *Niin*-sanasta ja alistussuhteesta [On the word *niin* and subordination]. *Virittäjä* 55: 92–5.

Ikola, Osmo 1977. *Nykysuomen käsikirja* [Handbook of Modern Finnish], revised edition. Helsinki: Weilin & Göös.

Itkonen, Terho 1982. *Kieliopas* [Language Guide], 2nd edition. Helsinki: Kirjayhtymä.

Ivars, Ann-Marie 1993. Så-konstruktonen i finlandssvenskt talspråk [The 'so' construction in Finland Swedish speech]. *Språk och social kontext*. Meddeland en från institutionen för nordiska språk och nordisk litteratur vid Helsingfors universitet. Serie B: 15.

Kannisto, Artturi 1901. *Lauseopillisia havaintoja läntisen etelä-Hämeen kielimurteesta* [Syntactic observations on the dialect of Southwestern Häme]. Helsinki: Suomal. Kirjall. Seuran kirjapainon osakeyhtiö.

Kettunen, Lauri 1949. *Hyvää ja vapaata suomea* [Good and free Finnish]. Jyväskylä: K.J. Gummerus Oy.

Latvala, Salu 1899. *Lauseopillisia muistiinpanoja Pohjois-Savon murteesta* [Syntactic notes on the dialect of Northern Savo]. Helsinki: Suomalaisen Kirjallisuuden Seura.

Matthiessen, Christian and Thompson, Sandra A. 1988. The structure of discourse and 'subordination'. In: John Haiman and Sandra A. Thompson (eds), *Clause Combining in Grammar and Discourse*. Amsterdam/Philadelphia: John Benjamins.

Nykysuomen sanakirja 1963 [Dictionary of Modern Finnish], 5th edition. Porvoo and Helsinki: WSOY.

Paunonen, Heikki 1995 [1982]. *Suomen kieli Helsingissä. Huomioita Helsingin puhekielen historiallisesta taustasta ja nykyvariaatiosta* [Finnish in Helsinki.

THE PARTICLE NI IN FINNISH

Observations on historical background and present-day variation]. Helsinki: Department of Finnish, University of Helsinki.

Rainio, Ritva 1968. *Asiatyyli ja viestintä* [Style and Communication]. Tietolipas 56. Helsinki: Suomalaisen kirjallisuuden seura.

Räisänen, Alpo 1987. *Sotkamon murretta* [Sotkamo Dialect]. Suomen kielen näytteitä 28. Helsinki: Kotimaisten kielten tutkimuskeskus.

Saarimaa, E.A. 1930. *Hyvää ja huonoa suomea* [Good and bad Finnish]. Porvoo: Werner Söderström Osakeyhtiö.

Saarimaa, E.A. 1941. Väärin rakennettuja virkkeitä [Misconstructed sentences]. *Virittäjä* 45: 394–6.

Saarimma, E.A. 1943. Väärin rakennettuja lauseyhdistyksiä [Misconstructed clause combinations]. *Virittäjä* 47: 121–3.

Saarimaa, E.A. 1947. *Kielenopas* [Language guide]. Porvoo: Werner Söderström Osakeyhtiö.

Saarimaa, E.A. 1951. Edellisen johdosta [Reply to Ikola 1951]. *Virittäjä* 55: 96.

Saukkonen, Pauli 1972: Kokeellisia havaintoja puhekielen ja kirjakielen tyylieroista [Experimental observations on the differences between spoken and written language]. In: Esko Vierikko (ed.), *Puhekieli ja ilmaisu*. Helsinki: WSOY, 13–32.

Setälä, E.N. [E.N.S.] 1880. *Suomen kielen lause-oppi. Oppikirjan koe* [Finnish syntax. An experimental textbook]. Helsinki: K.E. Holm.

Setälä, E.N. 1883. *Lauseopillinen tutkimus Koillis-Satakunnan kansankielestä* [A syntactic study on the vernacular of Northeastern Satakunta]. Helsinki: Suomalaisen kirjallisuuden seura.

Setälä, E.N. 1973. *Suomen kielen lauseoppi* [Finnish syntax], 16th edition, revised by Matti Sadeniemi. Keuruu: Otava.

Sirelius, U.T. 1894. *Lauseopillinen tutkimus Jääsken ja Kirvun kielimurteesta* [A syntactic study on the dialect of Jääski and Kirvu]. Helsinki: Suomalaisen kirjallisuuden seura.

Sorjonen, Marja-Leena 1996. Recipient activities: Particles *nii(n)* and *joo* as responses in Finnish conversations. PhD dissertation, University of California at Los Angeles.

Vilkuna, Maria 1989. *Free Word Order in Finnish. Its syntax and discourse functions*. Helsinki: Suomalaisen kirjallisuuden seura.

Vilkuna, Maria 1991. Constituent order and constituent length in written Finnish. In: John A. Hawkins and Anna Siewierska (eds), *Performance Principles of Word Order*. ESF EUROTYP Working Paper II, 2. Amsterdam.

CHAPTER 5

Involvement in 'standard' and 'nonstandard' English

Jenny Cheshire

5.1 The origins of standard English

In this chapter I consider the term 'standard English' as referring to a set of norms about English, to which speakers – and writers – conform to a greater or lesser extent. This is in line with Milroy and Milroy's account of standardization and standard language (1985: 22–3) and with Downes's (1984: 34) conception of a standard language as a complex of beliefs and behaviour towards language, which evolves historically. Standard English, in this sense of the term, has its origins in public, written language, arising initially from the need for a uniform variety of the language to be used in printing (Milroy and Milroy 1985: 36; Leith and Graddol 1996: 141). Written language has continued to be the reference point for standard English, with grammarians during the eighteenth century codifying the forms used in writing (Cheshire and Milroy 1993: 7) and with literacy remaining the major influence in promoting consciousness of the standard today (Milroy and Milroy 1985: 36–7). During the nineteenth century the term 'standard English' began to be used to refer to speech as well as to writing (Leith and Graddol 1996: 161), reflecting, perhaps, the fact that those people who spent much of their lives reading and writing tended to use in their speech the forms that had been codified as standard. For present-day English a link is now accepted between public written English and the spoken English of 'the educated' (Cheshire and Milroy 1993: 11), reflected in definitions of standard English as 'educated English' (Quirk *et al.* 1985: 18) or as the English used in print and in the speech of the educated (Trudgill 1984: 32). The notion of 'the educated' would of course be more accurately expressed as those who consider themselves to be educated, or who wish to appear educated.

When standard English was codified in dictionaries and grammars one of the aims was to minimize variation, with a single meaning attributed to a single linguistic form (Milroy and Milroy 1985). For morphological features this was relatively easy to implement, and the result has been a reduction of morphological variation in present-day standard English. For example, the verb SEE now has a single past tense form, *saw*, in standard English, whereas in nonstandard varieties of English, such as that spoken in Reading, Berkshire, there are still five different past tense forms: *saw, seen, sawed, seed* and *see* (Cheshire 1982). Differences of this kind between standard and nonstandard English can be described in a straightforward way. For other syntactic features, however, the principle of one form, one meaning has interacted in a complex way with the development of the standard from a primarily written variety. The result is that in present-day English a single form may occur in a range of linguistic structures with essentially the same function in each one, but its presence in some of those structures – particularly those associated with speech – has not been codified as standard. Instead, grammarians have variously designated these occurrences as nonstandard, colloquial or regional. I will illustrate this aspect of English syntax with two features of present-day English, *never* and *that*. I have analysed each of these features in detail elsewhere (Cheshire 1995, 1996); in this chapter, however, I focus specifically on the standard and nonstandard dimension of their use in order to show the interrelationship between codification, written language, and beliefs about standard English.

5.2 Never

The use of *never* as a negative form in English continues a cycle of language change that has been repeated over the centuries by successive generations of English speakers but which has now been interrupted by the process of standardization. The cycle is a common phenomenon in European languages, consisting of using a universal temporal quantifier, meaning 'ever' or 'on any occasion' to reinforce a negative expression that has become weakened through frequent use. Thus present-day English *no* derives from Old English *ne a*, 'not ever' (Jespersen 1917: 18), and the present-day negator *not* has its origins in Old English *ne a wiht*, literally 'not ever anything' (Traugott 1972: 94). In its turn *not* has now become phonetically weakened through rapid speech to the clitic *–nt*, first in spoken English and now, in present-day English, in some written texts too.

Not did not only become phonetically reduced; it soon became semantically weakened also, no longer interpreted as referring to universal time. We can see from early texts that writers – and presumably speakers too – continued the cycle by turning once more to the universal temporal negator to reinforce the expression of negation: examples (1) and (2) contain *naeure* and *neuer*, both from *ne aefre*, via *naefre*, literally 'not ever' or 'never':

TAMING THE VERNACULAR

(1) ði moder was an hore, for nuste heo naeure ðene mon ðat ðe streonde hire on.
(Lazamon's *Brut*, 1205)
'Thy mother was a whore because she didn't know the man who begot thee.'

(2) He asked what that was and his wiff said she wost neuer.
(*The Book of The Knight of La Tour-Brandy*, 1450)
'He asked what that was and his wife said that she didn't know.'

In present-day English *never* continues to be used as a negative marker, sometimes with the literal meaning of universal temporal negation, as in (3), and sometimes without a universal interpretation, as in (4) to (7) (unless otherwise specified, all examples in this chapter are taken from my own recordings of spontaneous conversation):

(3) Sally's a vegetarian . . . she never eats meat (i.e. on all occasions that Sally is offered meat, she will refuse it).

(4) You'll never catch that train tonight. (Quirk *et al.* 1985: 601)

(5) Well I've never seen Batman so I wouldn't know.

(6) I never went to school today.

(7) Benny: . . . we all went up there and jumped on him.
Nobby: you never . . . you you hit him with a stick and then booted him.

If the process of standardization had not intervened we could expect the cycle to have continued, with *never* eventually replacing *not* as the conventional marker of negation. We could expect *never*, in its turn, to become phonetically reduced through rapid speech processes, and to lose its expressive force through frequent use. In fact there is evidence that the phonetic form of *never* did become reduced. The spelling in examples (1) and (2) indicates that the intervocalic consonant in forms resulting from *ne aefre* was probably lost by the fourteenth century; and the spelling *ne'er* in the representation of speech in nineteenth-century novels suggests how *never* must have been pronounced at that time. With standardization, however, came the desire for the speech of the educated to resemble the form of the written language. During the nineteenth century short forms such as *howe'er*, *e'er* – and presumably also *ne'er* – were branded as vulgar by schoolmasters (Jespersen 1982 [1905]: 219), presumably because they did not preserve the *v* of the written form and perhaps also because they were used by social groups from whom speakers who considered themselves to be educated wished to disassociate themselves. We can compare the schoolmasters' view with some of the prescriptive views heard today which relate spoken forms to their spellings. 'Dropped h' is stigmatized in pronunciations of words such as *hospital* as [ospɪtəl]; and many people object to what they see as 'lazy' pronunciations of words like *butter* as [bʌʔə], where there is a glottal stop in place of the *t* of the written form (Cheshire and Edwards 1991). Today the short forms of *never* have disappeared from most varieties of English, surviving only in some rural dialects.

The evolution of a standard has affected the form of *never*, then. It has also interrupted its semantic weakening. We have seen that *never* can refer both to all possible occasions, as in *Sally never eats meat*, and to one occasion in the past, as in *I never went to school today*. This use of a single form, *never*, to express two meanings which appear to be completely incompatible offends against the principle whereby one form should express one meaning; not surprisingly, therefore, prescriptivists have attempted to restrict the contexts in which *never* can be used. The first record of a prescription concerning *never* relates to a context where it refers to a period of past time, and dates from the mid-eighteenth century:

> Wiseman, C. 1764. (*A complete English grammar on a new plan. For the use of foreigners, and such natives as would acquire a scientifical knowledge of their own tongue.* London.)
> *Never* should be replaced by *not* in 'What, and did never anyone come to relieve you before then?' (Sundby *et al.* 1991)

Prescriptions against using *never* to refer to past time have gathered momentum during the course of the twentieth century, with the majority of guides to good usage now warning against using *never* in this way, especially when a verb has the simple past form. The prescriptions have become progressively more severe as time has gone on, as the following extracts show: for Partridge, writing in 1948, the use of *never* to refer to the past requires only 'care', but for Wood, writing in 1981, this use is 'incorrect'.

> ... in serious writing, it should only be used after careful consideration.
> (Partridge 1948)

> This [use of *never*], however illogical, is idiomatic, at least colloquially.
> (Fowler 1965, *Modern English Usage*)

> In good usage, *never* is not used with simple past tenses to mean *not*.
> (*Collins Dictionary of the English Language* 1981)

> *Never* means 'not ever, on no occasion'. It is common to hear sentences such as *I never saw you at the party*. It is, however, incorrect to use *never* when referring to one occasion. *Never* can only be used in continuous context:
> Bob: *I didn't see you at the party, Jim.*
> Jim: *I've never been to any of Sue's parties.*
> (Wood 1981, *Current English Usage*)

We can see from these few extracts that prescriptivists favour the retention of *not* as the all-purpose English negator, and attempt to restrict *never* to fixed linguistic contexts. They implicitly insist on preserving the time reference of *never*, and on restricting this time reference to either all time (example (1) seems to be unquestionably 'standard') or, failing that, to a continuous period of time. But *never* continues to be used in a wider range of linguistic contexts in spoken English, some of which are seen as 'colloquial', others as 'incorrect'. This is preventing the development of a conventionalized, routine use of *never* to convey simple negation in all contexts.

Interestingly, one context that has become recognized as colloquial and that has escaped censure is when *never* refers to a single occasion in the future: *never* in example (4) (*you'll never catch that train tonight*) is termed a negative marker by Quirk *et al.* (1985: 601), who explain that the presence of the adverbial *tonight* 'rules out' the temporal meaning of *never*. Here *never* has apparently become a conventionalized, routine marker of negation. However, when it refers to a single occasion in the past, as in (6) and (7) above, *never* has become routine only for those speakers of English who have been unaffected by the doctrine of correctness. So-called preterite *never* is very widespread, reported in all countries of the world where English is spoken natively; in Britain it was one of the most widely reported features in our Survey of British Dialect Grammar (Cheshire *et al.* 1989).

What effect have the efforts of prescriptivists had on the beliefs of educated speakers of English about the contexts in which *never* can be used as a marker of negation? In 1986 I investigated this question by surveying some teaching staff and students at the University of Bath and the University of Reading, England. One hundred lecturers in non-language subjects were sent a postal questionnaire with nine sentences containing *never*, as in Table 5.1, and were asked to tick those sentences that they thought they might use themselves in speech and in writing. A total of 54 questionnaires were returned. The same questionnaire was distributed to 65 students of European studies at the end of a lecture at the University of Bath: all these questionnaires were completed and returned (thereby showing the advantages of using a captive population for research based on questionnaires!).

There are, of course, problems in drawing conclusions from a questionnaire about language. One problem that became immediately clear was that the majority of the participants did not like the word *bother*, so that several of them refused to give an answer for sentence 4, or ticked it but also crossed out *bother* and replaced it with a stronger expletive. Despite such problems it is interesting to note that the two age groups have the same pattern of responses, with both groups thinking they are most likely to use *never* in sentence 1, where the negation can extend to the widest period of time. Both groups claim that they would be less likely to use *never* in writing sentence 2, where the time reference is to a continuous period of past time – including the present – and where it cannot be to 'all time'. They claim to be still less likely to use sentence 3

Table 5.1: Acceptability of *never*

	Lecturers (N = 54)		Students (N = 65)	
	% might use in speech	% might use in writing	% might use in speech	% might use in writing
1. Sally never eats meat	97	93	98	95
2. John has never been to Baghdad	93	73	100	80
3. You'll never catch that train tonight	81	62	98	43
4. Bother! I never let the cat out	49		50	
5. John never stole that car	41	14	49	10
6. John never went to school today	25	5	20	3
7. Well I never!	51		45	
8. You trod on my toe. – No I never!	7		20	
9. John went to work today but I never	1		0	

in writing, where the time reference is to a single occasion in the future – thereby confirming that this use may indeed be typical of spoken colloquial styles of 'educated' English. The use of *never* with reference to an occasion in the past, as in sentence 5, is thought to be less likely still; and where the past occasion is clearly specified, by *today* in sentence 6, they judge their use of *never* to be least likely of all.

Thus the views of these educated speakers correspond exactly to the uses recommended by the handbooks of good usage. There is variability in their responses, with some claiming to use *never* and others claiming that they would not, but the variability is regularly patterned, with their estimated usage decreasing as the time period to which *never* refers becomes increasingly restricted. It is possible that the variation indicates that the codification of *never* and its resulting restriction to certain linguistic contexts is still in progress. It is impossible to predict whether the contexts in which *never* occurs will eventually separate out into a clear cut 'standard' versus 'nonstandard' usage, but the survey certainly confirms that the historical cycle of reinforcement of a weakened negative marker by the universal temporal negator has been interrupted, at least for these educated speakers of English.

At this point it is useful to consider the reasons why speakers of English should turn to the universal quantifier as a way of reinforcing a weakened negative marker. We cannot know for sure how we create meanings when we are speaking to each other, but it is usually assumed that speakers aim to guide their addressees in the interpretation of their utterances (Hopper and Traugott 1993: 64). Their interpretation consists, in part at least, in hearers drawing appropriate inferences: thus Sacks 1965 (1992) considers converters as 'inference-making machines' – although the work we do in conversation is surely less mechanical than Sacks's metaphor implies. These complex procedures of inference and deduction mean that speakers work together to produce meanings as the discourse unfolds (Bublitz 1992: 560). Chafe (1982) and Tannen (1989) use the term 'involvement' to refer to the way in which we ensure this collaboration through the linguistic features that we use. Thus Chafe (1982) identifies some of the ways in which speakers demonstrate their own involvement in what they are saying, for example through frequent reference to themselves or to their mental processes (using verbs such *I think* or *I believe*); he claims that we may also seek to involve the involvement of our interlocutor by directly addressing them with forms such as *you know*. The use of a quantifier by a speaker is a more sophisticated way of securing interpersonal involvement and the collaborative production of discourse, for it indicates to the addressee the kinds of inferences that they should draw: they must determine its scope. We can see how this might work by considering examples (3)–(7) in detail. In (3), the literal meaning of *never*, 'not on any occasion', can readily apply: the present tense verb *eats* can refer to 'all time' (Palmer 1974) and we could gloss the utterance as 'there is no occasion when, should meat be on offer, Sally will eat it'. In examples (4) to (7), however, it is logically impossible for *never* to refer to any occasion. The verb tenses and time adverbials specify the time reference of the utterance, so that in (4) the contracted *will* specifies that the reference is not to all time but only to all possible occurrences in the future. In (5) the present perfect form *have seen* indicates that reference is to occasions during a period of past time up to and including the present. Similarly, in (6) the past tense form *went* and the adverbial *today* unambiguously indicate reference to time that is past, and in (7) the preterite *jumped* serves the same purpose, although here it is also necessary to infer that the rest of the predicate in Barney's ellipted phrase *you never* is Nobby's preceding *jumped on him*.

Since the time reference of *never* is clear from the linguistic context of these utterances, there is no risk that addressees will fail to infer an appropriate meaning for the utterance in which *never* occurs. They may, however, have to work a little harder when they interpret an utterance containing *never* than with an equivalent utterance containing *not*, for with *not* they do not have to scan the linguistic context in order to determine whether or not the meaning of universal time can apply. This cognitive work has a function, however. When *never* cannot refer to universal time, its use enhances what Hopper and Traugott have termed 'expressivity' (1993: 65): speakers can emphasize the negative through overstatement, by referring to 'all time' when it is clear from the surrounding linguistic context that only a specific period of time or a specific occasion is at issue.

This means that when speakers use *never* they directly engage their addressee in the construction of meaning; *never* is a very effective strategy for creating interpersonal involvement. We can think of it as a joint focus of attention for the speaker and the addressee, like the discourse marker *oh* (Schiffrin 1987). However, an important difference between *oh* and *never* is that *never* is integrated into clause structure and therefore requires more complex linguistic processing than *oh*. It is particularly effective as a strategy for expressing interpersonal involvement when inferences must be drawn across speaker turns, as in example (7) above, since in this case the addressee has to infer the links between the utterances of different speakers, and is led therefore to see the overall coherence of the conversation.

Once speakers begin to use *never* frequently in this way it becomes a routine expression, losing its expressivity and no longer requiring addressees to do complex cognitive processing work in order to interpret it. In pragmatic terms we could say that the first time we hear *never* used with its non-literal meaning it gives rise to conversational implicatures, requiring us to do inferencing work; but that these implicatures become conventionalized as we continue to associate the same form with the expression of negation (as has now happened with *not*). The history of different languages contains many examples of this type of semantic 'weakening', where a form begins to be used in a way that appears to contradict its literal meaning and eventually takes on this non-literal meaning as one of its routine, conventional senses (see Cole 1975 for a discussion in these terms of the development of *lets* from a first person form to a second person imperative marker). This may well have happened for some speakers of English who habitually use *never* in a wide range of linguistic contexts. For other speakers, however, such as those who took part in my survey, the use of *never* to refer to a single occasion in the past has not become conventionalized. In principle this should mean that *never* in contexts such as this can still function as a way of creating interpersonal involvement. However, its association with 'incorrect' speech means that, for speakers who think of themselves as educated, the restricted sense of *never* has now become a social marker, symbolizing membership of what is for them an out-group. If they need to draw on conversational implicatures in order to interpret the use of *never* in a simple past context the cognitive work they have to do will make *never* cognitively salient, and it will function all the more effectively as a social marker. This social marking will then prevent them from using *never* to create harmonious interpersonal involvement. The historical cycle of negation, then, has been interrupted by the codification that is part of the process of standardization. The result is that there is now a sociolinguistic barrier between speakers of the same language: those who have adopted the standard norms and those who have not.

Meanwhile speakers of English have alternative ways of reinforcing a weakened negative. Hopper and Traugott (1993: 121) mention *no way*, as in *no way we're taking this stuff*. In my recordings of educated spoken English *not* frequently co-occurs with intensifying phrases, as in *we're definitely not going out tonight* or *I don't want anything at all to eat thanks* or *I don't like her a bit*. Affixes are also used, as in *it's a not unusual occasion*. And in nonstandardised varieties of English there is always the possibility of multiple negation.

5.3 That

My discussion of 'standard' and 'nonstandard' uses of *that* will be briefer than my discussion of *never*, because unlike *never*, *that* rarely appears in guides to good usage, nor does its use provoke such severe reactions from commentators on English. Those complaints that have been made about *that* are revealing, however, for they again illustrate the preference for using a single form in a restricted range of linguistic contexts. Addison, writing in *The Spectator* in 1711, devised the sentence given below as (8) to support his objection to *that* being used as a relative pronoun in place of his preferred *wh-* forms. His sentence aims to illustrate the potential problems that could be caused by the multiple functions of *that*: here it acts as a pronoun, a relative pronoun, a conjunction and a demonstrative:

(8) That that I say is this: that that that that gentleman has advanced, is not that, that he should have proved.

Arthur Sefton, a headteacher of a British school, devised a similar example nearly three hundred years later to show that *that* already has enough 'legitimate' functions without the 'illegitimate' one that he wished to complain about. The legitimate uses, he claims, are to join and to demonstrate, as illustrated in his sentence:

(9) On the day that I came, I saw that that that that man did was wrong.
     (1984, *Times Education Supplement*)

For him the illegitimate use of *that* is when it is an intensifier, as in (10):

(10) I was that ill... it was awful... I couldn't even stand up... I was off work for a week.

Quirk *et al.* (1985: 447) class this use of *that* as nonstandard; elsewhere it is seen as regional, typical of Northern varieties of English in particular (see, for example, Beal 1993: 209). The speaker who provided example (10) during a conversation was in fact from Yorkshire (in the North of England) so it may not be unreasonable to see his usage as a regional form. According to the definitions that are usually given for standard English, however, which link the standard with the speech of 'the educated', his usage should be seen as standard rather than nonstandard, since he was a university lecturer, and therefore, presumably, 'educated'. The label is unimportant however: what I would like to draw attention to is the expressivity of *that* in (10), as well as in (11) and (12), where *that* is used in a way to which Sefton also objects:

(11) You could go there by train ... it doesn't cost that much.

(12) Sadie: Well ... she usually walks home actually ... it isn't that far
Barbara: Oh I thought it was a couple of miles.

In negative contexts such as those of (11) and (12) the use of *that* is considered by Quirk *et al.* to be not nonstandard but typical of informal styles of English (1985: 447). We have here, then, in examples (10)–(12), some uses of *that* which fall on the borderline between nonstandard, dialect and colloquial varieties of English.

Although Sefton considers these uses to be illegitimate they in fact differ very little, if at all, from those that he counts as legitimate. His 'legitimate' example in *that man* contains a demonstrative *that*, pointing out the specific man to which the writer is referring. It is difficult, as I mentioned earlier, to say for sure what any form means in the context in which it occurs, but we can sometimes use the methods of conversation analysis to see from speakers' responses how they appear to have interpreted the utterance in the previous turn. In (11) and (12) it seems that *that* points something out, just as in Sefton's legitimate cases, but this time what is pointed out is an attitude: Sadie's *it isn't that far* implies 'it isn't as far as you might think it is', and her *actually* further implies that she is contradicting an assumption that she assumes Barbara to have. This interpretation is confirmed by Barbara's reply, where she makes her assumption explicit.

We can also obtain an idea of the function of *that* in contexts such as these by adopting a structural approach, contrasting it with other intensifiers that could have occurred, such as *very*. Unlike *very*, which merely intensifies the meaning of the item with which it is in construction, *that* requires some additional conversational inferences to be drawn, contrasting the speaker's view with what the speaker appears to think the addressee's view might be. Thus, in example (11), someone who says *it costs very little* is clearly stating their own point of view; if they use the negative expression *it doesn't cost much*, however, there is a hint that they believe their addressee could disagree; and if they say *it doesn't cost that much* there is more than a hint – the implication is that the price is not as great as the addressee might think it is.

In the same way we can contrast *that* in example (10), *I was that ill*, with other words that can occur in this context such as, here, the intensifier *so*. Like *so*, *that* intensifies the force of the item with which it is in construction, inviting the addressee to 'scale up' its force (Quirk *et al.* 1985: 590–1); unlike *so*, however, *that* implies that the addressee might disbelieve the strength of the assertion that the speaker is making. Thus in example (10) the speaker, who had just returned to work after a bad attack of influenza, goes on to give further details of the severity of his illness after his phrase *I was that ill*, as if to say that he was more ill than we might reasonably be expected to have imagined.

It is worth stressing that in example (10), just as in (11) and (12), *that* appears to refer to an assumed view that the speaker believes the addressee to have, but it is a view that the speaker does not explicitly state. These uses create interpersonal involvement because they refer to assumptions that the speaker is making about the attitudes of the addressee. Naturally we can only make assumptions of this kind about people whom we know relatively well, so it is hardly surprising if these uses of *that* have developed in relaxed face-to-face communication between social intimates, who know each other well enough to believe that they can predict the other's views and attitudes. We might expect these uses, therefore, to become markers of spoken varieties of English – whether colloquial, nonstandard or dialect English (see also Melchers, this volume).

These uses have much in common with the functions of *that* in set-marking tags, such as example (13):

(13)　Russell and that . . . they were down there making a camp . . . you know with some other boys . . . they was messing about (Wendy).

Everyone Wendy was talking to knew Russell and knew who his friends were, so she was able to refer to the whole set of friends by naming just one of them. Here the interlocutors are involved in the creation of the discourse by having to draw the necessary inferences about the people to whom Wendy is referring. But she has also drawn attention to the knowledge that she shares with her interlocutors about the membership of this group of friends, thereby reinforcing the expression of affective meaning. Other detailed studies of set-marking tags suggest that this is a common function of set-marking tags: for example, Dubois (1992) found that their reference tends to be ephemeral and context-dependent, based on culturally and individually related concepts, on the association of nuances and on shared knowledge specific to the participants (*op. cit.*: 182).

In informal conversation it is often more important to communicate a common understanding and a shared perspective on the topic of conversation than to communicate precise information about the topic. This is not the case with written language, however, especially the public written language that has been the basis for the development of standard English. I have not investigated the acceptability of the involved uses of *that*, other than to consult Quirk *et al.* (1985). However, Dines (1980) reports on a study that she carried out into the antagonism caused by various nonstandard features of English among groups of working-class and middle-class mothers in Australia. She concluded that set-marking tags were salient across the Australian speech community as stigmatized forms. As with the involved uses of *never*, it seems that uses of *that* which create interpersonal involvement become social markers, symbolizing uneducated or incorrect speech for speakers of English who see themselves as members of the more educated sections of society. A further factor at work in the divergence between standard and non-standard uses of a feature, then, is the desire of members of 'polite' society to mark themselves out as 'educated' (Stein and Tieken-Boon van Ostade 1994). The result is that forms that are appropriate and useful for creating interpersonal involvement in face-to-face communication are likely to become stigmatized by speakers who wish to present themselves as 'educated'. When the same forms are used in contexts where they can have a function appropriate for the explicit argumentation of written prose, it is these contexts that become considered as standard, and all other uses are then believed to be deviant.

5.4 Conclusion

My brief analysis of just two features of present-day English has identified a number of characteristics of standard English that can be related to its origins in public formal writing. These characteristics are interrelated, but it is useful to separate them out for discussion.

First, written language is often taken as the model for the standard. This can be seen in present-day *never*, which survives today in its full form while the phonetically reduced *ne'er* has been banished from the standard. It can also be seen in the contexts that have been outlawed: educated speakers consider *never* to be more nonstandard in utterances where they have to infer its scope across clause boundaries or across speaker turns, and many speakers stigmatize set-marking tags with referents that would need to be explicitly mentioned in writing, though not in the face-to-face context of speech.

Secondly, standardization involves codification, and codification favours the principle of one form, one function. Grammarians codifying English have disregarded the function of creating interpersonal involvement, which is characteristic of informal face-to-face communication rather than of explicit prose, and have tried instead to identify a single meaning for both *never* (time reference to a continuous period) and *that* (demonstrating or referring). This has interrupted the evolution of *never* as an all-purpose negator, and has outlawed *that* in contexts where it can create interpersonal involvement by referring to attitudes, beliefs or shared knowledge.

Thirdly, the more involved uses of both *never* and *that* require speakers to draw conversational inferences in order to interpret the utterances in which they occur. This cognitive work may make the forms salient when they occur in these contexts, and thus susceptible of becoming a marker of social groups with which self-consciously 'educated' speakers do not wish to be identified. The result is that 'polite' society no longer uses a form in the contexts that are particularly associated with the demands of face-to-face communication, while the rest of society continues to use the form in its full range of contexts.

Finally, the link between standard English and formal written prose means that prescriptivists and linguists alike tend to allocate a fixed meaning to a form that seems to fit the way it is used in formal written prose, and with our educated intuitions, but that does not fit the way it is used in face-to-face communication. This fixed meaning then makes it difficult for linguists to observe structural regularities, and we fail to see that a form may have essentially the same function in all the contexts in which it occurs. The standard puts blinkers on us, and we must try to see round them.

References

Beal, Joan 1993. The grammar of Tyneside and Northumbrian England. In: J. Milroy and L. Milroy (eds), *Real English: The Grammar of English Dialects in the British Isles*. London: Longman, pp. 187–213.

Bublitz, Wolfram 1992. Transferred Negation and Modality. *Journal of Pragmatics* 18: 551–77.

Chafe, Wallace 1982. Integration and involvement in speaking, writing, and oral literature. In: Deborah Tannen (ed.), *Spoken and Written Language: Exploring Orality and Literacy*. Norwood, N.J.: Ablex, pp. 35–54.

Cheshire, Jenny 1982. *Variation in an English Dialect*. Cambridge: Cambridge University Press.

Cheshire, Jenny 1995. Negation from an interactional perspective. In: L. Mondada (ed.), *Formes linguistiques et dynamiques interactionelles*. Lausanne: Cahiers de l'Institut de Linguistique et des Sciences du Langage, pp. 71–94.

Cheshire, Jenny 1996. That jacksprat: An interactional perspective on English *that*. *Journal of Pragmatics* 25: 369–93.

Cheshire, Jenny and Edwards, Viv 1991. School children as sociolinguistic researchers. *Linguistics and Education* 3(3): 225–50.
Cheshire, Jenny and Milroy, James 1993. Syntactic variation in nonstandard dialects: background issues. In J. Milroy and L. Milroy (eds), *Real English: The Grammar of English Dialects in the British Isles*. London: Longman, pp. 3–33.
Cheshire, J., Edwards, Viv and Whittle, Pamela 1989. Urban British Dialect Grammar: the question of dialect levelling. *English Worldwide* 10: 185–225.
Cole, Peter 1975. The synchronic and diachronic status of conversational implicature. In: Cole, Peter and Jerry L. Morgan (eds), *Speech Acts* (Syntax and Semantics volume 3). New York: Academic Press, pp. 257–88.
Dines, Elizabeth 1980. Variation in discourse – 'and stuff like that'. *Language in Society* 9: 13–31.
Downes, William 1984. *Language and Society*. London: Fontana.
Dubois, S. 1992. Extension particles, etc. *Language Variation and Change* 4: 179–203.
Fowler, H.W. (1965). *Modern English Usage*, 2nd edition. London: Oxford University Press.
Hopper, Paul J. and Traugott, Elizabeth Closs 1993. *Grammaticalization*. Cambridge: Cambridge University Press.
Jespersen, O. 1917. *Negation in English and Other Languages*. Copenhagen: Andre Høst and Sons.
Jespersen, O. (1982 [1905]). *Growth and Structure of the English Language*. London: Edward Arnold.
Leith, Dick and Graddol, David 1996. Modernity and English as a national language. In: David Graddol, Dick Leith and Joan Swann (eds), *English: History, Diversity and Change*. London: Routledge, pp. 136–66.
Levinson, S. (1983). *Pragmatics*. Cambridge: Cambridge University Press.
Milroy, James and Milroy, Lesley 1985. *Authority in Language: Investigating Language Prescription and Standardisation*. London: Routledge.
Palmer, F.R. 1974. *The English Verb*. London: Longman.
Partridge, E. 1948. *Usage and Abusage*. London: Allen and Unwin.
Quirk, R., Greenbaum, S., Leech, G. and Svartvik, J. (1985). *A Comprehensive Grammar of the English Language*. London: Longman.
Sacks, H. 1965 (1992). *Lectures on Conversation*. Ed. by Gail Jefferson. Oxford: Oxford University Press.
Schiffrin, Deborah, 1987. *Discourse Markers*. Cambridge: Cambridge University Press.
Stein, Dieter and Tieken-Boon van Ostade, Ingrid (eds) 1994. *Towards a Standard English (1600–1800)*. Berlin: Walter de Gruyter, pp. 115–33.
Sundby, B., Bjørge, A.K. and Haugland, K.E. (1991) *A Dictionary of English Normative Grammar 1700–1800*. Amsterdam: John Benjamins.

Tannen, D. (1989). *Talking Voices: Repetition, Dialogue and Imagery in Conversational Discourse*. Cambridge: Cambridge University Press.

Traugott, Elizabeth Closs 1972. *A History of English Syntax*. New York: Holt, Rinehart and Winston.

Trudgill, P. (1984). Standard English in England. In: P. Trudgill (ed.), *Language in the British Isles*. Cambridge: Cambridge University Press, pp. 32–44.

Wood, F.T. (1981). *Current English Usage*. London: Macmillan.

CHAPTER 6

This, that, yon: on 'three-dimensional' deictic systems

Gunnel Melchers

6.1 Introduction

In standard English, demonstrative pronouns and determiners expressing 'pure deixis', i.e. 'referring to the locutionary agent and the addressee without conveying any additional information about them' (Lyons 1981: 232), are indisputably characterized by a bipartite system: *this/these* (proximal) vs *that/those* (distal). In certain nonstandard dialects, however, a 'three-way' system appears to exist, having the potential of specifically referring to objects and concepts even more distant than those referred to by *that/those*. The most widely known realization of such an additional degree of remoteness (extra-distal) is *yon*, as found in Scotland and Northern England, but other forms occur, such as the analogous *thon* (Northumberland, Scotland, Ireland) and the West Country *thicky*.

In a worldwide typological perspective, an explicit three-term system is by no means unique; nor is it restricted to nonstandard varieties. Bloomfield (1933: 259) brings up Latin *hic/iste/ille* ('nearest the speaker'/ 'nearest the hearer'/'farthest away') and presents even more elaborate systems, as in Cree, which has a special lexical item for denoting 'something recently present but now out of sight', or Eskimo, through whose deictic pronouns cardinal points can be expressed. According to Weissenborn and Klein (1982), such diverse varieties as Japanese, Czech, Spanish and Rhineland dialects feature systems resembling the *this/that/yon* type, as do certain Swedish dialects.

The starting point of this chapter is an inventory and discussion of the alleged three-term system as realized in nonstandard English, in particular Northern English and Scottish varieties. Special attention will be paid to the functions of *yon* – or the regional variants *thon/thicky* – since these forms are claimed to express the additional dimension. It goes without saying, however, that the deictic function of *yon* is an interesting linguistic issue only when it is part of a system, i.e. contrasting with tokens of *this/that* (in two-term or three-term contrasts). The actual maintenance of a three-term system will be assessed on the basis of data from the *Survey of English Dialects* (*SED*), the *Linguistic Survey of Scotland* (*LSS*), my own current fieldwork for a project on Shetland dialect (see, for example, Melchers 1983), recent research on demonstrative adjectives and pronouns in the dialect of South Zeal, Devonshire (Harris 1991) and studies of demonstratives within the framework of the *Survey of British Dialect Grammar* (Cheshire et al. 1993).

The scope of the discussion is then widened into an attempt to explain why the seemingly useful and 'economical' three-way system is not found in standard English. The following questions will be addressed:

1 Is there evidence of stigmatization by grammarians and teachers?
2 Does the absence of an explicit three-way system in the standard language reflect a typical difference between spoken-oriented and written-oriented varieties?
3 To what extent can the character of deictic systems be related to the concept of conversational involvement (cf. Tannen 1989)?

6.2 The dialect evidence

6.2.1 Various claims put forward in the literature

In an important overall inventory of grammatical characteristics of non-standard dialects of English in the British Isles which was compiled with a view to suggesting research areas (Edwards and Weltens 1984), it is simply pointed out that 'in Scotland and N. England an extra dimension is available in the form of *yon* (singular plural), referring to objects even more distant than those referred to by *that/those*' (p. 37). It appears, however, according to another comprehensive publication in the field of linguistic geography (Kirk et al. 1985), that there are no recent studies dealing with the item *yon*.

Aitken (1984), writing for the monumental textbook *Language in the British Isles*, adds a sociolinguistic dimension by claiming that the three-term deictic system realized as *this* (pl. *thir*)/ *that* (pl. *thae*)/*yon, thon* (unchanged in the plural) is fully used only by his groups 3 and 4, i.e. working-class speakers, especially from rural areas, in speaking informally, and mono-dialectal speakers.

Macafee (1983: 51) states that *yon* 'expresses a further degree of conceptual or physical distance'. To illustrate this point she provides the following examples from her Glasgow texts:

(1)   We got yon way we'd started just going round to the wee school.
(2)   Heh, Ah hope he gies us wan i yon stories, eh?

It would appear that (1) refers to something not quite observable to speaker or hearer, and (2) is a vague type of reference, not really speaker- or hearer-pivoted either. Instances of *yon* are, however, scarce in

Macafee's vast text collections. It is a pity that it is only presented as a lexical item and not contrasted with the other 'members' of the system; could it, for example, be replaced by a form of *that* in the two examples quoted above?

Admittedly, the purpose of Macafee's 'grammar of Glasgow speech' is only to provide some background to the study of her text collection. What is more alarming is the lack of conclusive examples in the existing major dictionaries and grammars.

The word *yon* is derived from Old English *geon*, signifying 'that... over there'. Not until the Middle English period did it become frequent, but by the end of the fifteenth century it is documented in most British dialects. In grammars and dictionaries of Middle English and Late Modern English, *yon* is defined in much the same way as by Edwards and Veltens, as quoted above. There are, however, some indications that the 'distant-remote' distinction began to disappear in Middle English. Examples tend to be few and too much out of context.

Joseph Wright, in his *English Dialect Grammar* (appended to the *Dictionary*), lists an overwhelming number of forms of demonstratives but makes no claims whatsoever as to a three-term system. A further surprise is that this is not mentioned in the *Manual of Modern Scots* (Grant and Dixon 1921) either.

In *The English Dialect Dictionary*, on the other hand, *yon* is defined by Wright as 'that, those', but said to be 'especially used of a person or thing a little way off but within sight'. As always in this dictionary, examples are plentiful and drawn from diverse sources. Consider the following selection from various parts of Northern Britain:

(3) Turn down by yon house.
(4) He wanted you to say something to yon folks.
(5) Ye wouldna let me gie half-a-crown for yon lace.

Taking a critical view of these examples as they relate to Wright's own definition, we might argue that neither (4) nor (5) necessarily implies that the concept preceded by *yon* is 'within sight'.

Although *The Scottish National Dictionary* gives the same general definition of *yon* as other handbooks, it differs from the others in its careful selection of examples. These clearly suggest remoteness in time and space and sometimes demonstrate the whole system, as in the following quotation from Burns:

(6) Tho' this was fair, and that was braw, And yon the toast of a' the town.

It is also pointed out that *yon* tends to be used in phrases with euphemistic or depreciatory force. Thus *yon kind* is said to mean 'ill-conditioned', 'not quite the thing'. In fact, as many of the examples show, this attitudinal dimension of *yon* is not restricted to fixed phrases. As a matter of

TAMING THE VERNACULAR

curiosity, it could be mentioned that a special entry for *yon* defines it as being a euphemistic name for seasickness in fishermen's taboo language.

Finally, consider the description of Shetland usage, from Robertson and Graham (1991: 5):

> Generally speaking, *yun* is used of things near in time and place, while *dat* is used of things past or more remote. 'Yun's my bit o' land oot benoort, an dat wis my bridder's croft at du saa apo da tidder side o' da voe.'

As the reader will have observed, this contrasts with the alleged usage elsewhere.

Perhaps the point that emerges most consistently from this brief survey of the literature is that there could be an attitudinal sense associated with *yon*, though this is not usually explicitly discussed by scholars.

6.2.2 SED and LSS data on demonstrative pronouns

In Book IX of the *SED* Questionnaire (cf. Orton *et al*. 1962–71), a whole section (10) is devoted to 'PRONOUNS: DEMONSTRATIVE'. This section is the last but one; its first question is No. 1322 in the total 'battery', which is worth thinking about in assessing the informants' performance. Since it is essential to understand the 'deictic setting', the questions asked and the instructions to the fieldworker will be quoted in full. Key answers, i.e. 'the notions to be named', are emboldened.

> In asking the next questions, you must stand at the informant's side.
> 1. Here are two coins (put one close to him and the other a little further away). Say which you'll have. You'll have (point) . . . **that**.
> 2. Not (point) . . . **this**.
> 3. Now look! We have three coins (put the third some distance from him). Now you will choose, not (point) this, nor (point) that, but (point) . . . **that over there**.
> Next put two coins at each place.
> 4. Now you can choose (point) . . . **those**.
> 5. Or (point) . . . **these**.
> 6. Or (point) . . . **those over there**.
> 7. If I asked you how you fold your arms, you'd probably show me and say: Well, I just do it . . . **in this way**.

The results, as listed in Part 3 of the *Basic Material* (Orton *et al*. 1962–71), show a profusion of forms, especially in response to questions 3 and 6. This goes for all the volumes, i.e. for every part of the country. It would seem that there is great variation in expressing a distal dimension. In Volume I, *The Six Northern Counties and the Isle of Man*, for example, the following answers to question 3 are listed:

> THAT (ONE), THAT (ONE/OVER/) THERE, THAT OVER THERE/
> THONDER/YON/YONDER, THON (ONE), TOTHER, YON (/AT FARREST AWAY/ + FAR
> + ONE/TOTHER/), YON OVER YON/YONDER/, YOND

'THREE-DIMENSIONAL' DEICTIC SYSTEMS

The form *yon* is also used by many informants in replying to questions 1 and 4, i.e. when there is an explicit contrast between two items only.

The only replies selected for mapping in the *Linguistic Atlas of England* (1978) were tokens of *those* and *these*. *Yon* is not even mentioned in the key, and the only really interesting thing about the maps is that they demonstrate the extension of *them* as a deictic pronoun.

A more interesting issue, considering the data, would be the following: to what extent do informants produce a three-term system as searched for in questions 2/1/3 or 5/4/6? In order to investigate that, we should look at individual speakers rather than produce an overall mapping. Here are, for example, the replies to 2/1/3 by three Northern speakers and one informant from the South:

Yorkshire 16 (Easingwold): **this one/that one/yon one**;
Yorkshire 24 (Cawood): **this/that/yon over yonder**;
Man 2 (Ronague): **this/that/that one there**;
Cornwall 2: **thicky/that/thicky over there**.

In fact, it turns out that *all* informants all over England use different expressions, if not explicit, i.e. simple, forms, for 2, 1 and 3. This demonstrates the extremely enforced character of the questionnaire, investigating 'pure deixis' at its purest, not really even having a 'normal' speaker–hearer dimension but rather the fieldworker breathing down the informant's neck, acting as a sort of 'deputy pointer'. Admittedly, owing to the need for deictic context, it is extremely difficult to elicit systems of demonstratives, but the *SED* line of questioning must be regarded as unnecessarily crude. Yet the overall aim, as expressed only in a note on question 1 in Volume IV (Southern), was '... to elicit general differences in meaning and usage between the pronouns *that* and *this*, or their synonyms'.

In the *Linguistic Survey of Scotland*, demonstratives and a few other pronouns were elicited as part of the phonological(!) questionnaire, the reason probably being that it was found necessary to ask these questions in a face-to-face situation; lexical items were otherwise chiefly elicited by means of postal questionnaires. The data from these particular questions have as yet not been published. As in the *SED*, they come at the very end of the questionnaire. It is not quite clear what the fieldworker's instructions were. The type of question is that of a fill-in exercise, where the 'key form' is here written in capitals:

1401. THIS book in my hand
1402. THAT book in your hand
1403. THAT book I was telling you about.
1404. THAT house just opposite.
1405. THAT house away over there (visible)
1406. THAT house away beyond the hill (invisible)
1407–1412 deal with plural forms in the same framework.

The *LSS* directors have graciously allowed me to take extracts from the fieldworkers' records of the ten Shetland localities investigated. It appears that most informants basically make the distinction *this* (realized as *dis*)/*yon*. One informant, representing Dunrossness on South Mainland, showed great insecurity as to 1404 and suggested *dis* as well as *dat* and *yon*. The assumed distinction between 1405 and 1406 was not corroborated.

Do the findings from the *SED* and *LSS* suggest that a three-term system really exists in natural discourse? An obvious step towards investigating this would be to consult and search corpora of spoken nonstandard varieties, such as the Helsinki dialect corpus collected by Ihalainen and his colleagues, which draws heavily on transcriptions of recordings made for the *SED*. However, the results of such searches turn out to be extremely disappointing. Forms of *this* and *that* occur in much the same way as in standard English, and there is only one single example of *yon*, found in a recording from the West Riding of Yorkshire. The near-absence of *yon* may at first seem puzzling, since the word was obviously known by the *SED* informants, who did not hesitate to use it in answering the questionnaire. In many cases, these informants were identical with the people who produced the corpora texts. The reason for the discrepancy is, however, undoubtedly to be found in the character of the texts, which derive from interviews focusing on 'rural customs in the old days'. Such texts do not lend themselves easily to studies of spatio-temporal relationships or attitudinal expressions.

6.2.3 Focusing on demonstratives in discourse: some recent work

It follows from the above that alternative procedures must be chosen for the investigation of deictic systems. After having – unsuccessfully – subjected my Shetland informants to questions of the *LSS* type, I have come to the conclusion that the most rewarding way of investigating the matter is participant observation. Another worthwhile strategy has been adopted from Brown and Yule (1983), who designed experiments, including series of pictures, for the structured elicitation of reference systems. A third method, which is not to be neglected, is to have linguistic discussions with the informants themselves.

One result of such discussions has been the finding that young informants do not seem to master or acknowledge a three-dimensional system at all. They claim that *dat* and *yon*(*yun*) are 'the same'. Most adult speakers are aware of a difference, but seldom agree with the 'visibility' criterion. They would explain the Robertson–Graham example (cf. 6.2.1) as relating to time rather than place.

From participant observation carried out over a period of five years, I feel safe in arguing that there exists a three-term system in Shetland dialect, although, as we have seen, apparent-time observations, i.e.

considering different age groups, suggest that the system is crumbling. A maintained system, as realized by middle-aged and older informants, is characterized as follows.

The usage of *this* offers no surprises (cf. also Harris 1991). As to a *dat/ yon* distinction, a few tentative claims and distinctions could be put forward. *Dat* is used in idiomatic expressions and in anaphoric reference to unspecified, especially abstract, major units. As a determiner it often carries more stress than *yon*. From an attitudinal point of view, it is characterized by less involvement. *Yon*, on the other hand, is much more of a 'loaded' word, an indexical or marker of identity. It is used as a covert prestige form and quickly acquired by incomers who want to identify with Shetlanders, to the same extent as they start using the indexical *peerie* for 'small'. In mentioning this, I do not wish to suggest that incomers master the system, which would contradict the claim that the system is subject to change; the phenomenon is merely mentioned to demonstrate *yon*'s strong position as an indexical. The most powerful connotation of *yon*, however, is as a signal of emotional distance and foreignness, based on shared knowledge among the speakers. Walterston (1984), an extremely popular collection of cartoons describing Shetland in the oil age, abounds with examples of the type *yon oil company, yon muckle Concorde, yun flarestack* (referring to the oil terminal at Sullom Voe, with its eternal flame).

In his work on demonstrative adjectives and pronouns in the dialect of South Zeal, a village on the northern edge of Dartmoor, Harris found certain evidence, in conversational data, of a three-way system, often realized as *this/that/thicky*; differences in the actual phonetic realization will not be considered here. First of all, it appeared that *thicky* was extremely rare as a pronoun, although as an adjective it almost outnumbered *this* and *that* together (Harris 1991: 22). Turning to the actual functions of the forms, Harris states (p. 23f) that 'the role of *this* is similar to "this" in Standard English . . . , but any attempt to differentiate *that* and *thicky* proves extremely difficult'. He is, for example, puzzled by the sentence 'If you was to put *that* stick in across *thicky* pony . . .', where he finds that 'the two forms seem to fill the same function'. Yet, had a wider context been provided, an attitudinal-referential difference as observed in the Shetland material, might well have been perceived.

Harris, too, has found it useful to test acceptability and exchange of forms on the speakers themselves. *That/thicky* were often claimed to be equally acceptable. It should be mentioned that age is not mentioned as a factor in Harris's data, of which the principal supplier is quite aged. It is therefore difficult to make any claims as to possible changes in usage. Some details of the semantics of the forms are given: *that*, for example, is used when actually indicating a size with the hands, and *thicky* is used in contrast with *tother*. In the adjective plural, *thicky* is found only with numerals. Most of the occurrences of *that* as a pronoun do not refer to a specific antecedent. 'First compounds', i.e. having *here* or *there* as a second element (*this here*, etc.) 'refer to items which have not been mentioned before, and which are not adjacent to the speaker; they are thus referentially distinct from the normal use of Standard English "this"' (p. 25f). In all, Harris's analysis of his data focuses on grammatical rather than discourse functions, but the fact that *thick* and *thicky* were often claimed as equally acceptable suggests a parallel with *dat* and *yon* in Shetland and the possible existence of a similar attitudinal sense which is below the level of speakers' awareness.

The *Survey of British Dialect Grammar* (cf. Cheshire *et al.* 1993) is exclusively based on a questionnaire given to schoolchildren, which was presented and completed in writing. Thirteen questions related to demonstratives. Since this is a study of young people's usage, it is of special importance in considering changes in usage. The most significant results had to do with the widely reported use of demonstrative *them*. The only schools that did not report demonstrative *them* were the two schools in Glasgow, where *thon* as well as *yon* were elicited (p. 65). Schools in the North of England did not report 'first compounds', i.e. *this here, that there*. The discussion of the status of demonstratives in Britain today, establishes that *them* is the preferred demonstrative form in the urban centres of England; it is further suggested that other historical forms of the demonstrative adjective may now survive only in regions that are relatively independent of the urban centres. There is evidence here, then, that the three-way system is in decline, or has already declined, in mainstream English dialects.

6.3 Why is a three-way system not present in standard English?

The pronouns/demonstrative adjectives *yon* (*yond*), like the adverb *yonder*, alleged to express the 'extra-distal' dimension, are listed in the most recent edition of the *Oxford English Dictionary*, but marked as 'archaic', 'dialectal' or 'literary'. They do not surface in present-day grammars of English. In Old and Middle English, however, the forms are well documented (cf. section 6.2 above). Why then, are neither these forms nor, for that matter, 'first compound' forms (see, for example, Harris 1991), part of present-day standard English?

There seems to be no evidence of condemnation by grammarians. In Dr Johnson's dictionary, all the forms quoted in the *OED* are listed; nothing is said about their currency or acceptability, but any examples are taken from fiction (Shakespeare, Milton, Pope, etc.).

A more well-founded answer to the question posed above has to do with the commonplace that 'dialects are characteristically spoken'. Among salient differences between speech and writing as subtly analysed in

Biber (1988), demonstratives are highlighted and typically associated with informal, unplanned types of discourse, such as conversational interaction. A powerful element in such interaction is the concept of 'involvement', 'an internal, even emotional connection individuals feel which binds them to other people as well as to places, things, activities, ideas, memories, and words' (Tannen 1989: 12). Although not really substantiated by the Middle English textual evidence, *yon* may well have had an attitudinal sense in the spoken language of the period. The affective, 'involved' senses of the demonstratives may have been below speaker awareness and hence not picked up by descriptive grammars or dictionaries (see also Cheshire, this volume). The maintenance of a three-way system as still evidenced in Shetland dialect today indicates that it is above all of an emotional–attitudinal character. To some extent, it can be said to be a case of 'de-grammaticalization', in that a morphemic–syntagmatic distinctive marker once developed has returned to being a lexical item, albeit a multi-faceted one.

References

Aitken, A.J. 1984. Scots and English. In: P. Trudgill (ed.), *Language in the British Isles*, Cambridge: CUP, pp. 517–32.

Biber, D. 1988. *Variation across Speech and Writing*. Cambridge: CUP.

Bloomfield, L. 1933. *Language*. London: Allen and Unwin.

Brown, G. and Yule, G. 1983. *Discourse Analysis*. Cambridge: CUP.

Cheshire, J., Edwards, V. and Whittle, P. 1993. Non-standard English and dialect levelling. In: J. and L. Milroy (eds), *Real English*, London: Longman, pp. 53–96.

Edwards, V. and Weltens, B. 1984. Research on non-standard dialects of British English: Progress and prospects. In: W. Viereck (ed.), *Focus on: England and Wales*. Amsterdam: Benjamins, pp. 97–139.

Grant, W. and Dixon, J.M. 1921. *Manual of Modern Scots*. Cambridge: CUP.

Grant, W. and Murison, D.D. (eds) 1931–76. *The Scottish National Dictionary*. Edinburgh: Scottish National Dictionary Association Ltd.

Harris, M. 1991. Demonstrative adjectives and pronouns in a Devonshire dialect. In: P. Trudgill and J.K. Chambers (eds), *Dialects of English*. London: Longman, pp. 20–8.

Kirk, J., Sanderson, S. and Widdowson, J.D.A. (eds) 1985. *Studies in Linguistic Geography*. London: Croom Helm.

Lyons, J. 1981. *Language, Meaning and Context*. London: Fontana.

Macafee, C. 1983. *Glasgow*. Varieties of English around the World, T. 3. Amsterdam: Benjamins.

Melchers, G. 1983. *NORN. The Scandinavian Element in Shetland Dialect*. Stockholm University: Department of English.

Orton, H. *et al.* 1962–71. *Survey of English Dialects*. Introduction and 4 vols. Leeds: E.J. Arnold.
Robertson, T.A. and Graham, J.J. 1991. *Grammar and Usage of the Shetland Dialect*. Lerwick: The Shetland Times Ltd.
Tannen, D. 1989. *Talking Voices*. Cambridge: CUP.
Walterston, F.S. 1984. *Gaf it Aff*. Lerwick: The Shetland Times Ltd.
Weissenborn, J. and Klein, W. (eds) 1982. *Here and There. Cross-linguistic Studies on Deixis and Demonstration*. Amsterdam: Benjamins.
Wright, J. (ed.) 1898–1905. *The English Dialect Dictionary*. London: CUP.

CHAPTER 7

Grammatical variation and the avoidance of stress clashes in Northern Low German

Günter Rohdenburg

7.1 Introduction

In an article written over sixty years ago, the Dutch grammarian Overdiep (1933–34) stressed the special role played by phonology in dialect syntax. In particular, he pointed out that redundant syntactic material may be redeployed or exapted for rhythmical purposes.[1] Such a change involves the negative particle *ne* or *en*, which has been ousted by lexically strengthened versions in virtually all West Germanic languages. In certain Dutch dialects, however, it has been preserved as a purely prosodic filler in subordinate clauses. Overdiep's analysis, which cannot be presented here in any greater detail, is based on examples like those in (1):

(1) a. Toe   ze   nae huis   (en) ginge ete, ...
       when they to   house   went eat
       'When they went home to have dinner, ...'

    b. Et regende, toe   ze   nae huis   *(en) ginge.
       it rained   when they to   house   went
       'It was raining when they went home.'

While the meaningless particle is optional in (1a), it proves to be obligatory in (1b).

Prompted by Overdiep's research and also by Dieter Stein's (1986) work on *do*-support in Early Modern English, I investigated some years ago a number of grammatical variation phenomena in Northern Low German dialects. In many cases, it was discovered that the choice of the variants in question is largely determined by general phonological tendencies. Some of these earlier findings include the following phenomena:

1. *Doon-support in subordinate clauses* (Rohdenburg 1986). Here it was found that the selection of the older simple form is (in some dialects) favoured by tense stem vowels but disfavoured by short vowels preceding fricatives. Consider:

(2) a. ? He mutt oppassen, dat he noch wat krich.
 he must take care that he still somewhat gets
 'He'd better make sure he still gets something.'

 b. He mutt oppassen, dat he noch wat kriegen
 he must take care that he still somewhat get
 deit.
 does
 'He'd better make sure he still gets something.'

2. (*Earlier weak*) *feminine nouns with or without redundant case inflections.* In certain dialects the earlier object case inflections may now be used to mark strongly stressed items (Rohdenburg 1989a).[2] Compare the examples in (3).

 (3) a. He hüng sien Mütz op'n Nagel, ...
 'He hung his cap on a nail, ...'

 b. Denn steiht Vadder op un langt na sien Mützen.
 then stands Father up and reaches for his cap
 'Then Father got up and reached for his cap.'

3. *The deletion of oblique inflections with (weak) masculine nouns or pronouns* (Rohdenburg 1989b, 1993). Conversely, morphological or syntactic positions involving reduced stress favour the deletion of the object case inflections. Accordingly, these inflections are more likely to be lost in compound-final position than in the corresponding simple nouns.

There do not appear to be any comparable phonological influences at work in standard German. At any rate, what both Overdiep's and my data suggest is that the grammars of nonstandard varieties are generally more sensitive to phonological factors than standard languages. The hypothesis is also supported in English by the bit of evidence we have concerning relevant dialect phenomena and historical grammaticalization processes (cf., for instance, Wolfram 1976 and Stein 1986).

In this chapter I would like to strengthen the hypothesis by investigating the pronounced tendency shared by both English and Low German to avoid the occurrence of stress clashes (cf., for instance, van Draat 1910, Bolinger 1965: 139ff, Couper-Kuhlen 1986, Bollmann 1942: 6). Discounting the introduction of pauses, the devices used by English and Low German turn out to be very different. Unlike Low German, English boasts a large number of end-stressed words such as *in'tact*, *Chi'nese* and *in'creased* whose stress is regularly or potentially shifted to an earlier syllable in prenominal or attributive uses like those in (4).

(4) a. It still is an 'intact system.
 b. They had a meal in a 'Chinese restaurant.
 c. Owing to 'increased prices ...

However, there are hardly any grammatical variation phenomena left in English which could be said to function in a similar way. Notice that the type of contrast illustrated by (adjectivalized) participles like those in (5) has become fully grammaticalized (Bolinger 1965: 139ff).

(5) the drunken sailor – the sailor is drunk

The longer variant simply has to be used in attributive position even in cases where the short alternative would not have produced any stress clash.

In contrast to English, Northern Low German dialects feature a large number of grammatical alternatives which are – at least in part – exploited for the purpose of avoiding any stress clashes. In the following, I shall try to give an overview of the relevant variation phenomena. The analysis is based on a corpus of roughly 100 published books produced by 30 authors in as many dialects.[3] For our purposes at least, these texts may be regarded as satisfactory representations of spoken Low German (actually, quite a few of them were broadcast on radio).

7.2 Marked and unmarked infinitives

7.2.1 *The insertion of* to

In Northern Low German dialects, most verb-dependent infinitival uses generally involve either the infinitive marked by a preceding *to* (corresponding to English *to* and standard German *zu*) or the unmarked infinitive exclusively. However, the restrictions on the occurrence of unmarked infinitives are not as absolute as in the standard language, and one occasionally comes across infinitives marked by an extra *to* which cannot be accounted for in syntactic or semantic terms. Such insertions tend to be motivated phonologically, and in particular by the need to avoid a potential stress clash. Let us take a brief look at two cases in point.

(6) So geiht se   all   fröh an sien Bedd to stohn un
     so goes she already early to his bed   to stand and
     seggt: .... (Seidensticker 4, 46)
     says
     'So early in the morning she went up to his bed and said: ...'

(7) ... [he] hett nu   beide Hannen fast   um   dat Glas to
     he has now both hands   tightly round the glass to
     liggen, ... (Tenne 1, 89)
     lie
     '... now he had both hands tightly clasped round his glass ...'

In the corpus both construction types, *gohn + stohn/sitten/liggen* ('go + stand/sit/lie') or *hebben + stohn/sitten/liggen* ('have + stand/sit/lie') normally feature the unmarked infinitive, and apart from (6) and (7) this is how the type is realized in the authors concerned. No doubt, the regular construction would have produced a stress clash in both (6) and (7). The assumption that this explains the insertion of *to* is supported by the remaining unmarked infinitives of the construction *gohn* + *stohn* in Seidensticker: there are no stress clashes in the two other examples. For instance, compare (6) with (8):

(8)   De Schoolmester ... geiht no'n   Tiedlang achter Kríschan
        the schoolmaster   goes after a while   behind Christian
        stóhn, ... (Seidensticker, 2, 20)
        stand
        'After a while the schoolmaster went and stood behind Christian, ...'

Other insertions of *to* are found in elliptical constructions as in (9).

(9)   ..., un   he is säker'n   goden Jung. Man dén   to
        and he is certainly a good   boy. But that one/hím to
        fréen – .' (Rogge, Hinnerk mit'n Hoot, 89)
        marry
        '..., and he is certainly a good boy. But I don't know about marrying him – ...'

While the colloquial standard would probably use the unmarked infinitive in such cases, a surprising number of Low German examples as in (9) include the infinitive marker. The comparison of contrasting examples like those in (9) and (10) suggests that the extra *to* (as in (9)) is largely motivated by a desire to separate two strong stresses.

(10)   Man ik weet   nich rech, so'n   Schípper fréen,
         but   I   know not   quite, such a sailor   marry,
         de ... (*ibid.*, 91)
         who
         'But I'm not really sure about marrying a sailor like that, who ...'

7.2.2   The deletion of **to**

It has been known for a long time that many regionally modified varieties of the spoken standard show a pronounced tendency to drop the infinitive marker *zu* 'to' in constructions involving *brauchen* 'need' (cf., for instance, Pfeffer 1973). The tendency is comparatively weak in Northern Germany but very strong in Bavaria proper where the indigenous dialects do not use any *zu*-infinitives at all. In this respect, Low German dialects generally seem to be lagging far behind even the colloquial standard used in Northern Germany. If the various phenomena of *to*-insertion can be shown to be motivated phonologically, then we would expect the process of *to*-deletion to be also constrained by phonological

Table 7.1: The distribution of marked and unmarked infinitives associated with *bruken/höven* 'need' in (part of) the corpus

	I to	II Ø	III Total	IV Percentage of *to* (%)
1 All examples (excluding fronted infinitives)	293	31	324	90.4
2 Passive infinitives and other binary infinitival constructions	1	9	10	10
3 Particle verbs in authors employing the unmarked infinitive	41	13	54	75.9
4 Remaining verbs in authors employing the unmarked infinitive (excluding fronted or binary infinitival constructions)	115	9	124	92.7

needs. More precisely, we would predict *to*-deletion to be favoured in contexts where the retained *to* simply cannot serve as a buffer between two strong stresses. Examples (11) and (12) identify two general grammatical contexts of this kind.

(11) Dat bruukt nich glieks eten (to) warrn.
 that needs not at once eaten to become.
 'That needn't be eaten right away.'

(12) Ji   bruukt jem nich ut(to)trecken.
 you (pl.) need them not out to pull
 'You needn't take them off.'

Example (11) illustrates the class of passive infinitives. With these (and other binary infinitival constructions) a retained *to* generally follows an unstressed syllable such as the *-en* in (11) (*eten*), and it invariably precedes a stress-reduced syllable such as *warrn* in (11). Example (12) represents the class of particle verbs which invariably have the main stress on the particle itself (i.e. *ut*). In neither case could the optional *to* be used as a buffer between two strong stresses. As is shown in Table 7.1, both types of context do indeed favour the deletion of *to* to varying degrees.

7.3 Copied prepositions

This section draws attention to a curious construction related to and competing with preposition stranding. It involves the copying of a preposition in positions otherwise occupied by stranded prepositions (Meyer 1921: 85). Some typical examples illustrating the phenomenon include the following:

(13) Mit dissen ooln Fulwust harrn se em fix mit ansmeert. (Kinau 13, 68)
   with this old lazy sausage had they him strongly with cheated.
   'He had been really cheated with that lazy sausage.'

(14) Von beid' ward nich veel von snackt. (Seidensticker)
   of both is not much of talked
   'Not much is talked about either of them.'

(15) Mit'n Gewitterflog schall'n keen Spoß mit drieben. (Kinau)
   with a thunderstorm shall one no fun with drive
   'Thunderstorms are not something to joke about!'

(16) ... för dat Strafgeld will ick leewer Köhm un Beer för köpen! (Lemmermann)
   for the fine will I rather spirits and beer for buy.
   'I'd rather buy spirits and beer than pay a fine.'

While the two related constructions may serve very similar discourse functions all the available evidence suggests that the copied prepositions (such as *mit*, *von*, and *för* in (13)–(16)) are far more likely to be used as a buffer between two strong stresses. All of the examples given above display this function.

7.4 Prefixation

7.4.1 *The infinitival prefix* be-

With verbs of posture, most Northern Low German dialects boast two kinds of infinitives, simple unprefixed ones and others featuring the unstressed prefix *be-*. As a rule, the prefixed forms are restricted to combinations involving *blieben*, 'remain', as in (17).

(17) He bleew doar (be)sitten/(be)hangen.
   he remained there sit (inf.)/hang (inf.)
   'He remained seated/suspended there.'

Traditionally, the marked variant has been assigned a specific durative function: it is claimed to indicate either a markedly longer duration or the continuation of the states in question (Bernhard 1903: 14, Meyer 1921: 93, Harte 1981: 31–2, Saltveit 1983: 301). As is well known, the collocation *stehen bleiben* is two ways ambiguous in standard German and probably in most other varieties of German:

(18) a. Er mußte stehn bleiben.
   he must (Past) stand (inf.) remain (inf.)
   'He had to stop.'
   b. He had to stop (walking/running/driving, etc.).
   c. He had to remain standing.

In example (18a) we can distinguish between an inchoative reading as glossed in (18b) or a continuative interpretation as in (18c). The general assumption concerning cases like these seems to be that Northern Low German resolves or may resolve the ambiguity by restricting the prefixed infinitive to the continuative reading. My corpus analysis, however, suggests that any durative functions that the prefixed forms may have had are largely or nearly totally overshadowed by prosodic requirements: the prefix is mainly used as a buffer between two strong stresses. The tendency is illustrated in (19) and (20), which – despite the glosses provided – represent the inchoative reading of *stohn blieben*.

(19) ..., dennso blievt   mi doch   de Peer
   then   remain (pl.) me [particle] the horses
   bestohn. (Seidensticker)
   stand.
   '... then the horses stop.'

(20) De Wiehnachtsmann de bleev   op'n Stutz midden
   the Father Christmas he remained suddenly in the middle
   op de Brügg bestahn   un ... (Holschen 2, 69)
   on the bridge stand (inf.) and
   'Suddenly Father Christmas stopped in the middle of the bridge and ...'

Examples like these contrast with cases like (21) which do not involve any potential stress clashes.

(21) Mit eenen Gnuck bleev   de Wiehnachtsmann stahn
   with a   jerk   remained the Father Christmas stand (inf.)
   un ... (Holschen 2, 63)
   and
   'Father Christmas pulled up with a jerk and ...'

7.4.2 Alternatives involving ge-

Past participles in Northern Low German have generally dropped the prefix *ge-*, which is still characteristic of standard German or standard Dutch in this function. Some conservative dialects do, however, retain

TAMING THE VERNACULAR

a few of these prefixed participles in certain fixed collocations like that in (22).

(22) Dat is lich(t) gesegt. (Braasch, Kinau)
      'That is easily said.'

In (22) and similar cases the prefix serves to separate two strong stresses, and this undoubtedly accounts for its retention here. This assumption is supported by the fact that although these fixed phrases may be replaced entirely by some other expression they do not simply give up the buffer prefix alone.

Similar observations apply to the equivalent of standard German *genug* 'enough'. While most dialects are restricted to the unprefixed equivalent *noog*, some may occasionally use the extra prefix to avoid a potential stress clash. For example:

(23)   Ligt   jo   Kroom genoog an'n
        [there] lies [particle] stuff enough on the
        Grund. (Kinau 18, 52)
        ground
        'There's enough stuff lying on the ground.'

From the point of view of standard German, there are even examples of *ge-* insertion which may be used for the same purpose. A case in point is provided by *ruhig*, a loan from standard German, which is occasionally found with an extra prefix. Consider:

(24)   ...: Kannst ruhig wesen, ganz
        [You (sg.)]   can   quiet be,   quite
        geruhig. (Schmidt-Barrien)
        quiet
        'No need to worry.'

Admittedly, the prefix in *geruhig* is more commonly used to distinguish a semantically full adjective in the sense of 'quiet' from a bleached modal particle in the sense of '(just as) well/very well'.

7.5 Inflectional and other suffixes

7.5.1 *Attributive adjectives*

In Northern Low German, attributive adjectives modifying singular neuter nouns have traditionally been uninflected in the so-called strong declension. This concerns the indefinite article, the null determiner and (in most, though not all dialects) the possessive pronouns. In more recent times, however, forms featuring the suffix *-et* (or even *-es*) as in

Table 7.2: Attributive adjectives associated with neuter nouns (in the so-called strong inflection) in Seidensticker 1–3

	I -et	II -Ø	III Total	IV Percentage of -et (%)
1 *groot, lütt, good, ool*	1	54	55	1.8
2 Stereotyped uses	–	3	3	0
3 *fett, natt, swatt, witt*	2	5	7	28.6
4 Remaining adjectives:				
(a) All examples	15	49	64	23.4
(b) Monosyllabic adjectives	9	20	29	31.0
(c) Bisyllabic and trisyllabic adjectives	6	29	35	17.1
(d) Actual or potential stress clashes	9	10	19	47.4
(e) Other cases	6	39	45	13.6

(25a) have been gaining ground at the expense of the uninflected forms as in (25b) (cf., for instance, Heymann 1909: 129–30, Mackel 1907: 82, Meyer 1921: 161, Bunning 1934/5: 136–7, Harte 1981: 114–15).

(25) a. 'n/sien eischet Wurd
         a/his   nasty   word
     b. 'n/sien eisch Wurd
         a/his   nasty word

At any rate, the tendency is found to varying degrees in all of the dialects in the area lying between Hamburg and Bremen. Everywhere the distribution of the old and new forms seems to be subject to lexical as well as phonological constraints. Consider the data in Table 7.2, which deals with the language of a single author. As is shown in line 1, general and high-frequency adjectives (corresponding to *big, little, good* and *old* in English) are as yet hardly affected by the change. This holds also for many stereotyped phrases (represented in line 2) and perhaps even for most other adjectives ending in *t* itself (cf. line 3). In order not to prejudge a potential phonotactic issue, adjectives like these have been excluded from further consideration. Turning now to the remaining cases in lines 4b and 4c, we observe first of all that monosyllabic adjectives show a greater readiness to adopt the syllabic inflection than more complex items. Furthermore, as is indicated in lines 4d and 4e, this skewing may be largely attributed to the buffer function of the extra syllable. Compare example (26), in which the inflection separates two strong stresses, with (27), which does not involve a stress clash.

(26) ... so 'n ool mallet Jöken ... (Seidensticker)
'... such an old nasty itch...'

(27) ... mit sien ool klaterig Fohrrad ... (Seidensticker)
'... with his old rickety bike...'

An obviously related phenomenon concerns the equivalent of *last* in temporal phrases like *last year, last autumn* and so on. It is true that dialects clinging to the morphologically isolated participle *vledden* in (28) are not confronted with the problem of stress clashes.

(28) vledden Harst (cf. Dutch *verleden*)
    past   autumn
    'last autumn'

Difficulties may, however, arise in the case of the participle *vergohn*, as illustrated in (29).

(29) vergóhn'n Harst (cf. standard German *vergangen*)
    past   autumn
    'last autumn'

With masculine nouns like *Harst* 'autumn', the participle is inflected for the oblique case, which provides a syllabic nasal. With neuter (or feminine) nouns the participle would normally be uninflected. This could have produced a jarring stress clash in a number of extremely common collocations. However, what we find in certain areas at least is that the masculine inflection has exceptionally been extended to cases involving neuter and feminine nouns. Some of these extensions are illustrated in (30).[4]

(30) vergóhn'n Johr (n.)/Förjohr (n.)/Week (f.)
    past   year   /spring   /week
    'last year/spring/week'

The earlier extension of the oblique masculine inflection to nominative contexts in the strong declension should also be seen in this light. As a result of this change, examples like (31a) correspond to three different noun phrases in standard German (Rohdenburg 1989b, 1993).

(31) a. 'n söten Appel
      'a sweet apple'
   b. ein süßer Apfel (nom.)
   c. einem süßen Apfel (dat.)
   d. einen süßen Apfel (acc.)

Although the change is almost completed everywhere, a few fixed expressions as in (32) may have preserved the older and uninflected forms (Rohdenburg 1989b: 103–4).

STRESS CLASHES IN NORTHERN LOW GERMAN

(32) ..., do wor 't hellig Dag, ... (Braasch)
      then became it bright day
'..., then day dawned, ...'

However, what is remarkable about these relics is that they are never found to involve any stress clashes. In many cases, these adjectives contain the (unstressed) derivational suffix *-ig*, which may be lacking in the standard German equivalent. For instance, *hellig* (in (32)) corresponds to standard German *hell(er)*. Curiously enough, there are even some Low German dialects in which the use of *-ig* may – with some adjectives – be restricted to attributive position (Mackel 1907: 103). The situation is strongly reminiscent of the contrast between *drunken* and *drunk* referred to above (cf. example (5)).

Finally, it would appear that the phenomenon of gender variation, which is far more prominent in Low German than in the standard language, may also be exploited to some extent for similar purposes. Most dialects contain a number of nouns like *Sand* 'sand' or *Dook* '(piece of) cloth' which waver between the neuter and the masculine gender. Compare some representative choices involving *Dook* made by one particular author:

(33) De Lüüd harrn dat Dook (n.) woll mehr as Dekoratschoon
      the people had the cloth rather more as decoration
      brukt. (Schweitzer 2, 6)
      used
'The people had probably used the cloth more as decoration.'

(34) Doormals kunn he noch nich weeten, dat dat swatte
      then could he yet not know that the black
      Dook (n.) maal sien best 'Kaptaal' warrn
      cloth once his best capital become
      schull. (Schweitzer 2, 6)
      should
'In those days he was not to know that the black cloth might one day be his best asset.'

(35) Erstmaal fünn he [...] een beten grötter Stück swatten
      first of all found he a bit bigger piece black
      Dook (m.). (Schweitzer 2, 6)
      cloth
'First of all he found a slightly bigger piece of black cloth.'

In this dialect, the neuter gender, which may be due to pressure from standard German, represents the generally preferred choice. The masculine gender seems to be confined to cases like (35) where the extra syllable provided by the attributive adjective serves to avoid a stress clash.

7.5.2 Adverbs

Another inflectional extension in Low German involves certain intensifiers, which anticipate, as it were, the endings of attributive adjectives or nominalized adjectives (Bernhard 1903: 6). The phenomenon, which is paralleled in informal Dutch and many nonstandard forms of German (Henn-Memmesheimer 1986: 155ff), is particularly common with the intensifier *ganz* 'quite' preceding masculine noun phrases.[5] Consider, for instance:

(36) I He is 'n ganz(en) kloken Keerl.
he is a quite clever chap
'He is quite a clever chap.'

II He is 'n ganz(en) Kloken.
he is a quite clever one/clever clogs
'He is quite a clever clogs.'

There are two pieces of evidence suggesting that the use of inflected adverbs has been and still is encouraged by the tendency to separate two strong stresses. First of all, the inflection is restricted to monosyllabic intensifiers. Even such common adverbs like *bannig* 'very' are never found with the inflection. More important, the two grammatical uses illustrated in (36) show a markedly different behaviour, which seems to reflect different prosodic tendencies. While type II – without the inflection – would usually involve the clash of two strong stresses, the attributive adjective in type I is more likely to bear reduced stress. We would predict, then, that type II should represent a more advanced stage of the change in question. The prediction is clearly supported by the corpus evidence presented in Table 7.3. In all of the authors employing both types of constructions, type II shows a strikingly greater affinity with the inflection than type I.

In this connection, it is worth pointing out that in traditional Low German dialects numerals are usually modified by means of (inflected) attributive adjectives rather than (uninflected) adverbs as is generally the case in standard German. This tendency, which serves to eliminate any potential stress clashes, is illustrated in (37) and (38).

(37) ... 'n gode tweeunföfftig Johr ... (Bahr)
a good two and fifty year (sg.)
'... all of fifty-two years ...'

(38) ... ehre go'en veertig Wagens ... (Holschen)
their good forty carriages
'... at least forty floats of theirs ...'

Notice that this may create constructional ambiguities especially in cases like (38): apart from the intended reading (suggested by the parallel

Table 7.3: Inflected and uninflected occurrences of the adverb *ganz* 'quite' modifying masculine predicatives in part of the corpus

	I -Ø	II -*en*	III Total	IV Percentage of -*en* (%)
2 Behnken				
(a) attributive adjective	9	6	15	40
(b) nominalized adjective	1	5	6	83.3
6 Droste				
(a) attributive adjective	6	2	8	25
(b) nominalized adjective	2	6	8	75
13 Krämer				
(a) attributive adjective	3	6	9	66.7
(b) nominalized adjective	–	6	6	100
26 Seidensticker				
(a) attributive adjective	15	3	18	16.7
(b) nominalized adjective	3	6	9	66.7
Total				
(a) attributive adjective	33	17	50	34
(b) nominalized adjective	6	23	29	79.3

English type in example (37)) the adjective *go'en* in (38) could in theory be interpreted as a semantic modifier of the noun *Wagens*.

This brings us to a related problem concerning *equally* as a premodifier and its Low German equivalents *liek(e)*. In this function, *equally* has completely superseded the earlier adverb *alike*, which contained a final schwa or [ə] in Middle English. Notice that *equally* and the modified item tend to be strongly stressed. In addition, other uses of adverbial and adjectival *alike*, which do not involve any stress clashes, continue to flourish. This suggests that the replacement of *alike* by *equally* may have been encouraged by the tendency to separate two strongly stressed syllables. The assumption seems to be supported by ongoing developments in Northern Low German. The dialects spoken in the area between Hamburg and Bremen could have been expected to apocopate (or drop) the final syllable in Middle Low German *like*. Yet the expected form *liek* is found in few present-day dialects. While some retain the schwa [ə] in the final syllable, more and more dialects are adopting a strengthened, though semantically unmotivated ending -*er* as in (39).[6]

(39) Ji   beiden sünd lieke(r) duhn.
    you (pl.) both are equally drunk
    'You are both equally drunk.'

This effectively immunizes the form against the threat of apocopation.

7.5.3 Feminine nouns

As was pointed out in the introduction, certain dialects have preserved the semantically redundant object case inflection with some (weak) feminine nouns. Apart from simply signalling prosodically prominent items the extra syllable may also be used as a buffer between two strongly stressed syllables (Rohdenburg 1989a).

7.5.4 Lengthened infinitives

In a restricted area east of Bremen, a number of verbs with monosyllabic roots preserve the reflexes of the inflected infinitive.[7] For example:

(40) doon/to doon'n
    do /to do

The lengthened forms occur only under stress, and they typically retain the traditional association with the infinitive marker. Very occasionally, however, the extra syllable seems to be used simply to separate two stressed syllables. A relevant example is provided by (41).

(41) Un   as   Frollein Haubülten den armen Sünner dar   so trorig
    and when Miss   Hayheap the poor sinner there so sad
    vör   sik stahnen sehg – ... (Holschen)
    before her stand saw
    'And when Miss Hayheap saw the poor blighter standing there looking so miserable – ...'

7.6 Conclusion

We have seen, then, that Northern Low German dialects boast a wealth of grammatical variants whose distribution is largely determined by various phonological pressures. This distinguishes these dialects from standard German or standard English (and perhaps most European standard languages), where grammatical variation of the kind described seems to be controlled primarily by semantic, stylistic and possibly certain processing factors. In this chapter we have concentrated on what probably is the most important phonological constraint of all: the strong aversion to stress clashes. The buffer phenomena discussed represent a variety of function words (7.2.1–7.2.2, 7.3) and affixes (7.4.1–7.4.2, 7.5.1–7.5.4), which may be due to various insertion or deletion processes. In addition, a number of affixes which have become semantically redundant or are becoming so have also been exapted for phonological purposes. The morphological junk in question includes case inflections (7.5.3), inflected infinitives (7.5.4) and a few grammatical prefixes (7.4.1–7.4.2). Admittedly, phonologically motivated exaptation processes may also have occurred in standard languages like English (cf. the contrast between *drunk* and *drunken* in (5)). It may be assumed, however, that speakers of standard languages show a stronger tendency to reanalyse any such variation phenomena in semantic or syntactic terms.

Furthermore, there are even a few inflectional innovations whose main motivation seems to be phonological rather than semantic (7.5.1–7.5.2). While the bulk of the phenomena described are unlikely ever to be paralleled in standard German, some of them, such as the loss of certain nominal case inflections or the infinitive marker, may also be found in the standard language. But then the standard would tend to exploit such alternations for stylistic purposes. Owing to their reduced functional spectrum dialects generally lack this kind of stylistically motivated variation. What remains to be seen is whether and to what extent such phonological tendencies may be superimposed on the stylistically motivated variation phenomena in (regionally modified varieties of) the spoken standard.

Finally, it has to be conceded that Northern Low German dialects may also feature exaptive changes involving the redeployment of morphological junk for purely semantic purposes. For instance, while the reflex of the earlier dative in (42a) highlights the subject referent's personal involvement with the house in question (which presumably is his home), the uninflected neuter form in (42b) simply refers to a house *qua* building (which tends to be somebody else's home).

(42) a. He güng in 'n   Huus'.
      he went in the (dat.) house (dat.)
      'He went into his house.'

    b. He güng in dat/'t Huus.
      he went in the   house
      'He went into the house.'

It would appear, however, that (purely) semantically motivated exaptation tends to be confined to such variation phenomena which do not provide a potential buffer between strongly stressed syllables.

Notes

1 The concept of exaptation, which is also discussed in Vincent (1995), was first introduced to linguistics by Lass (1990).

2 The correlation appears to be iconic in the sense of natural morphology (cf., for instance, Mayerthaler 1981).
3 The corpus used for this paper is practically identical with that presented in Rohdenburg (1989b).
4 By contrast, the equivalent of *next*, which is based on the (otherwise defunct) present participle of *tókomen*, shows a totally different behaviour. There is no need here for any extra syllable. In fact, the second and unstressed syllable has been further eroded as is suggested by spellings like *tokum* or *tokern* among others.
5 Other assimilatory grammatical processes which are typically absent from (formal registers of) standard languages have been discussed in Rohdenburg (1988, 1991).
6 The change is implicitly recognized in Teut (1959, vol. 3: 49).
7 Unfortunately, this area has been overlooked in the most recent survey of the inflected infinitive presented by Keseling (1970).

References

Bernhard, J. 1903. Zur Syntax der gesprochenen Sprache. *Niederdeutsches Jahrbuch* 29: 1–25.
Bolinger, Dwight L. 1965. *Forms of English: Accent, Morpheme, Order.* Cambridge, Mass.: Harvard University Press.
Bollmann, Heinrich 1942. *Mundarten auf der Stader Geest.* Oldenburg: Stalling.
Bunning, H. 1934/35. Studien zur Geschichte der Bremischen Mundart. *Niederdeutsches Jahrbuch* 60/61: 63–147.
Couper-Kuhlen, Elizabeth 1986. *An Introduction to English Prosody.* Tübingen: Niemeyer.
Harte, Günter 1981. *Lebendiges Platt*, 3rd edition. Hamburg: Quickborn.
Henn-Memmesheimer, Beate 1986. *Nonstandardmuster. Ihre Beschreibung in der Syntax und das Problem der Arealität.* Tübingen: Niemeyer.
Heymann, W. 1909. *Das bremische Plattdeutsch.* Bremen: Gustav Winter.
Keseling, Gisbert 1970. Erwägungen zu einer überregionalen Syntax der niederdeutschen Mundarten. In: Dietrich Hofmann and Willy Sanders (eds), *Gedenkschrift für William Foerste.* Köln/Wien: Böhlau, pp. 354–65.
Lass, Roger 1990. How to do things with junk: exaptation in language evolution. *Journal of Linguistics* 26: 79–102.
Mackel, E. 1907. Die Mundart der Prignitz. *Niederdeutsches Jahrbuch* 33: 73–105.
Mayerthaler, Willi 1981. *Morphologische Natürlichkeit.* Wiesbaden: Athenaion.
Meyer, Gustav Friedrich 1921. *Unsere plattdeutsche Muttersprache.* Garding: Lühr & Dircks.

Overdiep, G.S. 1933-34. Dialectstudie en syntaxis: een overgangsklank. *Onze Taaltuin* 2: 44-5.
Pfeffer, J. Alan 1973. Brauchen als Vollverb, Hilfsmodal und Modalverb. *Wirkendes Wort* 23: 86-92.
Rohdenburg, Günter 1986. Phonologisch und morphologisch bedingte Variation in der Verbalsyntax des Nordniederdeutschen. *Niederdeutsches Jahrbuch* 109: 86-117.
Rohdenburg, Günter 1988. Flexionsangleichung von Substantiven an attributive Adjektive und verwandte Erscheinungen im Nordniedersächsischen. In: Heinrich Weber and Ryszard Zuber (eds), *Linguistik Parisette. Akten des 22. Linguistischen Kolloquiums, Paris 1987.* Tübingen: Niemeyer, pp. 277-88.
Rohdenburg, Günter 1989a. Prosodische Einflüsse in der Morphologie. Zur Variation von Kurz- und Langformen bei Feminina im Nordniedersächsischen. In: Norbert Reiter (ed.), *Sprechen und Hören, Akten des 23. Linguistischen Kolloquiums, Berlin 1988.* Tübingen: Niemeyer, pp. 59-71.
Rohdenburg, Günter 1989b. Zur Verdrängung des Nominativs durch den Obliquus im Nordniederdeutschen unter besonderer Berücksichtigung prosodischer Faktoren. *Kopenhagener Beiträge zur Germanistischen Linguistik* 25: 83-143.
Rohdenburg, Günter 1991. Formübertragungen, Assimilationen und Wiederaufnahmen in der Morphologie und Syntax des Nordniederdeutschen. *Korrespondenzblatt des Vereins für niederdeutsche Sprachforschung*, Heft 98: 35-42.
Rohdenburg, Günter 1993. Aspekte der Auflösung des Kasussystems im Nordniederdeutschen. In: Werner Abraham and Josef Bayer (eds), *Dialektsyntax (= Linguistische Berichte* Sonderheft 5). Opladen: Westdeutscher Verlag, pp. 213-229.
Saltveit, Laurits 1983. Syntax. In: Gerhard Cordes and Dieter Möhn (eds), *Handbuch zur niederdeutschen Sprach- und Literaturwissenschaft.* Berlin, pp. 279-333.
Stein, Dieter 1986. Syntactic variation and change: the case of DO in questions in Early Modern English. *Folia Linguistica Historica* 7: 121-49.
Teut, Heinrich 1959. *Hadeler Wörterbuch*, Vols. 1-4. Neumünster: Wachholtz.
van Draat, Fijn P. 1910. *Rhythm in English Prose.* Heidelberg: Winter.
Vincent, Nigel 1995. Exaptation and grammaticalization. In: Henning Andersen (ed.), *Historical Linguistics 1993.* Selected Papers from the 11th International Conference on Historical Linguistics, Los Angeles. Amsterdam: Benjamins, pp. 433-45.
Wolfram, Walt 1976. Toward a description of *a*-prefixing in Appalachian English. *American Speech* 51: 45-56.

CHAPTER 8

Norms made easy: case marking with modal verbs in Finnish

Lea Laitinen

8.1 Introduction

This chapter deals with the case-marking system of the central arguments in constructions containing modal verbs of necessity in standardized (written) and nonstandard (spoken) Finnish. The two systems are partly different. Even though it is very easy, the official norm, which dates from over a hundred years ago, has not been adopted in the spoken language. It ignores a large 'grey area', where the case alternation in nonstandard Finnish is hard to describe but not arbitrary. This alternation depends on the status of NPs on the person hierarchy, or on their degree of indexicality – a feature that is not easily standardized.

In an earlier work (Laitinen 1992), I analysed the case-marking system in colloquial Finnish, based on a corpus of about 5500 examples from all Finnish dialects, and of 200 examples from present-day educated language use which follow standard norms in most respects, other than the case marking discussed here. After presenting the main differences between the relevant case marking in standard and colloquial Finnish, I shall briefly describe how the standardized norm originally arose. This will be followed by a closer look at the semantics and at the historical background of the case-marking system in constructions of necessity of spoken Finnish.

8.1.1 Abbreviations used in this chapter

ADE = addessive case 'on'
ALL = allative case 'to'
COND = conditional
ESS = essive case 'as'
GEN = genitive case 'of'
ILL = illative case 'into'
INE = inessive case 'in'
INF = infinitive
NOM = nominative case
PAR = partitive case
PAST = past tense
PL = plural
PRS = present tense
PTC = participle
SAP = speech act pronoun
SG = singular

8.2 Constructions of necessity in Finnish

So-called *necessive* or *necessitative verbs* (henceforth: *nec-verbs*) in the Finnish grammatical tradition constitute a special group of 20 verbs among the modals in Finnish. They belong to the 'strong end' of the modal scale between possibility and necessity (e.g. Horn 1984), expressing obligation, compulsion, norms and suitability. The most common of them are *pitää* ('must, shall; have to') and *täytyy* ('must, have to'). They both have deontic and epistemic meanings, but *pitää*, the oldest nec-verb, has also developed other, mostly evidential functions.

In all these functions, the morphological form of the verb is third person singular. A nec-verb does not allow person or number agreement and it does not have passive inflection. Thus, in clauses with a nec-verb (henceforth: *nec-clauses*) there is no prototypical subject. Normally in Finnish, the subject is in the nominative and the finite verb agrees with it in person and number. A nec-verb can therefore be regarded as subjectless or impersonal.

On the other hand, nec-clauses do contain a subject-like argument, which can be in either the genitive or the nominative. In standard Finnish, the situation is relatively simple: according to the norm, this primary argument is in the genitive case in most instances:

(1) **Sinun** pitää tuoda lehmät kotiin.
you(GEN) must(3SG) bring(INF1) cow(PL NOM) home
'You must bring the cows home.'

(2) **Lehmien** pitää tulla kotiin.
cow(PL GEN) must(3SG) come(INF1) home
'The cows must come home.'

In examples (1) and (2), the nec-verb is *pitää*[1] and is in the 3rd person singular present and the complement (*tuoda, tulla*) is in a basic infinitive form. The noun phrase in the genitive (*sinun, lehmien*) typically precedes the finite verb, and is understood as the subject of the infinitive. As for the object, it is in the nominative: case marking of objects in nec-clauses is similar to that of clauses without an overt subject in Finnish, for example, imperative and passive clauses.

It is also possible to leave out the genitive argument in nec-clauses, as in example (3).

(3) **Lehmät** pitää tuoda kotiin.
cow(PL NOM) must(3SG) bring(INF1) home
'The cows must be brought home.'

While the clause has been translated into English with a passive, the Finnish passive was not used in the original. However, like a Finnish passive, this genitiveless nec-clause indicates that the agent is human but non-specific, or arbitrary. This is especially true of cases like this, where the object comes in the preverbal slot, the unmarked place for the theme or topic. With subjectless clauses in Finnish, it is very common for something else to be put in its place or topicalized (see Vilkuna 1989). If an utterance begins with a nec-verb, the referent of its implied agent is normally understood to be the first person:

(4)   *Pitää*   *tuoda*   **lehmät**   *kotiin.*
    must(3SG) bring(INF1) cow(PL NOM) home
    'I/we must bring the cows home.'

Hence, as we have seen, in nec-clauses the normal case of the subject argument is genitive and that of the object is nominative. However, subjects can sometimes be in the nominative case as well. In standardized written Finnish the nominative case is allowed in existential nec-clauses, such as (5), in which the subject, 'cow', is post-verbal:

(5)   *Navetassa*   *pitää*   *olla*   **lehmä**.
    cowshed(INE) must(3SG) be(INF1) cow(SG NOM)
    'There must be a cow in the cowshed.'

Thus, existential subjects are marked in the same way as the object,[2] and all other subjects have genitive marking. In non-standard varieties – both in present-day urban varieties and in dialects – the case marking is more complex: a nominative subject often occurs in an ordinary (non-existential) intransitive clause, as in examples (6) and (7):

(6)   **Lehmät**   *pitää*   *tulla*   *kotiin.*
    cow(PL NOM) must(SG3) come(INF1) home
    'The cows must come home.'

(7)   **Lehmä**   *pitää*   *olla*   *navetassa.*
    cow(SG NOM) must(SG3) be(INF1) cowshed(SG INE)
    'The cow must be in the cowshed.'

While the intransitive examples (2) and (6) can be translated in the same way ('the cows must come home'), they are not exactly synonymous:

(2) *Lehmien pitää tulla kotiin.* 'The cows are obliged to come home.'
(6) *Lehmät pitää tulla kotiin.* 'It is necessary that the cows come home.'

These two clauses constitute a minimal pair; the difference in meaning between them is obvious but not easy to describe. The choice of case marking is dependent on several semantic-pragmatic variables interacting together. Factors that favour the nominative as opposed to the genitive include thematic role, modal function, and the status of NPs on the animacy or person hierarchy (for a detailed description, see Laitinen 1992).

The meaningful grammatical choices available in constructions of necessity are not the only ones that have been lost in the standardizing of modern Finnish. In fact, in Finnish dialects there is an even more complex system indexing the semantic-grammatical category of person that official norms – and linguistic descriptions – have failed to capture. Unfortunately, there is not space to discuss these patterns here, but the relationship of third person pronouns *hän* and *se* is touched on in section 8.5. The next section focuses on the standardization of nec-clauses in the nineteenth century, the time when modern Finnish was being developed.

8.3 History of the standard norm

Present-day standard Finnish was, to a large extent, constructed during the second half of the nineteenth century, at the time when a Finnish national identity was being created. This identity was especially based on the Finnish language. As late as a hundred years ago, the educated and upper class in Finland spoke Swedish or another European language, whereas the common people (the vast majority of the population) spoke a Finnish dialect. To bridge the cultural distance between these two groups, it was necessary to create a 'new' common language that had to be learned both by the Swedish-speaking upper class and the Finnish-speaking lower classes. Modern Finnish was first created in a written form: it was based on old written Finnish (mostly biblical and legal) dating back to the sixteenth century, but also took into account the requirements of both European civilization and Finnish peasant culture. Once the written language was constructed, people started to speak it.

During this process, scholars had to create thousands of new words, select phonological and morphological forms from different dialects and so on. The most difficult decisions to make were morphosyntactic, because syntax was – and still is – the least studied area of Finnish dialects.

The case-marking norm with nec-verbs in standard Finnish, illustrated in examples (1), (2) and (5), was put forward by E.N. Setälä in 1880 in the first version of his Finnish syntax, and it has been repeated in subsequent editions. For almost a hundred years, this book was the canonical grammar of Finnish, both in a prescriptive and in a descriptive sense (see also Vilkuna, this volume). However, grammarians of the time were aware that something more subtle was going on in these constructions. Before Setälä, in fact, Yrjö Koskinen (1860) had mentioned the pattern illustrated in (6)–(7) in his syntax of the Finnish language (which was written in Swedish). He introduced the non-existential examples (8)–(9), in which the infinitive complement is a reflexive verb,[3] and he found them acceptable:

(8)   **Suuret   muutokset**   *pitää*   *tapahtuman.*
      big(PL NOM) change(PL NOM) shall(SG3)   happen(INF3)
      'There must/shall be big changes.'

(9) **Taivas** *pitää muuttuman.*
sky(SG NOM) shall(SG3) change(INF3)
'The sky must/shall change.'

As is obvious from a later study on a western dialect, Setälä (1883) was – or soon became – aware of this pattern (i.e. nominative in intransitive nec-clauses) in spoken Finnish. However, he omitted it from all editions of his grammar. In spite of this, the nominative subject illustrated in examples (6)–(9) has still maintained its status in nonstandard Finnish for over a hundred years. There is no evidence that its use is either increasing or decreasing. Nonstandard nominatives can even appear in writing and in elaborated speech:

(10) *Kolmessa kuukaudessa täytyy olla* **ne poikaset**
three(INE) month(SG INE) must(SG3) be(INF1) those young(PL NOM)
valmiita lähtemään maailmalle.
ready(PL PAR) go(INF1) world(SG ALL)
'In three months the young must be ready to go into the world [i.e. leave the squirrel's nest].' (Radio program 1980)

(11) *Vuosilomaan oikeuttava 15 vuoden*
annual holiday(SG ILL) entitling 15 year(SG GEN)
***palvelus** tulee täyttyä ennen*
service(SG NOM) must(SG3) complete(INF) before
lomakauden alkamista.
holiday period (SG GEN) start(SG PAR)
'The 15-year service required for (extended) annual holidays must be completed before the start of the holiday period.' (Administrative directions)

Nevertheless, in present-day Finnish, this nominative has a somewhat nonstandard flavour: school teachers usually correct it in students' writing and this option is not mentioned in grammars. Speakers are normally not aware of using it and, if it is brought to their notice, they consider it a mistake. Thus, speakers are not consciously aware of the differences in meaning between (2) and (6), but unconsciously make use of these two forms to convey meaningful distinctions in a systematic way.

8.4 Modal and role semantic factors

Setälä's dialect study (1883) mentioned earlier was published after he had spent some time collecting dialect data to improve his Finnish syntax. This study includes *inter alia* a description of the semantic difference between genitive and nominative subjects with nec-verbs in what would now be described as role semantic terms. The nominative is in place in 'situations, in which the contents of the infinitive are not carried out as a result of the action by the entity [referred by the nominative] itself' (Setälä 1883: 138). One of his examples is given in (12):

(12) Isäntä käski, että auringonlaskun aikaan viimeistäänkin
'The master ordered that at sunset at the latest
pitää **lehmät** kotona olla.
must(SG3) cow(PL NOM) home be(INF1)
the cows must be home' [i.e. 'you should get the cows home by then'].

As Setälä comments, it is not the cows who are responsible for bringing about the desired state of affairs (being home by sunset), but someone else, perhaps the implicated addressee. If the agent is the controller of the situation, it is marked with the genitive *lehmien*, just as in example (2). A non-controlling, non-responsible agent *lehmät* (as in (12) and (6)) is in the nominative.

A second example from Setälä (13) shows that the referent of the nominative subject can even be human:

(13) Silloin sitte päätettiin, että kyllä **vaimot**
at that time then it was decided that indeed wife(PL NOM)
pitää olla emäntänä
must(SG3) be(INF1) hostess(SG ESS)
'Then they decided that the wives should be hostesses.'

The case marking in these examples, once again, resembles that of objects (examples (3) and (4)) and existential subjects (5), and for this reason the system is considered ergative by Itkonen (1979). However, this split in the case marking of intransitive nec-clauses is semantically conditioned and similar to the system in certain so-called active-stative or split-ergative languages, where control, volition or primary responsibility is marked by the ergative and its absence by the absolutive. (It should be added that, in contrast to some other languages, the Finnish case alternation is not lexically conditioned by the class of the infinitival verbs; see Laitinen and Vilkuna 1993.)

A role semantic analysis nicely complements a modal semantic analysis. If we look at these examples in the light of the modal functions of the nec-verbs, we can see that the so-called deontic and dynamic interpretations of necessity correlate with the 'agent-oriented' cases where subjects are treated as responsible and controlling agents of norms and duties or intentional experiencers of obligations. In these contexts, the subject is in the genitive. However, in the examples with nominative subjects (10)–(13), the modality cannot be understood as prototypically deontic or dynamic necessity. Rather, it represents so-called *practical necessity*, which has not been given as much attention in linguistics as it has in modal logic (von Wright 1972).

Practical necessity resembles epistemic necessity because it is also based on reasoning, the so-called practical syllogism. On the other hand, it is rather close to deontic modality because it produces norms – so-called technical norms – and, like dynamic necessity, it always leads to action. However, it differs from all of these functions: something is necessary, because it is regarded as expedient, practical and appropriate for someone who is implied in the context. In my data, a large number of nominative subjects belong to the scope of this kind of necessity.

The rest of the nominatives are used in epistemic (i.e. inferential) or other evidential contexts, for example, with *pitää* expressing hearsay or reported information as in example (14); in this use, it resembles the German verb *sollen* and Swedish *skall*.

(14) **Lehmäp**   piti   tulleen   kotios sitteh hyvin.
     cow(PL NOM) shall(SG3 PAST) come(PTC) home then well
     'The cows should have got home well then; they say the cows got home well then.'

The nominative is also used with *pitää* when it is used emphatically in affective contexts; for instance, in expressions of wonder, lament or complaint:

(15) **Ne**   piti   ollak   korreita   sitte.
     they(NOM) must(SG3 PAST) be(INF1) pretty(PL PAR) then
     'My, were those [ribbons] pretty!'

As we know, so-called root modalities and epistemic interpretations have also formally moved into different directions in many languages. The case marking could now be seen in terms of either role or modal semantics, indicating the difference between agent-oriented or speaker-oriented expressions. The genitive belongs to the scope of deontic and dynamic necessity, where the event is obligatory for the agent or the experiencer of the situation. In these cases the referent of the subject-NP is an intentional being, whose actions or reactions are affected by some obligation – either by norms or somebody else's will (deontic interpretations) or by inner compulsion or outer circumstances (dynamic interpretations). The nominative is usual in contexts of practical necessity or in evidential contexts where the modal verb indicates that the state of affairs is inferenced, heard or evaluated by the speaker. In these cases, the role of the nominative subject or its own consciousness, intention or will is not relevant.

8.5 Persons, non-persons and indexicality

The intentionality or at least the animateness of the subject-NP's referent seems to be a crucial factor in the case-marking choices in nec-clauses.

This is also confirmed by my data from Finnish dialects. As many as 95 per cent of the genitive subjects in that corpus are referentially human or at least animate. Inanimate NPs, by contrast, clearly favour nominative subjects in intransitive clauses: 75 per cent of the nominatives are inanimate. As many as a quarter of the nominative subjects are thus referentially animate. This means that it is mainly animate NPs that can have either nominative or genitive marking, depending on the modal or role semantic interpretation (as in the minimal pair in (2) and (6)). They can, in other words, be treated as inanimate (or non-personal) entities, even in situations where they are, in fact, acting intentionally.

There is, however, an important 'exception' to this picture. The speech act pronouns, which are always referentially human, are marked with the genitive in all contexts. It is not possible to choose the nominative, regardless of whether the modal function of the verb of necessity is practical, epistemic, affective, or hearsay. Example (16) represents the modal function of *pitää* indicating reported speech; as illustrated, the first person subject (*mun*) is in the genitive:

(16) **Mun** piti   sanoneen nim mutta em   minä
I(GEN) shall(SG3 PAST) say(PTC) so   but   not(1SG) I(NOM)
nin sanonu   ollenkan.
so   say(PTC) at all
'They say that I said so but I didn't say so at all.'

Thus, the choice between nominative and genitive in nec-constructions is only possible in the case marking of third person animate NPs, whereas speech act pronouns are always in the genitive.

Interestingly, the third person pronoun *hän* ('he or she') is to be included in the group of speech act pronouns. The third person in colloquial Finnish has, in fact, split into two pronouns. Standardized written Finnish has adopted the same system as, for instance, in Swedish: the pronoun *se* ('it') is used for non-human entities and the personal pronoun *hän* ('he, she') can only refer to humans. However, in informal spoken Finnish the situation is different: the pronoun *se* ('it' in the standard language) refers to people as well ('she' or 'he') and the pronoun *hän* is used in dialects in a more restricted sense. In all Finnish dialects, *hän* refers to the speaker in reported speech: it is the 'I' of an earlier speech act – a speaker:

(17) **Se**   sano   että **hän**   on   väsynyt.
it(NOM) say(SG3 PAST) that s/he(NOM) be(SG3 PRS) tired
'S/he$_1$ said that s/he$_1$ was tired.' (S/he said: 'I'm tired.')

The pronoun *hän* can also refer to some participant in the actual speech act: it is used when its referent is present, either as a respected addressee or as a hearer in a situation where his or her thoughts or actions are interpreted for the benefit of the other participants. Just like the first and second person speech act pronouns, the pronoun *hän* is a referential index, indexing to a referent in a speech situation.[4] In nec-clauses, this pronoun is like a first or second person pronoun in that it is always marked with the genitive. In contrast, the pronoun *se*, as well as other NPs referring to human beings, can have either nominative or genitive marking.

Examples (18) and (19) can both be interpreted in terms of either deontic or dynamic necessity:[5]

(18) **Hänen** piti olla riihessä.
s/he(GEN) must(SG3 PAST) be(INF1) threshing house(SG INE)
'S/he had to be in the threshing house.'
[S/he told it me her/himself that s/he had to be there.]

(19) **Sem** piti olla riihessä.
s/he must(SG3 PAST) be(INF1) threshing house(SG INE)
'S/he had to be in the threshing house.'
[S/he did not tell it to me her/himself but I saw the situation, or heard about it from somebody else.]

Semantically, both modal and referential meanings of examples (18) and (19) are similar, but they differ in two respects. The evidential value of the utterances – the source of information – is different. So is their indexical value, based on the different speech act role of the referents of the pronouns: the referent of *hän* (in (18)) is an earlier speaker, the referent of *se* (in (19)) is not.

There is still the third possibility, given in the constructed example in (20), where the pronoun *se* is in the nominative. It can only appear in the scope of practical or epistemic necessity or with hearsay function. In this case the referent must be non-personal, for example, generic (referring to a category) or dead:

(20) **Se** piti olla riihessä.
s/he(it) must(SG3 PAST) be (INF1) threshing house(SG INE)
'It was necessary that s/he [e.g. the thresher, or the corpse of a dead person] was in the threshing house.'

In nec-clauses, *hän* 'he or she' (as well as its plural counterpart, the human *he* 'they') has a special status and is always marked by the genitive – by the same case as the speech act pronouns. This is natural, because *hän* is a kind of second-order speech act pronoun in colloquial Finnish. With the pronoun *se*, on the other hand, there are two options. If marked with the genitive, the referent of *se* is treated as a real person, a speaking subject, whereas the nominative case is used to categorize the referent as a non-person. Thus, the boundary between persons and non-persons seems to go in the middle of the third person – even if the category of person were to be based on the position of pronouns in the speech act (defined by Benveniste 1971: 195–223).

In fact, the case-marking system of all subject-like NPs in nec-constructions can be described on this basis: as dependent on their indexical status in the speech context, as outlined above. The system can be schematized as a continuum – or as a hierarchy – of NP-types, as in (21) below (Laitinen 1992):

(21) *Indexical hierarcy of NPs in the case marking of Necessives*
     personal pronouns   human,   vegetal,
     = SAPs   animate   inanimate, abstract
     persons ←-------------------------------→ non-persons
     GENITIVE   NOMINATIVE

In (21), the speech act pronouns (including *hän*) – SAPs – are always in the genitive, and referentially inanimate, non-personal NPs mostly in the nominative. If marked with the genitive, which also sometimes occurs, an inanimate NP can be metaphorically categorized as a person. However, it is mainly in the group of animate NPs in the middle of the hierarchy where case alternation occurs.

Like the so-called agentivity hierarchy, or more exactly the hierarchy of referential features of NP-types, suggested by Silverstein (1981), this continuum can be described in terms of indexicality. The leftmost NP-types are true indexical referentials, *shifters* in Jakobsonian terms (1956/1971), and the more we move to the right the less indexical the NP-types are. In the middle area, NPs can move to the right or to the left. Placed on the left-hand side, their referents are treated as (at least potential) speech act participants, capable of understanding and reacting intentionally to deontic norms or obligatory circumstances. This status is conveyed by the genitive. On the right-hand side, they are marked with the nominative, to indicate entities that have no access to the status of a speech act participant – that is, they can or may not speak, they are not to be addressed or even understood – but are only spoken about, described or evaluated. In the middle of this hierarchy, then, the case-marking options serve as a meaning potential for changes in the footing – or the indexical ground – of the utterance.

The alternation in case marking in the middle of the hierarchy belongs to the last phase in the semantic-grammatical history of nec-clauses. The following section gives a brief outline of earlier grammaticalization processes of nec-constructions (for a more detailed description, see Laitinen 1995).

8.6 Grammaticalization of necessity

During the past hundred years, Finnish linguists have developed a detailed hypothesis about the syntactic history of the so-called necessitative constructions. It is assumed to have resulted from a reanalysis and a restructuring process of the central morphosyntactic constituents. This process involved a gradual loss of person and number marking in the verb in its course from lexical to modal functions and analogical generalizations in the case marking of the arguments. (See, for example, Itkonen 1979.)

According to the reconstruction, what is analysed as the nominative object in modern Finnish was originally the subject of the source verb. The modal development began when this verb started to take transitive infinitival complements: *Lehmät pitää* 'the cows must' – *tuoda kotiin* 'to bring home' (cf. (3)). An optional argument in the genitive (interpreted as a directional case, the dative genitive) could also occur in prenecessitative clauses: *Lehmät pitää (meidän) tuoda kotiin* 'The cows are (for us) to be brought home' (cf. (1)).

The reanalysis began when the recipient of *pitää* ('we') – as it must have been analysed at that stage – was interpreted primarily as the agentive subject of the transitive verb (*tuoda*). Simultaneously, the intransitive subject of *pitää* ('the cows') was reanalysed as the object of the transitive verb, and, consequently, the genitive NP assumed the unmarked position of a prototypical nominative subject: *meidän pitää tuoda lehmät kotiin* (example (1)). At the next stage of development, the verb also started to take intransitive complements, first with nominative subjects (as in (6)): *Lehmät pitää tulla kotiin*, and then, analogically with the type shown in example (1), with genitives as well: *Lehmien pitää tulla kotiin* (as in (2)).

Though lacking a semantic analysis, this hypothesis is obviously close to the grammaticalization theories of today. Based on an extensive Finnish dialect data, I have developed it further (Laitinen 1992). The lexical sources of the nec-verbs are easy to find, because they still exist in actual use as semantically more concrete, independent predicates, usually intransitive verbs expressing change of place or state in the subject. The oldest nec-verb, *pitää*, probably originates out of the old intransitive meaning of *pitää* 'stick, get or be stuck'. The nec-verb *täytyy* ('must') has developed from a reflexive verb *täytyy* 'become full', which is derived from the adjective *täysi* 'full'; the lexical verb *täytyy* is still used in the eastern dialects with meanings such as 'become full, filled; become mature, ripe; become full-size, full-grown'.

Another common feature of the verbs from which nec-verbs developed is that they allow, or even favour, inanimate or non-personal subjects. This was virtually the only possibility in my data on the lexical verb *täytyy*: a container was filled; vegetal entities or other living resources (livestock, children) grew, ripened and matured. It is most likely that the nec-clause started from these kinds of specific, local contexts with third person singular subjects, especially with ones that referred to inanimate, vegetal or collective entities. Thus, the verb was third person singular from the beginning of the modal development. From this point of view, it is also only natural that the nec-verbs do not have passive inflection – the Finnish passive implies human actors.

Example (22), from a nineteenth-century dictionary, meets the requirement of inanimateness of the subject in pre-modal constructions of necessity.

(22) *Silmät   täytyi   puhjeta   itkuun.*
eye(PL NOM) must(PAST 3SG) burst(INF1) crying(ILL)
'The eyes had to burst into tears' (Lönnrot 1880: 'ögonen måste brista ut gråt').

The subject *silmät* 'eyes' could refer to the speaker's own eyes, expressing a kind of metonymical part–whole relationship. This is explicated in (23), which can be compared with the so-called 'habitive' sentences in Finnish (24).

(23) **Minun /minulla** *täytyi   silmät   puhjeta.*
I(GEN) /I(ADE)   must(PAST 3SG) eye(PL NOM) burst(INF1)
itkuun.
crying(ILL)
'My eyes had to burst into tears.'

(24) **Minulla/minulle/minun** *tuli   rakko.*
I(ADE   /ALL   /GEN)   come(3SG PAST) blister(SG NOM)
jalkaan.
foot(SG ILL)
'I had a blister on my foot.'

Habitive sentences in Finnish (24) contain a nominative subject in the third person and a clause-initial human possessor, marked by an outer locative case or by the genitive; as a contextually implied entity, the latter is often omitted (see Vilkuna 1989: 169–75). There is an implied relationship between these two entities: a relation of inalienable or alienable possession, control or kinship, etc. The nec-clause could have arisen from a similar kind of context, containing a displaced possessor (26).

(26) (*Meidän*) *täytyy   ruis   kaataa.*
(we(GEN)) täytyy(3SG PRS) rye(NOM) cut down(INF1)
'The rye (of ours) has ripened – to be cut down.'

This is not far from an agentive or control interpretation: 'The rye (of ours) has to be cut down' → 'We have to cut down the rye.'

There is a purposeful, inferential connection between the resulting state of an entity and the subjet's activity: the one is a necessary condition to the other. The rye is expected to become ready *enough* to be harvested; a girl is expected to mature enough to be married; a barn sufficiently filled for threshing, and so on. A possible pre-modal candidate for mediating between *täytyy* 'filling' or 'ripening' and *täytyy* 'necessity' is the meaning 'to be sufficient'. Example (27) is from a sixteenth-century text.

(27) *Leiuet   ei   teudhyisi   heidhen.*
      bread(PL NOM) Neg(3SG PRS) suffice(COND) 3PL GEN
      'The bread would not suffice for them' (Agricola; SKES s.v. *täytyä*).

The development from 'fulfilment' to 'sufficiency' is natural if the end point of the change of state is relevant for someone. When this end point is not only observed but even expected by somebody, for instance, by the speech act participants, then their practical reasoning produces the meaning of necessity. It seems to me that a referential-indexical starting point like this makes it easier to understand why the nonstandard case marking pattern in nec-clauses has been able to resist the standard norm for a hundred years.

8.7 Discussion

Why is the colloquial case-marking system of the subject-like arguments not included in Finnish grammars? If it was based on free variation, it would be easy to answer this question. Finnish grammars, which are generally still normative, do not often contain remarks on variation. However, the choice of the case marking with nec-verbs is not totally arbitrary or free. It is dependent on several semantic and pragmatic variables.

If the case marking was purely semantic in a referential way, it would not be so difficult to describe or even to standardize it. We could, for example, say that the genitive is the case of an animate NP in agent-oriented modal context and nominative of an inanimate NP and animate NP in speaker-oriented contexts. The personal pronouns could be mentioned as exceptions in that they must always be in genitive case.

The picture would be rather convenient for most purposes of grammar, but the phenomenon would, at the same time, lose something essential. The meaning of the genitive or the nominative does not exactly depend on the animateness of the NPs but on the status of the person. And the concept of person has, at least in Finnish, to do with the status of a speech act participant. The categorization of entities as persons, able to speak or to be addressed, or at least to be understood as intentional entities, is a pragmatic action, or – as I would prefer to say – an indexical process of signification. So is the categorization of non-persons, because of their necessary relationship to speaking subjects – a relationship of contiguity, available for metonymical operations, as outlined above.

Indexicality, as discussed in this chapter, is not seen as a single feature that referential NPs either can or cannot have. Neither can it be reduced to so-called 'pure', non-referential indexicality, expressing propositional attitudes of speakers. It is a pragmatically conditioned continuum of referential indexicality, which linguistics today has not yet been able to conceptualize in an adequate way.

Notes

1 Although *pitää* is used here, it could be replaced with *täytyy*. Both are common in standard Finnish. In dialects, there are some differences. As an implicative verb of strong necessity ('must, have to'), the eastern dialects use *pitää* and the western dialects *täytyy*. In the western dialects, *pitää* is a weaker, non-implicative modal verb of necessity ('shall, should, ought to').
2 Both the existential subject and the object can also be in partitive case, but this is not relevant to the present discussion.
3 As shown in examples (8) and (9), the nec-verb *pitää* ('shall, should') can take 3rd infinitive as a complement in western dialects. In these areas, other meanings (e.g. hearsay and future) of *pitää* are also possible. Yet, the case marking follows the same principles as in the eastern dialects and as with other nec-verbs in Finnish.
4 This old, fine-grained system of person in Finnish dialects was lost in the process of standardization. Today, Finns have learned the 'European' way of maintaining or indexing personal reference so well that to use *se* of people is considered impolite in many contexts. In dialects the division of labour between the pronouns *se* and *hän* is still living, but in urban speech *hän* is losing its status.
5 In western dialects, examples (18) and (19) can also indicate report or hearsay ((18): 's/he said that s/he was in the threshing house'; (19): s/he was said to be in the threshing house'). These interpretations do not change the grammatical picture presented here.

References

Benveniste, Emile 1971. *Problems in General Linguistics.* Miami Linguistics Series 9. Coral Gables, Florida: University of Miami Press.

Horn, Lawrence R. 1984. Toward a new taxonomy for pragmatic inference: Q-based and R-based implicature. In: Deborah Schiffrin (ed.), *Meaning, Form and Use in Context: Linguistic Applications.* Washington: Georgetown University Press.

Itkonen, Erkki, Joki, Aulis J. and Peltola, Reino (eds) 1975. *SKES* (= *Suomen kielen etymologinen sanakirja*). Helsinki: Lexica Societatis Fenno-ugricae XII, 5.

Itkonen, Terho 1979. Subject and object marking in Finnish: an inverted ergative system and 'ideal' ergative subsystem. In: Frans Plank (ed.), *Ergativity.* London: Academic Press.

Jakobson, Roman 1956/1971. Shifters, verbal categories, and the Russian verb. *Roman Jakobson, Selected Writings II*, pp. 130–147.

Koskinen, Yrjö 1860. *Finska språkets satslära*. Helsinki.

Laitinen, Lea 1992. *Välttämättömyys ja persoona: suomen murteiden nesessiivisten rakenteiden semantiikkaa ja kielioppia*. Helsinki: Finnish Literature Society.

Laitinen, Lea 1995. Metonymy and the grammaticalization of necessity in Finnish. *SKY 1995*, Yearbook of the Linguistic Association of Finland.

Laitinen, Lea and Vilkuna, Maria 1993. Case marking in necessitative constructions and split intransitivity. In: Anders Holmberg and Urpo Nikanne (eds), *Case and other Functional Categories in Finnish Syntax*. Studies in Generative Grammar 39. Berlin/New York: Mouton de Gruyter, pp. 23–48.

Lönnrot, Elias 1880. Suomalais-ruotsalainen sanakirja. *Finskt-svenskt lexicon II*. WSOY, Helsinki.

Setälä, E.N. 1880. *Suomen kielen lauseoppi*. Oppikirjan koe. Helsinki: K.E. Holm.

Setälä, E.N. 1883. Lauseopillinen tutkimus Koillis-Satakunnan kansankielestä. *Suomi III: 12*, Helsinki.

Silverstein, Michael 1976. Hierarchy of features and ergativity. In: R.M.W. Dixon (ed.), *Grammatical Categories in Australian Languages*. Canberra.

Silverstein, Michael 1981. Case marking and the nature of language. *Australian Journal of Linguistics* 1/1981.

Vilkuna, Maria 1989. *Free Word Order in Finnish*. Helsinki: SKS.

von Wright, Georg Henrik 1972. On so called practical inference. *Acta Sociologica* 15: 39–53.

CHAPTER 9

Articles and number in oral or close-to-oral varieties

Brigitte Schlieben-Lange

9.1 Introduction

My German friends often tease me when I use expressions of the type 'Hast Du **ein** Wasser?', 'Kannst Du mir **ein** Geld leihen?' In standard German this use of the indeterminate article combined with a mass noun is impossible, whereas it is completely usual in my oral variety which bears Bavarian substratum traces. So my everyday native speaker experiences brought me very early to reflect on the interplay between the semantic class of nouns on the one hand and number/determination on the other.

The relation between semantic class and number is one of the oldest and most central subjects with which traditional grammar deals. In the standard versions of traditional grammar (Donat, Priscian), that became the models for the whole European grammatical tradition, semantic class and number were both qualified as *accidentia* of the noun: *qualitas* and *numerus*. The category of *qualitas* summarizes a whole philosophical debate on the nature of words, as to whether they designate individuals or classes of individuals. One proposal had been to distinguish two different word classes: proper names and class nouns. The solution traditionally accepted was the one we find in the texts alluded to above, namely to assume only one word class and to treat the differences between proper name and class noun within this category and to do this under the heading of *qualitas* (cf. Borsche 1989). So the proper name vs class name distinction was the first one to be treated in the *qualitas* section of the grammars, but other distinctions were added: the abstract vs concrete distinction, the mass word vs count word distinction and, above all, the noun vs adjective distinction (as the separation of nouns and adjectives took place only very late). However, grammarians became aware that *qualitas* and *numerus* each had a distinct status: *qualitas* meant different semantic features inherent to nouns whereas *numerus* (as well as *casus*, *comparatio* and, to a lesser degree, *genus*) was a grammatical category to be combined with nouns. So gradually *qualitas* was given up as a separate category; but grammarians continued to comment on the different classes of nouns and, above all, on the interplay of semantic class and number. Unfortunately this stock of traditional reflection has mainly fallen into oblivion. Neo-grammarians discussed the problem, but mainly from the perspective of congruence (*logischer* vs *grammatischer Numerus*).

Louis Hjelmslev stated in 1939:

> Il est évident a priori que la conception traditionnelle, selon laquelle le nombre indique la quantité, le genre indique le sexe, et l'aspect indique le temps, est une erreur fondamentale. Ces faits ne constituent que des variantes qui se manifestent assez souvent il est vrai, mais qui par ailleurs ne se manifestent pas sans exceptions, et qui ne constituent qu'une seule des possibilités renfermées en germe dans la signification générale ou valeur des morphèmes en question.

> [It is clear, *a priori*, that the traditional ideas according to which number indicates quantity, gender indicates sex and aspect indicates time are fundamentally wrong. These phenomena are merely variations which occur fairly frequently, it is true, but which do not occur without exception. They express only one of the possibilities that exist in embryo form as part of the general meaning or value of the morphemes in question.]

The problems about number mainly arise from the interplay with semantic class. During the last few decades it is, above all, the mass word/count word distinction that has been discussed (Weinreich 1980). In my opinion, the most interesting approach to the type of problems I want to discuss here has been the Cologne Project on Universals (Seiler *et al*. 1982–1986).

Hansjakob Seiler and his collaborators treat the problems of number and gender from the perspective that languages must afford techniques providing the possibility of **apprehension**, that is, of subsuming the multiform reality under the categories of language. The group distinguishes several sub-types of apprehension techniques: abstraction, collection, classification. They state that there are two conflicting principles in apprehension: a generalizing principle (as coded grammatically in **gender**) and an individualizing principle (as coded grammatically in **number**). Languages have to organize their techniques of apprehension, and in fact their solutions are very different (one has only to think of noun class systems in African languages; of plural as unmarked opposed to individuative as marked in Irish and so on).[1] But even below the level of grammatical coding speakers can choose whether they prefer an individualizing or a collectivizing perspective on things: the task of apprehension is never definitely ended; it arises anew every time we speak.

Now my claim is the following: standard languages are largely oriented towards the model of logic, where the individual vs class distinction as well as (to a lesser degree) the discrete vs continuous distinction have mostly been discussed as if they were dichotomies. On the contrary, nonstandard varieties (and languages codified in opposition to already codified standard languages such as, for example, Catalan and Occitan or Creole languages – Schlieben-Lange 1991) are more open in this respect and may offer a greater variety of possibilities.

I want to develop this idea in three steps: first of all I shall draw a general tableau of the semantic class/number interplay (1). Afterwards I shall enlarge this tableau by discussing the behaviour of semantic noun classes combined with the indefinite article (2) and the definite article (3). I shall exclude from my considerations the gender problem which is – no doubt – related to the number relationship (see Seiler *et al.* 1982–1986). The languages I refer to will be written German and some Romance languages as well as oral varieties of these languages. Let me just add that I have done no empirical work on the issue so far, so my few examples are taken from personal experience and from already existing language descriptions.

9.2 Semantic class/number interplay

So, first, let us have a look at the semantic class/number interplay beginning with the possibility of forming a plural.

9.2.1 Proper names vs class nouns

Proper names don't have plural forms, because proper names are bound to specify individuals which, on the grounds of their being individual, cannot be multiplied. So when proper names are used with a plural form, they are generalized and are used as class nouns. This is a very common technique in languages when you have to denote inventions, for example:

Fr.: *la poubelle – les poubelles* (from: Poubelle, inventor of the dustbin)
G.: *der Ford – die Fords* etc.

But this technique is also available as a stylistic device, that occurs from time to time without implying a change in the status of the name:

G.: *all die kleinen Hitlers und Mussolinis* (all the small Hitlers and Mussolinis)
es gibt nicht viele Einsteins (there are not so many Einsteins)

In this case the proper name is employed as a class noun in order to denote a certain type of individual sharing some characteristic with the bearer of the original proper name.

9.2.2 Abstract nouns vs concrete nouns

Abstract nouns don't take plural endings; if they do so the meaning of the noun shifts towards concreteness. Languages differ in the extent to which they allow this type of concretization:

Fr.: *des beautés* (i.e. persons who are beautiful)
des libertés (i.e. concrete applications of liberty: e.g. la liberté de la presse)[2]
G.: *Er hat sich viele Freiheiten herausgenommen* (i.e. acts of liberty in a pejorative meaning)

whereas in English you employ a more explicit technique:

E.: **many pieces** of impudence

9.2.3 Mass words vs count words

Mass words generally don't take plural endings. If they do (i.e. in the language where the possibility exists and in the utterances where the possibility is actualized), the plural has an individualizing function. The individuals designated may be either real individuals

Fr.: *deux bières* (two beers)
Sp.: *dos cervezas*
G.: *zwei Bier or zwei Biere*

or, in some languages/contexts, classes of individuals. This is the case of the so-called 'Artenplural'

G.: *Wir haben heute zwei schöne Weine* (i.e. sorts of wine)
In diesem Restaurant gibt es 24 verschiedene Biere. (In this restaurant they have got 24 sorts of beer.)

The condition for countability is discontinuity.[3] So it is perfectly possible to have linguistic expressions which function like mass words, but are destined to designate ensembles formed by individuals in the real world. In these cases the linguistic perspective is a generalizing one. This is the case with collectives, such as *Vieh*, *Obst*. If they did have a plural form, which they in fact don't, it would be interpreted as an 'Artenplural'. Meisterfeld (1995) has shown in his excellent thesis that Portuguese has generalized this possibility of speaking about individuals in the form of mass words, without a plural:

P.: *muita moçaØ* (i.e. a great heap of girls)

He has claimed that this linguistic avoidance of discontinuity is widespread in ancient languages and may be found in nonstandard varieties much more often than one would suspect.

All the phenomena we have sketched so far may be explained by the same principle: plural formation is based on the possibility of counting discrete individuals. If there exists only one individual of one class, you cannot add one more; if you do so the proper noun no longer designates individuality, but typicality. On the other hand, abstract words and mass words lack the property of discreteness. If you nevertheless form plurals you convey the property of discreteness (either individual or of types) or, in the case of abstract nouns, of concreteness (you pin, so to speak, the abstract quality to a person or to an act). If, on the contrary, you use a noun normally designating discrete entities as a mass word, that is without a plural, you merge the discrete entities into a greater – continuous – unit.

9.3 Semantic class/indefinite article interplay

Let us now have a look at the behaviour of nouns of different semantic classes when combined with the indefinite article. We shall argue that it is very similar to their behaviour with respect to plural formation, discussed in the previous section. The function of the indefinite article which it shares with the numerals is above all the function of singling out discrete units.

9.3.1 Proper names vs class nouns

Proper names do not normally combine with the indefinite article, as individuals designated by proper names are already determined and individualized, so that further individualization is not required. If used with the indefinite article the proper nouns no longer designate unique individuals but representatives of a class. So the use of the indefinite article as well as the use of plural endings confers class character on proper nouns:

Fr.: *C'est* **un** *Don Juan.* (He is a Don Juan.)
It.: *Non si trova facilmente* **un** *Michelangelo.* (You don't find easily an artist like Michelangelo.)
G.: *Braucht Deutschland* **einen** *Mitterrand?* (Does Germany need a person like Mitterrand?)

9.3.2 Abstract nouns vs concrete nouns

Here we may observe a similar effect to the one discussed for the plural. Using the indefinite article with abstract nouns gives them a concrete meaning, that is you designate concrete entities to which the abstract quality applies

Fr.: *C'est* **un** *vrai malheur* (i.e. a case, an event) (This is a real case of misfortune)
It.: *Abbiamo avuto* **una** *pace durevole* (a period) (We have had a long period of peace)

9.3.3 Mass words vs count words

Mass words do not combine with the indefinite article, because no discrete unities are singled out. If they are combined, this has the effect of singling out discrete parts from the mass continuum, e.g.

Fr.: **une** *bière*
G.: **ein** *Bier*

Here we come to my initial example: nonstandard varieties may use this possibility in a less restricted way, such as

Bav.: *Kannst Du mir* **ein** *Geld leihen?* (Would you be so kind as to borrow me some money?)
(Perhaps also opposed to the negation: **kein** *Geld*.)

This use is different from the first one insofar as no concrete unit (e.g. a glass of wine/beer) is meant, but rather an indefinite part of the substance in question.

I think the necessity of speaking about parts of substances designated by mass words is frequent. Languages develop different devices to satisfy this necessity: numerals and quantifying nouns for definite units, indefinite pronouns for indefinite parts. French and (though not to the same extent) Italian have developed a special article for this purpose, the so-called partitive article, which corresponds largely to my Bavarian use of the indefinite article.

9.4 Semantic class/definite article interplay

Let us now consider the noun class/definite article interplay. Relations here differ from what we have seen so far. In this relationship the issue is not so much the singling out of individuals but determination or, even better, actualization.[4] Coseriu (1955) has developed an unfortunately not very well known hierarchy of procedures of determination (in a constant interaction with types of world knowledge). The lowest level of determination is the so-called actualization, generally expressed by means of the article (in the languages where this exists). Higher degrees of determination are those expressed by means of the demonstrative or the possessive pronouns. Generally one has to suppose that higher degrees of determination imply lower ones. So the demonstrative function would imply the actualizing function.

9.4.1 Proper names vs class nouns

On the basis of what has been said up to now it would seem quite natural that proper names do not combine with an actualizing procedure, being already actualized. Yet rules are quite complicated and quite arbitrary in different languages. Within our perspective the case of proper names is most interesting. Sometimes proper names are combined with the definite article in order to express esteem:

It.: **la** *Duse* (i.e. the one divine actress)

In other languages or varieties the use of the definite article with the Christian name connotes disdain; this is the case in Spanish, Portuguese, and standard German. In some varieties this combination is the normal one for informal exchange, as in Italian ('regionale con una sfumatura familiare') or in Southern German. Here, on the contrary, the omission of the article would connote distance and reproach. In French this combination is clearly impossible; in Catalan it is fully admitted (and is a typical interference in the Spanish spoken by Catalans).[5] So in the languages we haven't taken into account we have the following scale:

Art + Christian name:

Impossible	*Depreciative*	*Familiar*	*Normal*
French	Spanish	Italian	Catalan
	Portuguese	Southern German	
	Standard German		

As for the case of Catalan, one condition applies to which I referred above: standardization is partly oriented towards the distinction from Spanish. But I think there is another reason: Catalan disposes (just like Spanish *Don, Doña*) of an honorific: *En, Na*, used with Christian names. For phonetic reasons this honorific is partly replaced by the normal definite article:

Na Nuria → La Nuria
N'Antoni → L'Antoni

But how can I interpret the fact that in Southern German (and, I suppose, also in informal Italian) the *lack* of the article causes irritation? I suppose that the idea that proper names include actualization is a rather intellectual view of things. So, in some oral varieties the non-use of the article is felt as a lack of actualization. And this lack of actualization is interpreted as a lack of social integration, as speaking of a social outcast.

9.4.2   Abstract nouns vs concrete nouns

In this respect languages also differ. In most of the languages we are concerned with, abstract nouns are used with the definite article: in French and Italian the use is obligatory. The generic interpretation is the primary one (as opposed to the plural and indefinite article concretization effect). In German both possibilities exist:

G.:   *Freiheit ist ein hohes Gut.* (Liberty is a high value.)
      Die *Freiheit ist ein hohes Gut.*

In the first, the abstract noun seems to be used to denote something unique and indivisible. Something quite similar happens in the case of proper names: their use without an article confers on the abstract noun a note of distance and untouchability. An abstract quality might be supposed to be already actualized in its uniqueness. But it is felt as lacking actualization, that is integration in the everyday discourse world. There has been a broad use of the non-article form in the works of Adorno imitated in the German '68-movement, thus giving a quasi-sacred touch to abstract nouns, and this in an inflationary way. This little stylistic feature goes well with the moralistic aspects of the 1968 movement.

9.4.3   Mass words vs count words

The use of the definite article with mass words may, in different languages be individualizing and/or generic. In French and Italian the definite article is obligatory for both uses.[6] In German, on the contrary, you may, by this means, distinguish individual and generic meaning:

G.:   *Milch ist gesund.* (Milk is healthy.)
      Die *Milch ist verdorben.* (This milk is not good any more.)

9.5   Final remarks

I want to stop with these few remarks, as we are just entering into the vast field of generic expressions. My only aim in this sketch was to show that possibly oral or informal varieties are not submitted to the same constraints as the standard varieties – constraints that have to do with the idea that languages have to function like binary logic systems. So the individual/class distinction and the continuous/discrete distinction, as well as the idea that there is an implication hierarchy of determination, are partly suspended in oral varieties. I think that the Portuguese collective *muita moça*, the Bavarian partitive **ein** *Geld*, the article use with Christian names in Italian and Southern German are most revealing in this respect.

But let us state, on the other hand, that other digressions in our field belong to the higher stylistic varieties, e.g. the plural or indefinite article with proper names or abstract nouns without an article. So there is a little bit of freedom in the number/semantic class/article interplay at both poles of the variety spectrum. But let us state also that all this stylistic variety is deeply rooted in the functioning of semantic class, number and article and that language systems (be they standard or dialect systems) have already made certain choices which partly inhibit further freedom of variety (for example, the French article system).

Notes

1 Seiler *et al.* (1982–1986) discuss these problems; see, above all, Biermann (1982).
2 It is interesting to know that the plural use was the earlier one. Reinhart Koselleck has shown in several works that around 1800 there was a shift from plural use (liberté**s**, Geschicht**en**) to singular abstracts (**la** liberté, Geschichte).
3 Biermann (1982); see also Meisterfeld (1995) who stresses the importance of Damourette and Pichon's Grammar in this respect.
4 I refer to Coseriu (1955) and the preceding theories of actualization as formulated by Guillaume and Bally.
5 See Gauger and Cartagena (1989), Bd. II, p. 342.
6 See Guillaume's excellent 1919 exposition about the gradual shift from *puissance* to *effêt* during the history of French.

References

Bally, Charles 1950. *Grammaire générale et grammaire française*. Bern.
Biermann, Anna 1982. Die grammatische Kategorie Numerus. In: H. Seiler, C. Lehmann and F. J. Stachowiak (eds), *Apprehension* I, Tübingen, Gunter Narr, pp. 229–43.
Borsche, Tilman 1989. Quid est? Quot accidunt? Notizen zur Bedeutung und Entstehung des Begriffs der grammatischen Akzidentien bei Donatus. *Zeitschrift für Literaturwissenschaft und Linguistik* 76: 13–28.
Coseriu, Eugenio 1955. Determinación y entorno. Dos problemas de una lingüística del hablar. *Romanistisches Jahrbuch* 7: 29–54.
Damourette, Jacques and Pichon, Édouard 1911. *Des mots à la pensée. Essai de grammaire de la langue française*, Bd. I. Paris.
Gauger, Hans-Martin and Cartagena, Nelson 1989. *Vergleichende Grammatik Spanisch-Deutsch*. Mannheim, Dudenverlag.
Guillaume, Gustave 1919. *Le problème de l'article et sa solution dans la langue française*. Paris, Hachette.
Hjelmslev, Louis 1938. Essai d'une théorie des morphèmes. *Actes du Quatrième Congrès International de Linguistes, tenu à Copenhague du 27 août au 1 septembre 1936*. Kopenhagen, pp. 140–51.
Meisterfeld, Reinhard 1995. *Numerus und Nominalaspekt. Eine Studie aus Anlaß des Portugiesischen*. Dissertation, Universität Tübingen.

Schlieben-Lange, Brigitte 1991. Oralité et littéralité dans le domaine occitan. In: *LENGAS* 30: 15–27.

Seiler, Hansjakob, Lehmann, Christian and Stachowiak, Franz Josef (eds) 1982–1986. *Apprehension*, I–III. Tübingen, Gunter Narr.

Weinreich, Uriel 1980. *On Semantics*. Ed. by William Labov. University of Pennsylvania Press.

CHAPTER 10

Proscribed collocations with *shall* and *will*: the eighteenth-century (non-)standard reassessed*

Leslie K. Arnovick

The 'correct' use of *shall* and *will* has long confused English speakers. Codified by eighteenth-century prescriptivists, rules for the use of these auxiliaries – rightly or wrongly – have continued to appear in modern handbooks and grammars of the English language.[1] Despite the rules' long legacy, the structuralist grammarians of the early twentieth century rejected them on the basis that they had no precedent in real usage but were arbitrary inventions of the Academy. Indeed their codification proves telling in itself, and an understanding of the impetus behind the prescriptions sheds light on the corollary proscriptions of common usage. Essentially these eighteenth-century proscriptions support a 'standard' that made 'normal' usage 'nonstandard'. In this chapter, I will argue that the attempt to define a standard and to render the normal a nonstandard variety reveals much about how language change was viewed even while it was in progress. In broader perspective, the advent of the rules for *shall* and *will* might be understood as a reaction to diachronically derived synchronic fact.

Let me review the genealogy of the received rules before exploring the explicit and implicit rationale they bear.[2] In 1653, Bishop John Wallis formulated for the first time a set of definite rules for the use of *shall* and *will*. He explains that in order for a speaker to make a promise (1), he or she should use *will* in the first person and *shall* in the second and third persons. The forms for making a prediction (2) are reversed: *shall* in the first person, *will* in the second and third persons occur in predictive statements (Wallis 1972 [1653]: 339):

(1) To *promise*:
    I will ...   We will ...
    You shall ...   You shall ...
    He, she, it shall ...   They shall ...

(2) *To predict*:
    I shall ...   We shall ...
    You will ...   You will ...
    He, she, it will ... They will ...

Over the years that followed the publication of *Grammatica Linguae Anglicanae*, many other grammarians used Wallis's instructions in their own works. His statements proved so influential that while some handbooks merely repeated them and others elaborated on them, the collective seventeenth- and eighteenth-century dicta for future constructions using *shall* and *will* are commonly known as the 'Wallis Rules'. The most notable contributions to the bishop's original delineation were made over a century later. In 1765 William Ward's *Grammar of the English Language* provided an explanation for those rules based on the meanings of the auxiliaries themselves. By this time, the formulations had also been expanded by Bishop Robert Lowth in his 1762 edition of *A Short Introduction to English Grammar* to include questions and commands. Lowth stipulates that to question the desire or intention of one's hearer, the correct forms were *Shall I?*, *Will you?*, and *Shall he/she/it?*. In turn, *Will I?*, *Shall you?*, and *Will he/she/it?* are used to ask an addressee to state his or her expectation for the future.

Alongside these prescriptions is a set of corresponding proscriptions which also appear at the time. Not only do the grammarians tell people what to do with *shall* and *will*, they also tell them what not to do. The *Dictionary of English Normative Grammar 1700–1800* enumerates the common 'shall nots' for *shall* and *will* found during that period (Sundby *et al.* 1991: 190–2 *et passim*). The frequent error of co-occurrence (i.e. incompatibility between members of a grammatical construction) is earmarked along with the lesser sins of failed contraction and inflection. Fogg's 1796 lament typifies the grammarians' larger complaint:

> Our fellow citizens of North-Britain and Ireland, find much difficulty in these auxiliaries. Even such writers as Lord Kaim, Dr. Goldsmith, and Dr. Blair, are not always correct in them. . . . The main point of their error seems to be putting *will* for *shall* with the first person.
> (*Elementa Anglicana* 1796: II.129; quoted by Sundby *et al.* 1991: 191)

Use of the form *will* with the first person subject in utterances meant to foretell seems egregious to Fogg's contemporaries, who scold unwitting promisors. They particularly fault respected writers who ought to know better. Webster quotes Goldsmith's *faux pas*:

> If I draw a catgut or any other cord to a great length between my fingers, I *will* make it smaller than it was before.
> (*Dissertations* 1789: 237–8; emphasis mine; quoted by Sundby *et al.* 1991: 191)

Commentary collected by the *Dictionary* echoes the disapproval. In predictive contexts, first person *will* constructions are judged 'bad', 'improper', 'inaccurate', 'absurd', 'unidiomatic', and 'dialectal', or clearly 'Scotticism[s]' (cited by Sundby *et al.* 1991: 191).

Similarly, a third person subject proves incompatible with *shall* in acts of foretelling. Bayly observes the mistake Ascham commits, calling the usage 'obsolete':

> I know by good experience, that a child shall take more profit of two faults gently warned of, than of four things rightly hit; for then the master shall have good occasion to say ... which after this sort the master *shall* teach without error and the scholar *shall* learn without great pain.
> (*Plain and Complete Grammar* 1772: II.42; emphasis mine; quoted by Sundby *et al.* 1991: 190)

Providing another example, Webster cites the *Spectator*'s sentence, 'There is not a girl in town, but let her have her will in going to a mask, and she *shall* dress as a shepherdess' (*Dissertations* 1789: 239; emphasis mine; quoted by Sundby *et al.* 1991: 190). He, along with other arbiters of the polite, deems the construction 'improper' and 'unidiomatic' (cited by Sundby *et al.* 1991: 191).

Second person constructions fail to foretell when they contain *shall*, so they too are vanquished. Withers cites the 'Scotticism',

> You *shall* repent your Conduct.
> (*Aristarchus* 1790: 193; emphasis mine; quoted by Sundby *et al.* 1991: 192)

According to Dawson, even the Old Testament translation reads improperly in its prediction,

> But if ye *shall* still do wickedly, ye *shall* be consumed, both ye and your king.
> (*Prolepsis Philologiæ Anglicanæ* 1797: 16; emphasis mine; quoted by Sundby *et al.* 1991: 192)

Alternately, promissory or intentional utterances which require *shall* in the third person are violated by common use of *will*. Mennye seizes upon Swift's 'improper' structure:

> Whoever *will* examine the writings of all kinds, wherewith this ancient sect hath honoured the world, shall immediately find ... that the ideas of the authors have been altogether conversant.
> (*English Grammar* 1785: 81; emphasis mine; quoted by Sundby *et al.* 1991: 190)

The negative sanction accompanying these exemplary errors of co-occurrence must to large degree account for the emphatic force of their proscription. As Leonard points out, condemnations of 'common' and 'vulgar' constructions which violate grammatical rules are belied by an elitist agenda which must not be neglected. 'The multiplication of formal niceties ... was not without relation to the perpetuation of class differences' (Leonard 1929: 77). Class is often related to the sophistication of urbane southerners, moreover. 'No discussion of the *shall* and *will* matter in the latter part of the eighteenth century, as later, could get under way without condemnation' of the Scots and Irish 'for their misuses' (Leonard 1929: 178–9).[3] While it is not at all clear that failure to distinguish *shall* from *will* is tied to any one region or to Scots and Irish speakers of English, those who made 'mistakes' of usage were certainly victims of being identified as such. In other words, only vulgar provincials follow common usage.

Correct usage does not represent merely the cultivated refinement of those who knew it was important to know better. Because refined language also reveals the mind, or how the speaker perceived, it in turn reveals that individual's social status and 'worth' (Smith 1984: 21). Eighteenth-century divines interested themselves in usage for this reason. For Lowth, who proclaimed language a gift from heaven, linguistic correctness means using language in accordance with God's purpose (Smith 1984: 8). To the extent that deviance from polite usage proves unnatural and signifies moral and intellectual deficiency, *shall* and *will* prescriptions deliver an important mandate.

The doctrine of correctness persisted during the eighteenth century, although not all grammarians approved its mission of establishing usage. Dissenters like Campbell counter the imposition of usage from on high, arguing for a grammatical standard based in custom: 'from its conformity to these [customs] and from that alone, it derives all its authority and value' (1776: 340–1; cf. Webster 1789).[4] Samuel Johnson's treatment of the two auxiliaries in his *Dictionary* exemplifies a less rigidly prescriptive course of treatment. He attempts to represent the overlapping functions of *shall* and *will* by distinguishing a future-auxiliary use from a modal-auxiliary use (cf. Tieken-Boon van Ostade 1985: 127–30). Such mediation of the prescriptive with the descriptive turns out to be exceptional, however. Despite efforts like Johnson's, the contemporary grammatical description of the use of the two auxiliaries was overwhelmingly traditional, as Tieken-Boon van Ostade (1985) has shown.[5] The rules were prescriptive and in keeping with the prescriptive teaching grammars current at the time. It is ultimately the market for school grammars that favoured the received rules with influential reprintings, Tieken-Boon van Ostade argues (1985: 141–2). Reinforced by commercial forces in this way, ideological principles ensure the hegemony of the conventional rules.

It is important to bear in mind the great demand for clear formulations like the Wallis Rules. Jonathan Swift, for instance, believes that the extreme social, moral, and intellectual dangers of linguistic 'corruption' must be fought through regulated, precise usage. His *Proposal for Correcting, Improving and Ascertaining the English Tongue* articulates a cultural anxiety answered by the grammars in absence of an Academy (1957 [1712]). Swift's disquiet appears to be personal as well as societal, for his philosophical statements are made concrete in the usage problems he himself faced when writing English prose.[6] A comparison of textual variants (found between and among manuscript and printed versions of a work) illustrates not only the evolution of the dean's thinking about his subject, but also his continuing concern about that thought's expression. Swift's editorial process gives credence to the usage questions addressed in the grammars. His corrections indicate that he often re-evaluated earlier usage and abandoned previous choices while pursuing the form or structure that would convey his intended meaning. He replaces the relative pronoun 'who' with 'that', substitutes the adverb 'further' for 'farther', writes the past participle 'drunk' in place of 'drank', and discards the modal 'can' for 'may'.[7] In brief, he questions the same usage questioned by other writers of his time.

Swift's revisions prove especially relevant to the usage of *shall* and *will*. Modified drafts and printings of his humorous *Directions to Servants* exhibit Swift's change of heart in the use of one auxiliary instead of the other (1959: 209–10; vii–xxiii). For example, the original copy (*c*. 1738) by the amanuensis of the Forster Manuscript reads 'will have', a third person prediction allowed to stand when Swift himself emended the manuscript sometime later. That reading concurs with the one found in the third Dublin edition of the work (1751). On the other hand, Faulkner's 1745 edition, prepared from a copy text now incomplete, reads 'shall have'. The diction in this first edition (repeated in the second edition of 1746) agrees with the usage of the 1731 Rothschild autograph, a version which predates the Forster original. In his final versions of the *Directions*, then, Swift replaces 'shall' with 'will' in a third person construction meant to predict (1959: 13).[8] Reconsideration of the modal required in this construction leads Swift to substitute one form for the other: he rejects his original (common) usage to follow a 'correct' usage.

Another manuscript in the Victoria and Albert Forster Collection shows Swift's process of revision even more transparently, although it concerns the requisite modal in its conditional form (Swift 1955: 329–30). The autograph manuscript containing his 'Letter to the Archbishop of Dublin Concerning the Weavers' (dated 1729), includes Swift's own alterations and corrections to the text. In the standard edition prepared by Davis the sentence revised by Swift reads, 'What I have said may serve as an answer to the desire made me by the Corporation of Weavers, that I *would* offer my notions to the publick' (1955: 71; emphasis mine). Originally the manuscript read 'to offer', but the 'to' has been deleted and the phrase, 'that I should' has been inserted above the line. Subsequently this emendation appears itself to have been corrected: the phrase, 'that I would' is written in the left margin where other alterations appear. Clearly Swift has hesitated over the necessary modal and decided that *would* rather than *should* is required by the construction in this conditional context.[9]

Swift's struggle for precision is exemplified one final time by a collation of foul and fair copies of his political apology, 'An Enquiry into the

Behaviour of the Queen's Last Ministry' (1953: 215–31). Two times in the course of revising his first draft, a manuscript *A* from the Rothschild collection, he cancels particular modals. Their replacements appear in a second Rothschild manuscript, *B*, the fair copy of this corrected draft. Here an amanuensis renders the foul copy (prepared for the most part in Swift's hand) into a version which will become the copy text of the first (1765) printed edition. When preparing this memoir for publication, Swift verifies his new diction by leaving it unchanged when he himself corrected the fair copy. It is on the authority of Swift's own revisions, then, that in the Davis edition 'can' appears instead of the earlier 'will' (1953: 227, 166) and 'may' replaces the earlier 'shall' (1953: 208, 89).[10] Problems of co-occurrence apparently caused Swift to avoid the use of either *shall* or *will* and to replace them with other modals.

Swift's practice of revising and correcting questionable usage substantiates the usage quandaries troubling eighteenth-century writers. The dean's uncertainty also underscores the practical need shared by others writing English. Their requirement is satisfied by the grammars. Where common use is proscribed and sanctioned, correct use is prescribed and praised.

To Leonard's way of thinking, both proscription and prescription for *shall* and *will* boil down to one purpose. The insistent differentiation between the two auxiliaries manifests one of the eighteenth-century's main methods of handling usage. Promoting a singularity of form and function,

> they discarded one [word or phrase] and accepted another on the ground that any difference in structure means added exactness in discrimination and expression. (Leonard 1929: 75–6)

Indeed, the differentiation between constructions using the two modals preserves an important linguistic distinction. But this distinction is not merely a lexical one; nor is it a purely syntactic distinction of 'grammatical' compatibility. Rather, the rules distinguish larger semantic and pragmatic functions. As Wallis elaborates,

> In the first person *shall* simply indicates a prediction, whereas *will* is used for promising or threatening. In the second and third persons *shall* is used for promising or threatening, and *will* of a straightforward prediction. 'I shall burn', 'you will' ('thou wilt'), 'he will'; 'we shall', 'ye will', 'they will', 'burn' all simply predict what will happen; whereas 'I will', 'you shall' ('thou shalt'), 'he shall', 'we will', 'ye shall', 'they shall', 'burn' are used for guarantees or pledges of what will happen. (Wallis 1972 [1653]: 339)

While these rules may or may not have been arbitrary in origin, they certainly do possess an underlying rationale.[11] A careful examination of the Wallis Rules reveals the way in which they tell us 'how to do things with words'. The formulations indicate whether a speaker commands, promises, or predicts; they indicate whether the speaker is the agent of volition or prediction or whether he or she is the questioner of such agency. By distinguishing speaker attitude and speaker involvement the Wallis paradigm makes formal distinctions of modality which are central to the utterance of a speech act.

Let me examine the working of these rules in greater detail. Because their rationale is nothing if not rational, it can be used to deconstruct them. Looking at the paradigm outlined by Wallis, we note the primacy of the first person in determining the modal. As Lowth (1762: 64–5) explains,

> *Will* in the first Person singular and plural, promises or threatens; in the second and third Person, only fortells; *shall*, on the contrary, in the first Person only fortells; in the second and third Persons, promises, commands, or threatens.

In other words, first person *will* promises and commands, while second and third person *will* predicts. The division between the experiencer of intention or the imposer of obligation, *I*, and the goal of that intention or obligation, *you* or *he*, is explicitly signalled in the commissive by a switch in the modal auxiliary: *will* in the first person alternates with *shall* in the second and third persons.

The formalized distinction between the experiencer of volition and the grammatical subject and goal of the promise or command can be seen more clearly in Ward's illustration of compound sentences (1767: 121–3):[12]

(3) I resolve or determine that I will go.
     You resolve or determine that you will go.
     He resolves or determines that he will go.

But:

(4) a. I resolve or determine that I will go.
     I resolve or determine that you shall go.
     I resolve or determine that he shall go.

(5) a. I predict that I shall go.
     I predict that you will go.
     I predict that he will go.

Ward claims that when the first person clause is removed, the modal so clearly signalling the speaker's volition or prediction remains. The compound sentences in (4a) can be replaced by sentences meaning the same thing in (4b):

(4) b. I will go.
     You shall go.
     He shall go.

While the compounds in (5a) yield the simple predictions in (5b):

(5) b. I shall go.
You will go.
He will go.

There is little potential for confusion in this system, for Ward says that only the clause referring to the speaker can be eliminated without affecting the meaning of the sentence. *You will go* cannot mean a report about the subject *you*'s volition as it did in (3). *You will go* is only the speaker's prediction about the future action of *you*. Conversely, *you shall go* represents the speaker's assurance about that going (Ward 1767: 121–3).

When a speaker wishes to express intentions or desires for a future event affecting that speaker or another person, the auxiliary changes along with the personal pronoun to signal the co-referentiality or lack of co-referentiality between agent and goal. In the Wallis system, both modal auxiliaries and subject pronouns function as deictic markers that relate the utterance to the speaker and agent of the illocutionary act.

This correlation of form and meaning extends into the rules for predictions. *Shall* signals the non co-referentiality of goal and agent of volition in the paradigm for promises and commands. In predictions, on the other hand, volition is not involved in the utterance; nor is an agent of volition present. Therefore the auxiliary associated with volition in first person utterances, namely *will*, is also absent in first person predictions. In first person predictions, *shall* signals a separation between the grammatical subject of the utterance and the volition of its agent, even to the point of representing the absence of a deontic agent. In the first person, then, *shall* simply predicts, reflecting the expectation rather than the volition of the speaker. In predictions centred on second and third person subjects, a switch in auxiliaries to *will* occurs, paralleling the switch between the auxiliary in first person promises on the one hand and second and third person promises on the other. The auxiliary alternation in statements of belief also indicates the speaker's role in the speech act: in predictions, a first person speech act with an agent of belief co-referential to the sentence's grammatical subject is once again distinguished from utterances in which the subject is not co-referential with the speaker.

Most notable in this system, then, is the way that the speaker's attitude of volition or expectation is formally represented in the distinction between *shall* and *will*. Within the Wallis system there is an attempt to invest in promises and commands a deontic modality that distinguishes them from predictive statements of epistemic futurity. The 'correct' speaker who observes the Wallis distinctions, asserts his or her belief in declaratives which predict, asserts his or her intention in declaratives which promise, and asserts his or her desire in declaratives which command.

18TH-CENTURY (NON-)STANDARD REASSESSED

To restate the rationale, the clear delineation of prediction and volition is paralleled by the distinction between the agent of those attitudes and the object they affect. The alternation of modal auxiliaries and subject pronouns in the futurate paradigm signals the speaker's presence and attitude. Thus modality is encoded within the Wallis Rules.

In order to determine if similar rhyme or reason supports the interrogative paradigm, let me review the rules as set forth by Ward and Lowth. In Ward's grammar, his chapter 'of the difference between the Future by *Shall*, and that by *Will*', addresses interrogatives:

> When Questions are asked, *shall* denotes a State which the Person of whom the Question is asked foresees concerning himself, but determines concerning other Objects; *will* a State which he determines concerning himself, but foresees concerning others: Therefore 'shall you go?' is equivalent to 'do you expect to go?' but 'will you go?' to 'do you resolve or determine to go?' But 'shall I, he, they go?' are equivalent to 'do you determine that I, he, they may go?' or 'do you permit us to go?' and 'will I, he, they go?' to 'do you think or believe that I, he, they are determined to go?' or, 'in such a situation as that [is] our, his or their going ... likely to take place?' (Ward 1767: 121–3)

Lowth agrees that the interrogatives *Will I/we?*, *Shall you?*, and *Will he/they?* question the hearer about his prediction for the future act mentioned in the question's proposition. On the other hand, *Shall I/we?*, *Will you?*, and *Shall he/they?* question the hearer about his desire or intent regarding the future proposition.

The declarative paradigms demonstrate the conceptual and grammatical split between the agent of prediction or volition and the grammatical subject of the utterance. Yet in the interrogative, the paradigms ostensibly violate this division and fail to preserve the correlation between the co-referential *I* and the auxiliary directly associated with it in the indicative. For example, the auxiliary *shall*, which is elsewhere reserved for second and third person statements of volition, appears to question volition in the first person. In fact, the pronouns distinguishing agent from goal of modality and the auxiliaries distinguishing the direct from the indirect relationship between the speaker-agent and the subject still hold. The interrogative, however, affects and redefines which pronouns and auxiliaries are transparent (direct) or opaque (indirect) with respect to agency. Awaiting the hearer's response before he or she acts upon the proposition, the speaker (or agent of the question) transfers agency to the hearer who will in turn offer either a directive or a prediction. To signify the transfer, the speaker uses the auxiliary appropriate for the hearer's response, but changes the pronoun.

In interrogatives, both first person and third person pronouns behave as indirect or 'objective' subjects with regard to the agent of volition. Both take indirect verbal forms to question the agency of a hearer implicitly (indirectly) involved in the utterance. When the hearer is explicitly involved, when the speaker addresses a question to a person whom the speaker regards as *you*, the nature of the interrogative changes. Its paraphrase and its grammatical formation manifest this direct relationship. Instead of asking about another's will, the *you* is asked directly for an expression *of* will. Subject, agent, and hearer become co-referential. To signal a direct request and the expectation of a direct expression of desire, the direct modal verb form *will* is used in the question, *Will you?*.

The same sorts of distinctions found in the declarative paradigm operate among interrogatives. The involvement of the speaker is clearly established. *Shall I?* and *Shall he?* questions reveal the speaker as the questioner of a hearer's desire. *Will you?* questions establish the direct nature of the discourse.

Bishop Lowth claims that in questions asking for a simple prediction of future events, the sequence is reversed. *Will I?*, *Will he?*, and *Shall you?* request predictions according to a rationale consistent with that proffered by Ward. We can see further that the expected answers to such questions of expectation, namely the assertions of belief formulated by Wallis, actually repeat the modal found in the question: the questioner uses the modal appropriate for his respondent. The answer, *You will go* corresponds to the question, *Will I go?*; the response, *I shall go* satisfies the question, *Shall you go?*; the assertion, *He will go* constitutes a reply to the interrogative, *Will he go?*. In a like manner, the answers to the three phrases designed to question volition also repeat the question modal and entail the very assertions of volition outlined by Wallis.

The paradigm for questioning the hearer's expectation works in perfect opposition to the paradigm for questioning volition. Not more than one question in either paradigm has the same form and no ambiguity arises. Expected answers complement each question with equivalent singularity. When conducted through the interpretive lens of pragmatic analysis, a reading of the received rules for *shall* and *will* exposes an elaborate albeit consistent illocutionary rationale. The prescriptions dictate attitudinal and illocutionary distinctions which were considered fundamental and necessary.

Obvious questions arise in light of the rules' basic meaning: Why legislate those syntactic and pragmatic distinctions? Why make a distinction in usage and then bring negative sanction to bear on its defence? In other words, what is the vernacular against which the standard so forcibly reacts? What does actual usage look like at the time prescription and proscription are both applied? Briefly, vernacular usage was mixed, because increasingly epistemic modals were the raw material of both 'temporal' (epistemic) and 'modal' (deontic) utterances of futurity. Reference to a now famous article by Fries highlights larger patterns of usage. After surveying four hundred years of English drama along with later American plays, Fries concludes that the seventeenth- and eighteenth-century grammarians had set down rules that were without strong precedent in eighteenth-century usage. Fries determines that for independent declarative statements, *shall* occurs commonly with the second and third persons only early on (in sixteenth-century usage); by the nineteenth century, *will* had gradually replaced *shall*, so that *will* predominated in all three persons.

Certainly this common usage of *will* is established by the eighteenth century. Even the discovery of the prescribed paradigms (e.g. Hulbert 1947 and Taglicht 1970) in writing from the late seventeenth and the eighteenth centuries fails to contradict the diachronic pattern Fries identifies. Chafe's (1984) study of the effect of the Wallis prescriptions in written usage accounts for the presence of those structures as the result *of* prescription. Demonstrating the impact of prescription, he shows that it prompts an artificial but temporary usage which lasts until prescription has run its course and the proscribed feature re-emerges. He finds the simple future, 'I shall' secured in usage only in the late nineteenth century, generations after the prescription becomes standard. As prescribing diminishes, it begins to wane, until 'I will' futures predominate one hundred years later (Chafe 1984: 98). Thus the conventional paradigms for *shall* and *will* follow a typical development after their introduction into usage: when change is imposed from on high, it does not initiate much significant or permanent change in actual usage. On balance, then, Fries's evidence refutes widespread eighteenth-century practice of the Wallis Rule that a first person *will* corresponds to second and third person *shall*.

Turning to questions, Fries observes that '*shall* is almost always used with the first person and *will* with the second and third' (1925: 1024). He argues, therefore, that in questions asking for predictions of mere futurity, the Wallis paradigm is not used: *Shall I?* questions predominate in place of the *Will I?* forms required. Although *will* appears the majority of the time in third person constructions, the relative absence of *shall* in the second person suggests to Fries that the rule that *shall* is the normal auxiliary in second person questions of futurity does not seem to have a basis in usage.

Not surprisingly, the usage Fries reports is consistent with that seen in the larger development and grammaticalization of *shall* and *will*.[13] The net semantic effect of these changes is a shift in the modalities of *shall* and *will*. Over time a semantic alteration occurs wherein these, like all the other modals, exhibit an increase in epistemic meanings (Goossens 1984: 152; cf. Goossens 1982). In addition, these two modals display a movement 'from relatively weak subjective epistemicity to more strongly subjective epistemicity' (Traugott 1989: 43; cf. Traugott 1982; cf. Warner 1990). A clear weakening and decrease of deontic meanings occurs while epistemic meanings strengthen and increase.

Eventually the meanings of *shall* and *will* achieve their modern senses. The notion of pure futurity overshadows that of determination in Early

Modern English *will* (Visser 1969: 1582). In North American as well as British dialects of English the auxiliary conveys the 'uncertainty, doubt, and speculation' inherent in the very notion of futurity (Haegeman 1983: 166). As Modern English *shall* correspondingly loses its sense of obligation, neutral *will* displaces it in the majority of future constructions in Present-Day English. *Shall* survives as a 'purely... suppletive form of *will* which is used either in contexts where *will* might seem ambiguous or as a more formal variant' (Perkins 1982: 264).

The semantic changes have pragmatic implications which also need to be considered given the illocutionary purpose of the rules under scrutiny. During the Middle English period, deontic modals still occurred in commissive utterances and epistemic modals still predicted. Yet the exclusionary increase of epistemic meanings has illocutionary repercussions in later English, as I have shown elsewhere (Arnovick 1994; cf. Traugott and König 1991). By the modern period, another way of promising begins to supplement illocutions containing deontic modals. When promissory discourse contains temporal modals, it often expands beyond the length of a single utterance in order to emphasize the speaker's promissory intention.

The pragmatic repercussions of semantic change lie at the crux of the received rules' relationship to common Modern English usage. In light of the diachronic trajectory for temporal *will*, Fries ascertains that the conventional rules for *shall* and *will* are 'without a validity based upon the practice of the language' (1925: 1023). Furthermore, after analysing the grammars presenting them, he concludes (1925: 981) that these rules were artificial and arbitrary:

> In harmony with the common attitude toward correct language and the usual purposes of the 18th century grammarians, . . . [proponents of the Wallis Rules] definitely repudiate usage as the standard of correctness and attempt to regulate the practice of English speakers and writers by means of rules based on 'reason'.

Thus reads the commonly held view about the rules for *shall* and *will*. If we reflect on the artificial 'Wallis' variety of standard English and consider the nonstandard variety maintained in common usage, the prescriptions possess a larger meaning. The received rules encode modality in future constructions during a period when the modal auxiliaries have levelled in both form and function. The timing of their appearance is not insignificant. The impulse of distinguishing deontic from epistemic futurate utterances coincides with the levelling of such formal distinctions in the grammar. As is often the case, the traditional prescriptions are designed to fix and to maintain precisely those distinctions collapsing in real use. The prescriptions seem to have been devised with the modals of seventeenth- and eighteenth-century English, not those of Old English, in mind. By combining subject and auxiliary into a syntactic unit, they resurrect a meaning that the grammaticalized modals in themselves have lost. In the final analysis, perhaps the artificial variety entailed in the eighteenth-century standard tells us something important. Through its strictures, eighteenth-century grammarians maintain that basic illocutionary and semantic distinctions are worth making. Reaching beyond niceties of usage, they insist on a fundamental differentiation between deontic and epistemic utterances, between their agents and goals, and between promissory or predictive illocutionary force. The standard variety reveals the eighteenth-century awareness that English writers and speakers *do* things with words, even while it ignores the language's actual if less 'rational' means of pragmatic expression.

Notes

* This article was made possible in part through a grant from the Social Sciences and Humanities Research Council of Canada.
1 See, for example, *The Oxford Dictionary and Usage Guide to the English Language* (1995), a 'one-stop reference' published in both Oxford and New York and sold widely in Canada and the United States for an audience who most generally and idiomatically ignores the 'formal' use recommended in its formal writing.
2 For a fuller history of the treatment of *shall* and *will* with an exploration of descriptions supplementing the received rules, see Tieken-Boon van Ostade (1985); cf. Michael (1970); cf. Fries (1925). My historical sketch of the evolution of the conventional rules for *shall* and *will* appeared in a somewhat different version in Arnovick (1990).
3 Even St Patrick's illustrious dean was not immune to such criticism. In directions to Swift's London printer, his Dublin publisher warns that the text of *Directions to Servants*, unfinished before Swift's death, is 'consequently very incorrect. I believe you may see some Irishisms in it; if so, pray correct them...' (quoted by Davis in Swift 1959).
4 In fact, whatever their origin, rules generally tended to become prescriptive, once they were set down. The two streams of thought about linguistic usage may have produced a common result, then. Whether individual grammars utilized prescriptive or descriptive methodologies deriving from elitist or democratic ideologies, they shared the common assumption that language mattered and that people should be given the guidance they expected from these books. This outcome must not be taken as a given, however. Hudson's (1994) important work on writing and speech in the eighteenth century warns against underestimating the real dialectic of views on usage at the time. Prescriptivism was not unopposed even though it holds sway with regard to *shall* and *will*.

5 Wallis states that he offers rules for *shall* and *will* to foreigners who may not otherwise realize that English speakers do not use the two auxiliaries interchangeably (1972 [1653]: 339). Clearly he means to describe correct usage to that audience. Whether the basis of this description was actual usage or prescribed practice is less clear, for he remains silent on that question. In a letter written at age eighty he does account for a larger philosophy underlying his life's work. Answering a biographer's request for self-reflection, Wallis stresses his life-long attempt to moderate extremes in religion, education, and the public good. In his grammar, as in all else, is his guiding principle, 'if things could not be just, as I could wish, to make the best of what is' (Bodleian Ms Smith 31 dated 29 January 1696/7). While Wallis's methodology remains unknown, his formulations certainly serve a prescriptive function when they are codified in the eighteenth-century grammars. I would like to thank the Bodleian Library for giving me access to its collection of Wallis's correspondence.

6 For a detailed examination of Swift's fascination for and concern about English language as reflected in his life and works, see Kelly (1988). I would like to thank Susan Wright for alerting me to Swift's practice of revising his usage.

7 See, for example, Swift (1957: 289, 60; 1951: 241, 125; 1957: 297, 179; 1962: 349, 80).

8 On the authority of the later corrections, the text established by Davis now reads,

> But Ingenuity can do much, for prudent Servants have found out an effectual Remedy against this insupportable Grievance, by tying up the Pulley in such a Manner, that the weight of the Lead *will* have no Effect.
> (Swift 1959: 13, 210; emphasis mine)

9 On another occasion the related question of whether or not to use an indicative or a conditional form of the modal has caused Swift to alter his work. His first draft of 'A Letter on Maculla's Project' (on circulating copper notes) seems to be preserved partially in an autograph manuscript in the Forster Collection (Swift 1955: 332; see also Davis's introduction, xvii–xviii). It serves as the base for a 1765 edition printed by Deane Swift. A 1759 edition printed by Faulkner (presumably based on a draft corrected subsequent to the Forster manuscript) contains substantive changes and additions not found in the 1765 volume or its copy text. Because of these changes, the first edition is thought to be based on a corrected manuscript which has been lost. Lacking that corrected source, Deane Swift prints the earlier 'will be' in that line. The corrected version, which Faulkner printed, reads 'would be' in the sentence, 'But there are some points in his proposal, which I cannot well answer for, nor do I know whether he *would be* able to do it himself' (Swift 1955: 94, 333; emphasis mine).

While the choice of verbal mood may not be on the order of a choice between one modal or another, it typifies both the author's care for linguistic precision in face of uncertain usage and the related issues involved in modal use.

10 Although I have selected evidence treating *shall* and *will*, the meaning and use of other modals often troubles Swift. Revealing his confrontation of another typical usage problem, 'might' also occurs in place of 'could' in his revised 'Enquiry' (1953: 231, 179).
11 The following discussion of the illocutionary rationale for the rules appeared in a somewhat different version in Arnovick (1990).
12 Here I cite Ward's influential second edition (1767) of the *Grammar* for its concise explanation of the rules.
13 See Arnovick (1994) from which the following review is taken for a fuller discussion of the development of *shall* and *will*.

References

Arnovick, Leslie K. 1990. *The Development of Future Constructions in English: Modal and Temporal* Will *and* Shall *in Middle English*. New York: Peter Lang.
Arnovick, Leslie K. 1994. The expanding discourse of promises in present-day English: A case study in historical pragmatics. *Folia Linguistica Historica* 15(1): 175–91.
Chafe, Wallace 1984. Speaking, Writing, and Prescriptivism. *Georgetown University Round Table on Languages and Linguistics*, ed. Deborah Schiffrin, Washington, DC: Georgetown University Press, pp. 95–103.
Campbell, George 1776. *The Philosophy of Rhetoric*, vol. 1. London: W. Strahan.
Davis, Herbert s.v. Swift, Jonathan.
Fries, Charles C. 1925. The periphrastic future with *shall* and *will* in Modern English. *PMLA* 40: 963–1024.
Goossens, Louis 1982. On the development of the modals and of the epistemic function in English. In: Anders Ahlqvist (ed.), *Papers from the Fifth International Conference on Historical Linguistics*. Amsterdam: John Benjamins, pp. 74–84.
Goossens, Louis 1984. The Interplay of Syntax and Semantics in the Development of the English Modals. In: N.F. Blake and Charles Jones (eds), *English Historical Linguistics: Studies in Development*. Sheffield: Centre for English Cultural Tradition and Language, pp. 149–59.
Haegeman, Liliane 1983. *The Semantics of* Will *in Present-Day British English: A Unified Account*. Brussels: Verhandelingen van de Koninklijke Academie voor Wetenschappen.
Hudson, Nicholas 1994. *Writing and European Thought 1600–1830*. Cambridge: Cambridge University Press.

Hulbert, J.R. 1947. On the origin of the grammarians' rules for the use of *Shall* and *Will*. *PMLA* 62: 1178–82.
Johnson, Samuel 1755. *A Dictionary of the English Language*, facs. repr. 1968. Hildesheim: G. Olms.
Kelly, Ann Cline 1988. *Swift and the English Language*. Philadelphia: University of Pennsylvania Press.
Leonard, Sterling Andrus 1929. *The Doctrine of Correctness in English Usage 1700–1800*. Madison: University of Wisconsin.
Lowth, Robert A. 1762. *A Short Introduction to English Grammar*. London (publisher unknown).
Michael, Ian 1970. *English Grammatical Categories and the Tradition to 1800*. Cambridge: Cambridge University Press.
Perkins, Michael R. 1982. The core meanings of the English modals. *Journal of Linguistics* 18: 245–73.
Smith, Olivia 1984. *The Politics of Language 1791–1819*. Oxford: Clarendon Press.
Sundby, Bertil, Bjørge, Anne Kari and Haughland, Kari E. 1991. *A Dictionary of English Normative Grammar 1700–1800*. Amsterdam: John Benjamins.
Swift, Jonathan 1951. *The History of the Four Last Years of the Queen*, ed. Herbert Davis, repr. 1964. Oxford: Basil Blackwell.
Swift, Jonathan 1953. *Political Tracts 1713–1719*, ed. Herbert Davis and Irvin Ehrenpreis, repr. 1964. Oxford: Basil Blackwell.
Swift, Jonathan 1955. *Irish Tracts 1728–1733*, ed. Herbert Davis, repr. 1964. Oxford: Basil Blackwell.
Swift, Jonathan 1957. *A Proposal for Correcting the English Tongue, Polite Conversation, Etc.*, ed. Herbert Davis, repr. 1964. Oxford: Basil Blackwell.
Swift, Jonathan 1959. *Directions to Servants and Miscellaneous Pieces 1733–1742*, ed. Herbert Davis. Oxford: Basil Blackwell.
Swift, Jonathan 1962. *Miscellaneous and Autobiographical Pieces, Fragments, and Marginalia*, ed. Herbert Davis. Oxford: Basil Blackwell.
Taglicht, J. 1970. The genesis of the conventional rules for the use of *shall* and *will*. *English Studies* 51: 193–213.
Tieken-Boon van Ostade, Ingrid 1985. 'I will be drowned and no man shall save me': The conventional rules for *shall* and *will* in eighteenth-century English grammars. *English Studies* 2: 123–42.
Traugott, Elizabeth Closs 1982. From propositional to textual and expressive meanings: Some semantic-pragmatic aspects of grammaticalization. In: Winfred P. Lehmann and Yakov Malkiel (eds), *Perspectives on Historical Linguistics*. Amsterdam: John Benjamins, pp. 245–71.
Traugott, Elizabeth Closs 1989. On the rise of epistemic meanings in English: An example of subjectification in semantic change. *Language* 65(1): 31–55.
Traugott, Elizabeth Closs and König, Ekkehard 1991. The semantics-pragmatics of grammaticalization revisited. In: Elizabeth Closs Traugott

and Bernd Heine (eds), *Approaches to Grammaticalization*, vol. 1. Amsterdam: John Benjamins, pp. 189–218.

Visser, F.T. 1969. *An Historical Syntax of the English Language*, vol. 3. Leiden: E.J. Brill.

Wallis, John 1765. *Grammatica Linguae Anglicanae*, 6th edition. London: G. Bowlyer.

Wallis, John 1972. *Grammar of the English Language*, ed. and trans. J.A. Kemp. London: Longman.

Ward, William 1765. *Grammar of the English Language*. London: R. Horsfield.

Ward, William 1767. *Grammar of the English Language*. York: C. Etherington.

Warner, Anthony R. 1990. Reworking the history of English auxiliaries. In: Sylvia M. Adamson et al. (eds), *Papers from the Fifth International Conference on English Historical Linguistics*. Amsterdam: John Benjamins, pp. 537–58.

Webster, Noah 1789. *Dissertations on the English Language*. Boston: I. Thomas and Company.

CHAPTER 11

The genitives of the relative pronouns in present-day English

Aimo Seppänen[1]

11.1 Introduction

Within the system of its relative pronouns, present-day English displays a clear distinction between two levels of usage. So far as standard English is concerned, the available items are the three familiar pronouns:[2]

(1)   NOM/ACC   GEN
    who/who(m) whose
    which   –
    that   –

In the nonstandard regional forms of the language, these items are similarly found – *that* and *who* with varying degrees of frequency, *which* only rather sparingly – but there are three additional items that are used in this function. They are given here in the forms traditionally recorded, as in Wright's *English Dialect Dictionary* (henceforth *EDD*) and *English Dialect Grammar* (henceforth *EDG*) about a hundred years ago.

(2)   NOM/ACC   GEN
    at   –
    what   –
    as   –

The display of forms cited reveals a striking case of asymmetry in the total lack of genitives for all of the items except *who*. With a clear gap in the system, the need for circumlocutions obviously arises, and descriptions of the language have traditionally presented a number of 'genitive equivalents' available for that purpose. However, in more recent work dealing with the English of our own century, cases have been noted where the defective paradigm has been complemented by a genitive form not recorded from older usage. This clearly points to a morphological and syntactic change in twentieth-century English which seems to me well worth a closer study. In taking up the question of these genitives in the present chapter, I want to consider in particular the following general issues, each to be dealt with in its own section:

GENITIVES OF THE ENGLISH RELATIVE PRONOUNS

(1) What are these new genitives and what is their distribution in standard or non-standard varieties of the language?

(2) What are the individual changes involved in their appearance and what are the general forces responsible for them?

(3) What are the general implications that these genitives have for the grammatical analysis of the items concerned and for the interpretation of the differences between the relativization strategies applied in standard and nonstandard English?

11.2 The new genitive forms

11.2.1 The form that's

The best known of the new genitives is the form *that's* noted in a number of studies and associated in particular with Scotland. In Grant's *Scottish National Dictionary* (henceforth *SND*), it is illustrated by the following examples from 1972:

(3)   a. The woman *that's* sister mairriet the postie.
        b. The kye *that's* caur were born aa about the same time.

Sometimes viewed as a pure Scotticism, *that's* is in fact also recorded from many other parts of the English-speaking world. Harris (1993: 150) notes its occurrence in Ireland, as in (4), and from the modern dialects of England we have (5), recorded from Essex in Orton and Dieth's *Survey of English Dialects* (henceforth *SED*; III.iii.1327).

(4)   Remember the man *that's* house got burnt down?

(5)   That's the chap *that's* uncle was drowned.

In addition to these records from genuine regional usage, the form is also known to be used more generally in educated colloquial speech. Aitken (1970: 105) points out that *that's*, as in *the people that's houses were demolished*, is the favoured form, rather than *whose*, in what he calls Middle Class Scottish Standard English, and adds that this applies to the spoken but not the written language; and Romaine (1980: 227, 234, 236; cf. also Romaine 1982: 95) offers *the house that's roof was damaged* as a more recent illustration from spoken Scottish with a similar note about the non-occurrence of the form in her written material.

A situation not entirely different from the Scottish one appears to be reflected in records from other English-speaking countries. From England, Hudson (1990: 396) notes the form *the pencil that's lead is broken*, produced by his eleven-year-old daughter and considered to be acceptable by many other speakers from the south of England. From America, Stahlke (1976: 591), without noting any recorded instances of the form, reports that in a test about 20 per cent of his college students found *that's* in *the dog that's leg was broken* fully acceptable. The two authors do not directly refer to the variety of language concerned, but Seppänen and Kjellmer (1995: 395), repeating Stahlke's experiment with a limited number of British and American colleagues, found that when the context was explicitly specified as familiar conversation, the structure with *that's* + Noun was felt by the testees, British as well as American, to be even more generally acceptable than indicated by Stahlke's figures.

To this discussion, some genuine examples can be added which further illustrate the situation. Of the following cases, the examples under (6) come from the recorded spoken material of the Cobuild Corpus, while the quotation under (7) represents written usage, culled from an advertisement in *The Observer* (27 March 1988).

(6) a. they put new hair on the doll *thats* hair had fallen out or you'd pulled it off or something erm and they repair teddies and things as well
 b. so that's the phase angle (3) the angle *that's* tangent is omega CR over two (3) alright?
 c. down this increasing mass *that's* velocity is increasing
 d. colloquial forms, the kind of language *that's* use in . . . used by the native sp

(7) Back in 1976, JVC made a name for themselves by inventing the world's most popular home video format. Yes, you guessed it – VHS. Twelve years on, they have come up with another milestone in home video technology, the GR-45 camcorder. It delivers a VHS picture the like of which the world has never seen. A picture *that's* quality of detail, colour and resolution is unrivalled.

The source of (6a) is a face-to-face conversation between friends (British, from 1991), with a style which is clearly colloquial. The other examples under (6) are somewhat different in that they stem from what appear to be lectures on physics/mathematics or linguistics. Yet, although the texts represent serious expository prose in strictly standard English, the style would seem to be close to colloquial, and that is so even in the written example (cf. *Yes, you guessed it*). What is of interest here, however, is the fact that in (7) the form *that's* is used in print in a context where the message is directed not to a narrow circle of close associates but to the entire readership of a national quality paper.

In view of the development illustrated by this usage, it is of interest to further test speaker reactions to the new genitive with two different age groups. For this purpose, I added one sentence to a questionnaire dealing with other matters, and presented it to two groups of academic native informants: an older group consisting of university professors or lecturers from various language departments in Europe and North

America, and a younger group consisting of students of English at Manchester University. The example and the results were as follows.

(8) For heaven's sake wake up and face the facts: ours is the only house in the area *that's* value has not gone up during the last couple of years.

(9) | Results | No | No? | Yes? | Yes | Total |
|---|---|---|---|---|---|
| Older group | 12 | 3 | 5 | 1 | 21 |
| Younger group | 4 | 3 | 6 | 4 | 17 |

Limited in scope as the test is, the difference between the two groups seems to point to a growing acceptance of *that's*. But note that here too we are dealing with clearly colloquial language, and in fact several informants modified their acceptance (either Yes? or Yes) by adding that this applied only to spoken usage.

All in all, there is thus growing evidence available to show that the genitive *that's* has started to move from purely regional language to the colloquial variety of standard English. This usage is subject to some restrictions which will be dealt with later as they are shared by the other items to be considered, but one point specific to *that's* can be taken up here. In its regional use, *that's* is freely employed with animate as well as inanimate antecedents, as will readily appear from the quotations given earlier, but in all the cases noted from colloquial standard English it refers to an inanimate antecedent. In terms of the system of standard English pronouns, it is easy to suggest the reason for this. To fill the gap in the system created by the invariability of *which*, the usual genitive equivalents available as alternatives to *the pencil that's lead is broken* are *the pencil the lead of which is broken* and *the pencil whose lead is broken*, the first clumsy and strongly disfavoured in speech, and the second avoided by many speakers because of the human or animate associations of *who* (for a thorough discussion of present-day usage on this point, see Johansson 1995). In this situation, *that's* may be resorted to because it offers a way out, whereas there is no need for such an innovation with human antecedents where *whose* is readily available.

11.2.2 *The form* at's

The pronoun *at* is originally a weakened form of *that*, or possibly a loan from Old Norse where the corresponding weakening had already taken place (cf. Mustanoja 1960: 191, Romaine 1982: 70). As a relative it is chiefly used in Scotland and the northern counties of England (cf. *EDD*, Upton *et al*. 1994: 489). The earliest recorded occurrence of it in the genitive is quoted by Jespersen (1927: 111) from James A. Barrie, and thus goes back to the turn of the century, and other examples, recorded from the 1920s, are given in the *SND*.

TAMING THE VERNACULAR

(10) a. A wife *'at's* wrapper's never even on, an' wha doesna wash her mutch aince in a month.
   b. That's the man *'at's* hoose was brunt.
   c. The mannie *at's* doggie wis tint has disappear't.

To these Scottish examples we may add a modern example from the North of England, recorded from Cumberland, Lancashire and Yorkshire (*SED* III.iii.1085),[3] and additionally mention the occurrence of the form in Essex (information from David Wright, personal communication):

(11) That's the chap *at's* uncle was drownded.

11.2.3 *The forms* what'/what's

The pronoun *what* as a relative is recorded in the *EDD* as being in general use in regional English, and from more recent sources the word is known to be the favourite relative of nonstandard urban speech (Hughes and Trudgill 1987: 18, Cheshire *et al.* 1993: 68). The genitive of the pronoun is recorded in the *SED* in two forms: *what*, given by one informant in Essex, and *what's*, noted from Derbyshire, Essex and Somerset (*SED* II.iii.1072, III.iii.1327, IV.iii.1156).

(12) a. That's the chap *what* uncle was drowned.
   b. That's the chap *what's* uncle got drowned (was drownded, drowned self).

The more recent study of Cheshire *et al.* (1993: 69) notes only the form *what's*, as used in the following example, reported by them from a large number of informants from England and Scotland and similarly reported to me by a couple of informants from North Wales.

(13) That's the girl *what's* mum loves horror films.

The genitive *what'* (as I prefer to spell the zero form) is a survival of the Early Modern English pattern where the ending of the genitive could be dropped in prenominal position (e.g. *the king hand, oure unkill name, it importance*). Generally lost in standard English (on this, see Seppänen, forthcoming), it is preserved even today in some dialects (e.g. *this cow legs, it name*, cf. Upton *et al.* 1994: 484, 488), but the genitive form *what'* is not recorded in any source outside its one appearance in the *SED* material.

11.2.4 *The form* as'

The pronoun *as* in the relative function is well attested in the *EDD* and *SED* from different parts of Britain, and is noted in Cheshire *et al.* (1993: 68) with the additional observation that it is infrequent in modern urban dialects. A genitive form for the word is not explicitly recognized in any study known to me. However, the situation on this point is less straightforward than it at first appears, because the *SED* records contain the following form,

(14)   That's the chap /əz/ uncle was drowned (drownded)

The relative pronoun, given here in its phonetic form, must obviously be in the determiner position, and thus a genitive form. What, though, is the status of this form? Is it a genitive of *as*, with a zero genitive ending due either to its final sibilant or to the more general tendency of omitting the ending of the prenominal genitive, or is it perhaps just a strongly reduced pronunciation of *whose*? The *SED* editors are not explicit on this point: the form *as uncle* is not listed among their written representations (*SED* III.iii.1326; Upton *et al.* 1994: 489–90) and it might be that the form is meant to be included as one realization of the structure *whose uncle*. It seems to me, however, that there are two difficulties with that interpretation. First, the phonological form, identical with the nominative and accusative *as*, stands in contrast to all the weak forms of *who* and *whose* recorded in the *SED* from the same area, which all have a rounded back vowel. Second, the informants from whom this genitive form is recorded do not use *who* at all even as a subject pronoun in their other responses: in *I know a man ... can help you* the pronoun they suggest is *as* in 11 cases (the one remaining informant suggested *what*). These facts would clearly seem to favour the interpretation of the pronoun as the genitive of *as*, although they obviously do not count as conclusive evidence.

As the data provided in the *SED* are not sufficient to determine the appropriate interpretation of sentence (14), it would seem useful to approach the question by exploring how speakers who are familiar with the usage illustrated in (14) react to written sentences with an unambiguous *as'* in the relative function. I have attempted to study the question by means of a test of an admittedly rather limited scope, administered to primary school teachers in Leicestershire, who might be expected to have been exposed to the local dialect even if they do not originally come from the area. The purpose of the testing was thus not to examine the testees' own English but to find out to what extent they felt that the test sentences represented genuine regional usage. Excluding material not relevant to the present point, the sentences were as follows:

(15)   Of course it's true, every word of it. I heard it myself from a feller as goes to France once a month.

(16)   a. Well, it can't be the same bloke as' motor-bike got stolen last week.
       b. Didje hear the one about a girl as' boyfriend had a wooden leg?

c. The Williams boy? Not the brat as' father used to come and complain about our Jim's motor-bike, I hope.

Of the 14 informants who returned the questionnaire, 3 were unfamiliar even with the subject function of *as*, as in (15), and then equally unfamiliar with the genitive. Of the others, 7 informants were either unfamiliar with the genitive (3 of the 7) or at any rate doubtful about it (4 of the 7), while the remaining 4 informants recognized the genitive form and reported it as a genuine dialect feature. The evidence is very limited, and the same test sentences were therefore also presented to some informants from Lancashire who were familiar with the local dialect, and further to a number of colleagues with a general North of England background. In both cases the results were in agreement with the Leicestershire test, showing that to many of the informants the forms with *as'* in the genitive were familiar and/or fully natural regional forms, associated by some informants especially with the North.

There are some further data which are pertinent to the interpretation of the relative *as* but which must be left to be discussed in another context. It seems to me, however, that in the light of the data considered, it is justifiable to suggest that the form /əz/ in the determiner position recorded in the *SED* is to be interpreted as a genitive of the pronoun *as*, which can therefore be added to the list of new forms noted earlier.

11.3 Rise of the new genitives

11.3.1 On the diachrony of the change

In our discussion so far, the traditional list of relative pronoun genitives quoted in (1)–(2) has been complemented by adding to it the forms *that's, at's, what'/what's* and *as'*, so that ultimately *which* is left as the only pronoun in the list which has no genitive form.[4] On the other hand, it will be clear enough from our remarks that the use of these new forms is rather limited. It is significant that they are generally not recorded at all in recent studies of regional relatives (Ihalainen 1980, Polycansky 1982, Miller 1988, Poussa 1990, Van den Eynden 1990, Penhallurick 1991), and that even where they are recognized, as in the *SED* and Cheshire *et al.* (1993), they are generally recorded from a very limited subset of the informants who use the corresponding nominative and accusative forms in their responses. The results of the limited amount of testing on the use of *that's* and *as'* reported above are in full agreement with that finding, and from their extensive study Cheshire *et al.* (1993: 69) quote more reliable figures which confirm the same distributional pattern: *what* was reported by 86.3 per cent of their informants in subject function and by 78 per cent in object function, but by only 24.1 per cent in the genitive form.

It might seem natural to connect the restricted use of the genitives with the well-known fact that genitival relatives are generally rather infrequent and in many languages not found at all (cf. the low position of the genitive in the accessibility hierarchy of Keenan and Comrie 1977). However, this can be a partial explanation only of the non-occurrence of these forms in corpus-based studies and does not apply to the findings of research where the informants are prompted to produce a genitive, or are presented with a given genitive, but select a more traditional form in preference to the new genitives. In such cases of avoidance or rejection of our forms, the natural explanation for the informants' choice must be that we are dealing here with recent innovations which have not yet had time to come into more general use. In the records available, *at's* is known from one recorded instance about the turn of the century and is better attested from the 1920s on, while *that's* in our sources goes back only to the 1970s and *what'/what's* and *as'* only to the 1980s. Of course the forms as such will all be older than suggested by the earliest records available – indeed, in the case of *what's* it can be established from an unprinted source that the genitive form was used at least thirty years earlier.[5] But as these genitives are all absent even in the most careful studies of dialect from the nineteenth century and earliest twentieth century, such as Murray (1873), Wright (1892) and Wilson (1915), and the general surveys of the *EDD* and the *EDG* which make a point of noting available genitive equivalents, it seems likely enough that these genitives – including even *at's* – were not yet a normal part of regional usage at that time. All in all, it thus appears that we are here in the middle of an ongoing morphosyntactic change which is reflected in divided usage in different sections of the speech community.

11.3.2 *The nature of the change*

Leaving the question of chronology, let us now look more closely at the exact nature of the process involved. What precisely is the origin of these new genitives? If we assume that the items in question are pronouns, as we have been doing throughout our discussion, then the creation of a genitive must be seen as a natural process which brings the words into line with the normal inflectional pattern of the language, at least when they have human or animate reference, and perhaps even elsewhere, particularly since the items are freely used with both human and non-human antecedents. It is of interest to note a parallel nonstandard case showing such an extension of genitive inflection to pronouns not treated as case-variable in standard English: the dialectal inflection of *this* and *that* as deictics (e.g. *I like this's head best*; *Whose is that bonnet? – It's that's*; *EDG*). This generalizing tendency, due to analogical pressure from other, case-inflected NPs, must obviously be assumed as a general background against which the whole process of new genitive inflection must be seen.

Recognition of the general influence of analogy does not, however, exclude the possibility of other more specific factors having played a role in the process, and one such factor is of particular interest here: the so-called *his*-genitive recorded in Old English and used more commonly in Middle English and Early Modern English, especially in cases where a normal genitive inflection was not available (e.g. *Pharao the king of Egypt his sinne; whether of the two his death; Oxford English Dictionary (OED)* s.v. *his*). To see how this form can interact with the development of the genitive, consider the development of the so-called group genitive as outlined in the following sketch.

(17) a. þaes geongan mannes talu
b. the young man's tale
c. (the young man) 's tale

(18) a. the Man of Law his tale
b. the Man of Law 's tale
c. the Wife of Bath her tale
d. the Wife of Bath 's tale

While the genitive ending was originally attached to the noun, as is clear in (17a), the loss of the inflection of the premodifiers created the structure (17b) where the ending can be interpreted as being construed either with the noun or, alternatively, with the whole NP, as indicated in (17c). In theory this morphosyntactic development would be enough to explain the rise of the group genitive, but in actual fact there was another source for it: the *his*-genitive illustrated in (18a). Being unstressed, the form *his* was frequently phonologically weakened, ultimately to a mere -s which was cliticized to the preceding word. Semantically identical with the normal genitive ending, it could then be reanalysed as a genitive suffix, which here was clearly attached to the whole NP rather than the postmodifier. Once the reanalysis had created a group genitive, the form could be generalized even to other NPs, such as (18c), where there is no way of interpreting the ending as a weakened form of the appropriate possessive pronoun (for a fuller discussion, see Seppänen, forthcoming).

The development sketched above is from the earlier history of English, but it is highly relevant in an account of the development of the new genitives of the relative pronouns. Though still commonly used in Early Modern English, the *his*-genitive was an anomalous structure in the system because of its use of two separate coreferential NPs in one syntactic position, and as such it was an instance of what Ben Jonson (1640/1972: 72) called the error of 'superfluity of nouns', and gradually fell more and more into disuse. In present-day English, considerations of logic and correctness exclude it from careful formal English, but it is not entirely unknown in colloquial speech, as in (19), and is generally the natural genitive equivalent in regional dialects, as in (20).

(19) a. There's two fellows *that their* dads are millionaires. (Jespersen 1927: 110)
  b. I liked that fish that we saw at the Steinhart – the one *that its* tail wasn't like a fish. (Halliday 1985: 95)

(20) a. The crew *that their* boat wis vrackit are in Aiberdeen. (*SND*)
  b. The quine *at her* mither wis jil't turn't up in the Broch. (*SND*)
  c. That's the man *what his* son done it. (Hughes and Trudgill 1987: 18)
  d. That's th' chap *as his* uncle was hanged. (*EDG*)

Structures like those of (20) can easily be connected with the rise of the new genitive along the lines of our sketch of the group genitive, and a suggestion to that effect is indeed made in the *SND* discussion of the Scottish use of *that's* and *at's*: here too the possessive pronoun *his* was weakened to -*s*, and this form was later reanalysed as a genitive ending and could then also be used in connection with feminine, neuter and plural antecedents. The *SND* analysis is concerned only with the two words quoted, but it can obviously be generalized to *what's* and, taking into account the possibility of dropping the genitive ending in the prenominal position, also accounts for the genitives *what'* and *as'*.

In the *SND* description structures like *the chap that's (at's, what's, as') uncle*, often taken automatically to be genitives, are thus analysed as grammatically ambiguous forms, being either simple contracted forms of *that (at, what, as) + his*, or genitives proper. Looking back at our earlier quotations in the light of this distinction, we see that the material quoted contains structures like *the woman that's sister, the kye that's caur, the people that's houses, the house that's roof; a wife at's wrapper: the girl what's mum: a girl as' boyfriend* – all of them indicating that the -'*s* forms do indeed occur in contexts where they are unambiguous genitives. On the other hand, there is a clear imbalance in the material in that *the people that's houses*, quoted from Aitken's account of Scottish usage, is the only case of a plural antecedent. From informant reactions it emerges that this is not a coincidence: plurals like *the chaps that's brother* and *the girls that's brother* tend to be regarded as less natural than the singulars *the chap that's brother* and *the girl that's brother*, and this distinction appears to be shared in basically the same form by several informants who do not themselves use either form and likewise by at least some who are fully familiar with the genitive from regional speech.[6] With the genitives other than *that's*, the distinction between the singular and the plural seems to be far less clear but does not appear to be totally lacking. In terms of the *SND* account, it thus seems that while the reanalysed -*s* may be regarded as normal with feminine and neuter singular antecedents, its generalization to plural antecedents is partly checked by some disturbing factor or factors, in particular in connection with *that*.

In addition to the case pointed out in the *SND*, there is another structure where forms like *that's* must unambiguously be taken as genitives: the occurrence of the sequence *that's* + Noun, etc., in a non-subject position. The following set of examples will illustrate the crucial difference between the two types of structures involved.

(21)   a. the dog *that* the wolf broke *his* leg
        b. the woman *at* ye ken *her* son (*SND*)
        c. It is the bloke *what* Peter was courting *his* sister.
        d. A gentleman from India, *as* you see *his* name writ up. (*OED*)

(22)   a. the dog *that*'s leg the wolf broke
        b. the woman *at*'s son ye ken
        c. It's the bloke *what*'s sister Peter was courting.
        d. A gentleman from India, *as*' name you see writ up.

As the relative and the associated possessive are not contiguous in the structures of (21), there is no way of viewing the forms ending in -'s as contractions in (22): if the genitive is at least partly derived from a reinterpreted contraction, then that reinterpretation must have taken place in cases where the *that's* + Noun, etc., was used in subject position, and the occurrence of the structure in non-subject positions is then a later generalization.

What, then, is the status of structures like those of (22)? Looking back once more at our material, we see that the genitive + noun structures in all of our examples are used in subject function, and in actual fact the same observation holds without exception for all the material on the genitives recorded from unsolicited use in the *SND* or the Cobuild Corpus or any other source, or elicited by means of testing in the *SED* or Cheshire *et al.* (1993). The first scholar I know of who has considered the difference between subject and non-subject positions in the use of the new relative genitives is Stahlke (1976), who reported that while the form *the dog that's leg was broken* was accepted by 20 per cent of his (American) informants, the corresponding non-subject form *the dog that's leg the wolf broke* was unanimously rejected by all of them. On this point the test carried out by Seppänen and Kjellmer (1995: 395) gave a somewhat different result, showing that while the non-subject structure was indeed either rejected or regarded as doubtful by several informants who accepted *that's* + Noun in subject function, it could nevertheless also be treated as a fully normal construction in colloquial English with a regional flavour. The basic correctness of the finding in this modified form is shown by the results of further testing which I have carried out and which leads to two related conclusions: first, that the non-subject position is indeed accepted, but by fewer informants than the subject position, and, second, that even with the informants who either accept or reject both positions, there is nevertheless a fairly general tendency to regard *that's* + Noun, etc., as more natural in subject function than in non-subject function. Taken in conjunction with the evidence from recorded instances, these findings clearly suggest that the use of the genitive in non-subject function has not yet reached even the status which it has in subject function.

From the discussion above it emerges then that even though the rise of the genitives might as such be regarded as a fully straightforward analogical process, the syntactic restrictions on the use of the new forms that we have been discussing afford evidence suggesting that the immediate source of the *his*-genitive is at least partly to be sought in a reinterpretation of an earlier relative + *his* structure. In defence of this weaker formulation of the view of the *SND* editors, we may briefly add two further facts which point to the role of the *his*-genitive.

First, as noted in our discussion, the new genitives are forms that basically belong to nonstandard regional varieties of the language, but have also come to be used in colloquial standard speech, primarily in Scotland and to a lesser extent even elsewhere. In both its geographical and social aspect, this distribution is an exact reflection of the spread of the relative + possessive structures in present-day English, and thus again points to the role of the *his*-genitive in its development.

Second, as also noted earlier, *which* remains the only relative which does not have a genitive. Since *which* is not very much used in regional forms of English, this variety of the language will not normally contain the sequence *which his* which could be contracted and reanalysed as a genitive; typically, the instances of the structures relative + *his* recorded in the *SED* use all the other relatives, including even the combination *who his*, but not one occurrence of *which his*. Thus, while the one remaining gap in the inflectional system of the relative pronouns is striking, in terms of the history of the new genitives it is not entirely unexpected.

One final question to consider in this connection concerns the possible role of the standard language in the rise of the new genitives. As we have seen, the *his*-genitives disappeared from standard usage a few centuries ago, replaced by the normal genitive. When the same process of reanalysis is applied today to the *his*-genitives of regional speech, its effect is obviously comparable with the older change in that here too the *his*-genitive is beginning to give way to the genitive proper. Why should the old process be repeated now, a few centuries later? It seems to me that we are dealing here with a case of cultural lag. With the social structure of the preceding centuries, the traditional rural dialect could survive without being deeply affected by the norms of the upper-class standard speakers. In Victorian England, the general social development, and in particular the spread of schools even among the poorer part of the population, had created a situation where the old dialect speakers came in direct contact with the standard variety of the language as it was defined and maintained by the middle classes (cf. Stein 1994: 8), and with the advent of the new media of radio and television in the twentieth century, the standard language was brought directly into the homes of all speakers. In this situation, the old dialect speakers came more and more to be bilingual between the traditional dialect and a locally modified form of standard English (cf. *SED* Introduction, pp. 15, 18–19; Petyt 1992). This situation has generally led to a development where the various local accents are preserved but the dialect vocabulary and, what is more relevant in this connection, dialect morphology and syntax are more and more influenced by the forms of standard English (cf. Petyt 1992: 112–14). Viewed in this context, the rise of the new genitives is most naturally interpreted as a result of a growing adoption of the standard English norms in regional speech: even though the actual genitives are not identical with the forms of the standard language, because the pronouns themselves are not identical in the two varieties, as straightforward genitives they agree with the general morphological pattern of the language and encroach on the traditional domain of the *his*-genitives which deviate from the accepted standard language norms.

11.4 Relativization in standard and regional English

The development outlined in our remarks has important implications for the interpretation of relativization in different varieties of the language, and we shall close the discussion by briefly considering this more general aspect of the phenomenon. In discussions of the relative structures in English it has long been customary, particularly among generative grammarians (cf. Radford 1988: 480–92, Haegeman 1991: 155–9) but even more generally (cf. Lass 1987: 184–8, Huddleston 1984: 393–8, 1988: 155–9), to make a distinction between two radically different types of relative structures, or two modes of relativization: one relying on the use of straightforward *wh*-relativizers to introduce the clause, the other one a gapped variant which employs no overt relativizer but may be introduced by the conjunction/complementizer *that*, or in nonstandard English also by *at, as, what*, although these items are seldom taken note of. By distinguishing between the two types of clause, this view at the same posits a radical difference between formal English, which relies on the *wh*-strategy, and the colloquial/regional forms of the language, which favour the second strategy or employ it to the exclusion of the other alternative (for a particularly strong statement of this view, see Miller 1988).

A great many syntactic differences are assumed to distinguish the *wh*-pronouns and the non-pronominal complementizers from each other, one important distinction being the category of case: as pronouns, the *wh*-items are inflected for case, while case inflection obviously does not apply to the conjunctions: there are no genitives like **if's meaning*, *although's interest*, and if strings like these are put into sentences, they cannot be given any sensible interpretation. However, from the existence of the genitives *that's, at's, what's* and *as'*, it must then follow that these items must be pronouns and not conjunctions or complementizers, and the only item whose status as a pronoun would have to be questioned on the basis of the inflectional criterion is the fully indeclinable *which*. Furthermore, it is not possible to dismiss these genitives as having relevance only for the description of the particular dialects where they are actively employed, because they are very easily and naturally given the intended interpretation even by speakers who do not themselves use them or have not even ever heard them; they are simply not at all like the would-be genitives **if's meaning, *although's interest*. All in all, the rise of these new genitives in some varieties of the language and the way they are generally interpreted by all speakers thus point to a fundamental identity of the mode of relativization applied in all varieties of English.

Within a basic similarity between the two, the usage of formal vs colloquial/regional English is characterized by two less radical properties which distinguish between them: first, the selection of a different set of pronouns in the two varieties and, second, the ban on the older relative + possessive structure as a genitive equivalent in the formal variety, as opposed to its retention in the regional and, more marginally, the colloquial variety. This survival of the *his*-genitive in turn played a part in the development of a new regional vs standard difference because it made it easy to reanalyse the *his*-form as a genitive proper and then extend the new genitive beyond its original domain of singular masculine nouns – a development which seems to have aided the creation of new genitives even if the new inflection as such can be taken as a natural result of analogy from case-inflected pronouns. So far as can be ascertained, the new genitives are a relatively recent innovation, and at present they are characteristic only of a minority of dialect speakers. It is possible that the rise of these genitives is due to the general influence of standard English on dialect syntax. To some extent, however, the influence has also gone in the opposite direction in that the genitive of *that* – the only one of the relatives which is also used, in its non-genitive form, in standard English – has made some inroads into the colloquial variety of standard English.

Notes

1 I am greatly indebted to numerous colleagues and friends – in Sweden, Finland, Germany, Belgium, Britain, Ireland, the United States, Canada and Australia – who have helped me as informants by probing into their intuitions and discussing parts of the present study with me,

and am very grateful to several colleagues for valuable help with informant testing (David Denison for Manchester, Christopher Hall for Leicester, Jennifer Herriman for Lancashire and Lynn Savin for North Wales). Thanks are also due to Gunnar Bergh, Jennifer Herriman, Göran Kjellmer, Joe Trotta, David Wright and the editors of the present volume for helpful comments on an earlier version of the study.

2 In dialect studies it is sometimes assumed that certain uses of what look like personal pronouns are in fact to be analysed as relatives. If that view is accepted, then of course the list of relatives must be further extended to include *he, she, it* and *they*, with their inflected forms. I shall not here be concerned with these items (any more than with the so-called zero relatives), leaving them for a separate study.

3 These responses are recorded in the *SED* in their phonological form but the genitive *at's* is not recognized in the list of written forms, and in Upton *et al.* (1994: 490) *at's* is included among the recorded occurrences of *that's*. But since the nominative and accusative forms *at* and *that* are treated as separate pronouns in both studies, the genitives must surely be treated similarly. In Seppänen and Kjellmer (1995), *at* was taken to be a form of *that*, but it seems to me now preferable to deal with the various forms as belonging to two separate pronouns.

4 It might be added that *which* is actually recorded in the genitive (without any ending added to it) in Middle English (cf. Mustanoja 1960: 197), but that genitive seems to have been a rare form and has no bearing on the modern usage studied here.

5 Thanks are due to David Wright, who was able to date an incident where he heard the form (not necessarily for the first time) in Oxford in the 1950s in the sentence *When you look at me, you are looking at one what's rare – I am one what's voice has never broke.*

6 The remarks on the distinction between the singular and the plural go ultimately back to an observation which was made by John Payne in Manchester (13 March 1990, in connection with a guest lecture given by me on the grammatical status of the relative *that*) and which was readily accepted as valid by several of those present – this in an audience where no one present was actually familiar with this new genitive. With regard to the distinction, it might be added that Aitken's *the people that's houses*, and similarly *the men/women that's houses*, is generally felt to be more natural than *the fellows that's houses, the boys/girls that's names*, etc. Is it the presence of the same *s*-suffix in two different functions that is disturbing here, and thus also in *the fellers what's names, the chaps at's bikes*)? It might also be thought that if the plurality of an antecedent generally clashes with *that's*, then this is an indication that *that's* in the genitive, clearly marked as a nominal form, is somehow associated with the number contrast of the demonstrative *that/those* more clearly than the Nom/Acc *that* which is more naturally connected with the conjunction. Such an association seems

to exist for some speakers of British English for whom the genitive form is naturally pronounced with a full vowel, as distinct from the schwa of the Nom/Acc form, but in their judgements these speakers do not seem to differ from those who would use in both forms either a reduced vowel (apparently the majority of British speakers) or a full vowel (American speakers).

References

Aitken, A.J. 1970. Scottish speech: a historical view with special reference to the standard English of Scotland. In A.J. Aitken and T. McArthur (eds), *Languages of Scotland*. Edinburgh: Chambers, pp. 59–93.
Cheshire, J., Edwards, V. and Whittle, P. 1993. Nonstandard English and dialect levelling. In J. Milroy and L. Milroy (eds), pp. 53–94.
Grant, V. (ed.) 1934–1976. *The Scottish National Dictionary*. Edinburgh: The Scottish National Dictionary Foundation.
Haegeman, L. 1991. *Introduction to Government and Binding Theory*. Oxford: Blackwell.
Halliday, M.A.K. 1985. *An Introduction to Functional Grammar*. London: Edward Arnold.
Harris, J. 1993. The grammar of Irish English. In J. Milroy and L. Milroy (eds), pp. 138–86.
Huddleston, R. 1984. *Introduction to the Grammar of English*. Cambridge: Cambridge University Press.
Huddleston, R. 1988. *English Grammar: An Outline*. Cambridge: Cambridge University Press.
Hudson, R. 1990. *English Word Grammar*. Oxford: Blackwell.
Hughes, A. and Trudgill, P. 1987. *English Accents and Dialects: An Introduction to Social and Regional Varieties of British English*. London: Edward Arnold.
Ihalainen, O. 1980. Relative clauses in the dialect of Somerset. *Neuphilologische Mitteilungen* 81: 187–96.
Jespersen, O. 1927. *A Modern English Grammar on Historical Principles*, vol. III. London and Copenhagen: Unwin/Munksgaard.
Johansson, C. 1995. *The Relativizers 'whose' and 'of which' in Present-day English: Description and Theory*. Uppsala: Acta Universitatis Upsaliensis.
Jonson, B. 1640/1972. *The English Grammar*. Menston: Scolar Press.
Keenan, E.L. and Comrie, B. 1977. Noun phrase accessibility and universal grammar. *Linguistic Inquiry* 8: 63–99.
Lass, R. 1987. *The Shape of English: Structure and History*. London: Dent & Sons.
Miller, J. 1988. That: a relative pronoun? Sociolinguistics and syntactic analysis. *Edinburgh Studies in the English Language* 113–19.

Milroy, J. and Milroy, L. (eds) 1993. *Real English: The Grammar of English Dialects in the British Isles*. London: Longman.

Murray, J. 1873. *The Dialect of the Southern Counties of Scotland*. Oxford: Clarendon.

Murray, J.A.H. et al. (eds) 1933. *The Oxford English Dictionary*. Oxford: Clarendon Press.

Mustanoja, T.F. 1960. *A Middle English Syntax. Part I: Parts of Speech*. Helsinki: Société Néophilologique.

Orton, H. and Dieth, E. (eds) 1962–1971. *Survey of English Dialects*. Leeds: University of Leeds.

Penhallurick, R.J. 1991. *The Anglo-Welsh Dialects of North Wales: A Survey of Conservative Rural Spoken English in the Counties of Gwynedd and Clwyd*. Frankfurt am Main: Peter Lang.

Petyt, K.M. 1992. The influence of the standard variety on northern forms of British English. In J.A. Leuvensten and J. Berns (eds), *Dialect and Standard Language in the English, Dutch, German and Norwegian Language Areas*. Amsterdam: North Holland, pp. 106–18.

Polycansky, L. 1982. *Grammatical Variation in Belfast English*. Belfast Working Papers in Language and Linguistics 6.

Poussa, P. 1990. Norfolk relatives (Broadland). Paper read at the International Congress of Dialectologists, Bamberg, August 1990.

Radford, A. 1988. *Transformational Grammar: A First Course*. Cambridge: Cambridge University Press.

Romaine, S. 1980. The relative clause marker in Scots English: diffusion, complexity and style as dimensions of syntactic change. *Language in Society* 221–49.

Romaine, S. 1982. *Socio-Historical Linguistics: Its Status and Methodology*. Cambridge: Cambridge University Press.

Seppänen, A. (forthcoming). The genitive and the category of case in the history of English (to appear in the Festschrift for J. Fisiak, 1997).

Seppänen, A. and Kjellmer, G. 1995. The dog that's leg was broken: on the genitive of the relative pronoun. *English Studies* 38: 389–400.

Stahlke, H.W.F. 1976. Which 'that'? *Language* 52: 584–610.

Stein, D. 1994. Sorting out the variants: standardization and social factors in the English language 1600–1800. In D. Stein and I. Tieken-Boon van Ostade (eds), *Towards a Standard English 1600–1800*. Berlin: Mouton de Gruyter, pp. 1–17.

Upton, C., Parry, D. and Widdowson, J.D.A. 1994. *Survey of English Dialects: The Dictionary and Grammar*. London: Routledge.

Van den Eynden, N. 1990. Aspects of non-standard relativization. Paper presented at the *Sixth International Conference on Historical Linguistics*, Helsinki, May 1990.

Van der Auwera, J. 1985. Relative 'that' – a centennial dispute. *Language* 52: 584–610.

Wilson, J. 1915. *Lowland Scotch as spoken in the Lower Strathearn District of Perthshire*. Oxford: Oxford University Press.

Wright, J. 1892. *The Grammar of the Dialect of Windhill in the West Riding of Yorkshire*. London: Kegan Paul, Trench & Trubner.

Wright, J. (ed.) 1898. *The English Dialect Dictionary*. Oxford: Oxford University Press.

Wright, J. (ed.) 1905. *The English Dialect Grammar*. Oxford: Clarendon Press.

CHAPTER 12

'Ah'm going for to give youse a story today': remarks on second person plural pronouns in Englishes[1]

Susan Wright

12.1 Introduction

> In many dialects of English around the world, the historical loss of the second person singular/plural distinction that went with the loss of *thou/thee* has been repaired by the introduction of new second person plural pronouns, such as *youse*, which is found in North America, Australia, Scotland, England, and especially Ireland. The American South ... has *y'all*, and less widely, ... *you 'uns*. ... In these dialects, *you* is singular only.

Thus Trudgill and Chambers (1991: 8) illustrate one way in which we might distinguish the histories of standard varieties of English and 'mainstream nonstandard and traditional dialects'. This brief comment on the apparent resurgence of the number distinction in the second person pronoun in a variety of Englishes contains a number of important assumptions. The first is that the extra-territorial varieties of English (ETEs) referred to have a common ancestor, or ancestors whose pronominal systems share some of the same characteristics. The second is that each variety inherited a pronominal system in which the old second person singular pronoun was dead and buried. The third assumption is that the pronominal system of each new variety was, in some way, bereft of the number distinction, and recognizing this, its speakers 'repaired' the damage.

I want to consider these varieties of English together in order to understand better what appears to be a common strategy – the replacement of one pronoun (*you*) with two functions (singular and plural) by two pronouns each with its own function to create a match of formal and functional features. The strategy is one shared both by new Englishes, and by traditional dialectal and mainstream nonstandard varieties in England.

SECOND PERSON PLURAL PRONOUNS IN ENGLISHES

Let us survey very briefly some present-day varieties that distinguish formally between singular and plural second person subject pronouns:[2]

	SINGULAR	PLURAL
Irish English	you/ye	youse[3]
Scottish English	you	yous, yous yins
Australian English	you	youse
South African English	you	yous
L1 Zimbabwe English	you	you 'uns
Southern US English	you	y'all/you 'uns
Northern US English	you	youse

The first thing to notice about this list is that there is a strong resemblance of the variant forms across varieties as historically different as Scottish English (Broad Scots), Southern US English, and first language (L1) Zimbabwe English on the one hand, and between South African English, Irish English and Scottish English on the other. This might be taken as strong evidence for an underlying tendency for varieties to innovate on existing forms in the language, in this case, the base form *you*. In addition, or alternatively, the presence of the same or similar forms in present-day nonstandard (mainly extra-territorial) varieties might be one consequence of the historical influence of the same older nonstandard varieties.

I will focus on the second person plural pronoun in a small group of native-speaker Englishes. This pronoun is an expression which seems to me to highlight the robustness of the internal (structural) regularities of a wide range of (not always related) nonstandard Englishes. The frequency with which this feature appears in non-English varieties with different settlement histories and contrasting socio-historical situations suggests that we need to consider carefully the relative roles of universal tendencies (and logical systems) and social factors in the grammars of new (nonstandard) English dialects.

12.2 Reconstructing inputs: social and linguistic

I will follow Lass (1987 and elsewhere) in adopting a division based on periods of settlement, between northern hemisphere Englishes, which include Irish, Scottish and Southern US varieties of English, and southern hemisphere Englishes, into which category Australian, South African and first language (L1) Zimbabwe Englishes fall. These groups contrast in certain typological[4] and geographical characteristics; they also differ from one another in their relationships to the mainland (superstrate) variety (which provided their initial inputs). It is also just possible that the historical differences between the two groups will tolerate the speculation that some features of a variety which it is tempting to consider a very early Extra Territorial English (Irish or Hiberno-English) filter into later new varieties through contact. This, of course, depends on our being able to establish that these features are established early enough and that they occur sufficiently regularly to be able to serve as input or even target features.

12.3 Northern hemisphere varieties: Irish, Scots and southern US

Let's start with the northern hemisphere varieties of Englishes; both mainland and extra-territorial (though this is not to say such labels are unproblematic). The members of the northern hemisphere bunch are heterogeneous (disparate) in a number of ways. Lass observes that 'Scotland has had a peculiar and in some ways unique history, which has led to radical discontinuities between its speech and that of the rest of the English-speaking world' (1987: 251). The same might be said for Ireland. Modern Hiberno-English bears some substratal Irish marks, but it is also strongly imprinted with the characters of 'various types of English and Scots that were brought to Ireland during the peak years of English and Scottish colonization in the sixteenth and seventeenth centuries' (Harris 1993: 140). Of course, the speech of both English and Scots settlers in these periods would, to a greater or lesser extent, have had the number distinction expressed in the contrast of *thou/thee* with *ye/you*. This means that whether the 'planters' were landowners (very few were) or labourers and traders (many were), their dialects were likely to have some formal realization, albeit variable, of the number distinction in the second person (see Kallen 1994: 156 on the complex settlement pattern of seventeenth-century Ulster). This means that the residual *thou/you* contrast of (southern, London) standardizing Early Modern English is likely to have mingled with Scots and other English dialectal realizations of the distinction and provided one set of inputs to the new varieties of English in Ulster and Southern Ireland. The question is when and indeed how this traditional realization of the number distinction gives way to the division based on different forms of *you*.

Here it might be useful to consider formally attested usages of the plural pronoun current in the nonstandard varieties of English spoken in the North (notably Belfast) and in the South of Ireland.[5] The *OED* covers the attestation in (specifically Southern) Irish English for two variant forms of an overtly marked second person plural with two correspondingly separate entries; one for *yous* and one for *yez*.[6] The earliest Irish English citation for *yous* is a literary one:

(1) <Mahon> That man marrying a decent and moneyed girl! Is it mad yous are? Is it a crazy-house for females that I'm landed now? (1907, J.M. Synge, *Playboy of the Western World*, III.63)

This would seem to be quite late; but note that it is a representation of speech. Synge notes in his preface to the play that the language is based on that of the 'herds and fishermen along the coast from Kerry to Mayo, or from beggar-women and ballad-singers nearer Dublin'. It is clear that though his characters are ostensibly peasants, their language is not typical exclusively of traditional rural dialect. The alternate form, *yez*, is treated explicitly as being characteristic of 'Anglo-Irish' dialect. It is attested in a text produced more than fifty years earlier than Synge's:

(2) a. Who are yiz at all, gintlemin?
(1842, Samuel Lover, *Handy Andy: A Tale of Irish Life*, xxxiv.280)

Again, this form occurs in prose fiction intended to convey the flavours of Irish speech, and it is not unreasonable to assume that the writer is here attempting some sort of representation of speech. Not only does the writer employ a particular form of pronoun, he appears to be trying for a particular rendition of vowel pronunciation too. James Joyce's own letters (anticipating the deployment of the pronoun in his fiction), also supply instances of *yez*:

(2) b. I will send him very gladly if that will make yiz all happy and loving.
(1908, J. Joyce, *Letters*, 8 December (1966), II.226)
c. Now yiz are in the Willingdone Museyroom.
(1939, *Finnegan's Wake*, 8)

It is probably sensible to assume that the contrast in the dates of attestation for the two forms is barely significant. After all, the variants imprint a phonetic contrast, between stressed (*yous*) and unstressed (*yez, yiz*), rather than one of semantic substance. What can we infer from the sources quoted by the *OED*? Mainly that the form must have been sufficiently established in speech by the 1840s, if it could be uttered in a phonetically unstressed form. Henry's treatment of the properties of *youse* in her comparative study of the syntax of present-day Belfast English and standard English indicates that the plural second person pronoun is (at least by now) entirely integrated into the urban dialect. She observes (1995: 38) that 'for some speakers, [*youse*] permits singular concord and can occur after the particle in verb–particle constructions', as in the following:

(3) a. Youse is really stupid.
b. I'll phone up youse.

The interesting thing to note is that the two properties are present or absent together; Henry suggests that those speakers who reject (3a) are likely to reject (3b) too.

If the plural second person pronoun is well established in Irish English by the second half of the nineteenth century, it is worth considering its origins in urban varieties of Broad Scots (like the Glasgow dialect). The available evidence suggests that *youse* appears to have entered Scots as late as the beginning of the twentieth century. The personal pronoun system in most varieties of Scots has retained the number distinction in the second person pronoun, albeit in different forms. McClure (1994: 69) reports that '*thou* used as a familiar singular survived in all dialects until the nineteenth century, to at least the beginning of the twentieth in the west, and in peripheral dialects is still to be heard'.[7] However, in the present-day dialects of the west and the central belt, particularly in *urban* working-class speech, this traditional realization of the number distinction has disappeared. Instead, the singular is realized in the old plural form *you*, and the plural is expressed in the innovation *yous* (written <yiz>, <yese>, <yous>, pronounced /jiz/, and /juz/ when stressed). There is another variant of the second person plural in present-day Scots, *yous yins*, which resembles the forms of this pronoun in other, quite historically distinct varieties. According to McClure (70), *yous* is 'first attested in the early twentieth century'. The *OED* produces only the following, a citation for *yez*, which can be attributed to a Scottish source:

(4) Yez ur gitn a rare day.
     (1962, D. Phillips, Lichty Nichts, 30).

The apparent distance between the first formally attested Irish English and Scottish instances cannot tell us any more than that the pronoun is perhaps associated earlier with Irish than Scottish varieties.

Interestingly, it does not seem to be the case that the Scottish settlements of Ulster contributed to the innovation of *yous/yez*; it is a development that is too late for this direction of influence to be a real possibility. If there is any influence, it is an Irish one on Scots, but it is equally likely that Scots *yous/yez* is entirely independent of the Irish pronoun.

Sources (like Harris and Miller) for the present-day use of *yous(e)* in Irish English and Scots focus on the non-traditional, nonstandard urban varieties. So Harris comments on *youse* in Belfast, and Miller on its usage in Glasgow. It may well be that *youse* in both Irish varieties and Scottish varieties is a particularly *urban* working-class innovation, generated in the hiatus created by the separation from the old rural dialect traditions in the continual migration from the countryside to the towns of Ireland by the second half of the nineteenth century, and of Scotland in the course of the second half of the nineteenth century. It may be that the new urban working classes stigmatized the old singular, avoiding its use in favour of singular and plural *you*. If this shift left a formal gap, the formal-functional mismatch might have encouraged the innovatory plural *youse*.

There is evidence from late nineteenth-century American English to support the suggestion that the form was entrenched in nonstandard

Irish English by the second half of the nineteenth century. Stephen Crane's tale of life in the tenements of New York's Bowery, *Maggie: A Girl of the Streets*, is marked by locutions which Crane's editor, Fredson Bowers, labels (naively from a linguistic point of view) rather simply as 'dialect'. In fact, the dialect of Crane's character recalls some of the features of Synge's speakers, among them, the plural second person *youse/yehs*:

(5) a. 'Ah, where d'hell was yehs when I was doin' all d'fightin'?' he demanded. 'Youse kids makes me tired.'
(1893, S. Crane, *Maggie*, i.9)
b. 'Ah, Jimmie, youse bin fightin' agin.' (*ibid.* p. 11)

By the close of the nineteenth century the pronoun must have been quite well established in what Mencken calls 'Bowerese, later Brooklynese' since its reference includes singular as well as plural. The consistent appearance of the pronoun in this kind of determinedly realist writing suggests that Crane was hearing a reasonably strong marker of Bowery speech. Crane's characters are Irish American, and their dialect seems to me to resemble aspects of modern working-class Irish English. And this plural second person pronoun must have been a salient marker of Irish English by the beginning of mass Irish migration to America in order to be remarkable in the urban language of (new) Americans at the close of the century. McDavid (1979: 172) reports the reduced form (transcribed /jɪz/) in nonstandard varieties spoken in urban communities (less often in rural ones); Mencken (1948: 380) remarks (merely in passing) that *yous* is Northern.

The realization of the plural second person pronoun in Southern US English is quite different from that in Northern US English, and indeed from that in Irish and Scottish Englishes. The plural form *y'all* is attested in the English spoken by white Southerners in the US as early as 1824, when Henry C. Knight (pseudonym Arthur Singleton) writes that *you all* is one of the 'odd phrases that white southern children learned from slaves' (cited by Dillard 1992: 96). Edwards (1974) considers the semantic and functional parallels between the use of *y'all* in the 'white plantation English of Lousiana' and *unu* of the slaves, concluding that the 'use of *y'all* (semantically *unu*) was probably learned by white children from black mammies and children in familiar domestic situations'. He also notes the occasional use of *unuaal* (*unu + all*). The form *you-all* is attested in fiction as early as 1864, in R.M. Johnson's *Georgia Sketches* (republished in 1871 with the title *Dukesborough Tales*):

(6) You all little fellows was . . . skeered.
(1871, R.M. Johnson, *Dukesborough Tales*, vii.95)

The orthographic (and perhaps also phonetic) variant *y'all* is given a separate *OED* entry, which cites references such as the journal *Dialect*

Notes (1909) and *Scribler's Magazine* (1935). The pattern of citation is becoming restricted to description rather than the incidence of actual usage. However, by 1982, it is beginning to look stereotypical:

(7) Yes, Doctor. You'll be in the breakfast room. Y'all have a nice day.
(1982, J.S. Borthwick, *Case of Hook-Billed Kites*, xxxiv.114)

The alternative form *you'uns* is first attested about a decade earlier than *y'all/you all*, in a traveller's journal:

(8) a. Youns is a word I have heard several times, but what it means I don't know.
(1810, M.V.H. Dwight, *Journal* 10 Nov., in *Journey to Ohio* [1912], 37)

The next citation offered is dated 1869, when a Northerner called Socrates Hyacinth compares *you-all* with *you'uns* in an essay on southwestern slang in the *Overland Monthly*:

(8) b. During the war we all heard enough of 'we-uns' and 'you-uns', but 'you-alls' was to me something fresh.
(1969, *Overland Monthly*, Aug. 131)

By 1885, Mary Murfree, writing under the pseudonym C.E. Craddock, adopts *you-uns* as a marker of early American white (dialectal) speech in the Southern states:

(8) c. I hev no call ter spen' words 'bout sech ez that, with a free-spoken man like you-uns.
(1885, 'C.E. Craddock', *The Prophet of the Great Smokey Mountains*, 7)

That this form continues to be used into the twentieth century is confirmed by its note in an affectionate (not to say patronizing) report of the usage in Murphy, North Carolina in 1927 (8d), and by Faulkner's use of it in the 1930s (8e):

(8) d. After a night's rest, the paterfamilias questioned solicitously: 'Did you uns sleep good last night?' Later on, after we had been up for several minutes, he said: 'You uns can come to breakfast now. Jist hep yerselves, sich as it is.'
(1927, *American Speech*, II.345)

e. Why did you uns have to stop here?
(1934, W. Faulkner, *Dr Martino*, 341)

It is sufficiently entrenched in common perceptions of the dialect (if not actual use) to provide a model for the humorous representation of rural, good old boy, speech:

(8) f. 'Proud to know ye!' Sam will beam. 'Why, you-uns be a-comin' in ter th' fire an' set a spell.'
(1941, *American Mercury*, June 660/2)

The salient markers in this quotation are current in African American English – the invariant form of *be*, but the affix *a-* is by contrast archaic, perhaps intended to represent the idiolect of an old man. What we get is a caricature of southern, and certainly early African American English.

It happens that *y'all* as one form of the second person plural pronoun persists in Southern English of the US, as well as in African American Vernacular English (AAVE). Whatley examines the impact of the exodus of African Americans from the south-east to the north-east and elsewhere in the early twentieth century. She argues that in the ghettoes of New York, Detroit, Chicago, and Philadelphia, 'the restricted social environment of Blacks fostered continuation of features of Black speech brought from the South and promoted the development of linguistic traits distinctive to urban life' (1981: 93). One of the features which flourished was *y'all*. This pronoun has not disappeared from Southern speech. It is typical of the region's vernacular, crossing ethnic and class boundaries. The use of *y'all* does not identify its speaker as urban or rural, but as a Southerner. As a marker of solidarity and Southern identity, it is subject to pragmatic manipulation, so that it may be used as a familiar singular as well as a plural. Whereas educated Irish and Scottish speakers generally avoid *youse*, Southerners avoid *y'all* only in formal situations. So its use is situationally conditioned rather than being restricted to the idiolects of particular, socially-categorized groups of speakers.

The journal *American Speech* (founded in 1925) is a treasury of contemporary anecdote and (mostly folk) theories on the origins and occurrence of the plural second person pronoun. Judging from the range of papers produced from 1926 onwards, the pronoun and its variants are spread pretty widely across the Southern states; relevant comment includes the following:

(9) In Florida and North Carolina ... the plural of *you* was *you all*, with the stress on *you*. *You all* was used, and I believe is still used, by cultivated people....

Occasionally we heard the plural form *you uns* (*you ones*), but this form was considered vulgar. If I remember rightly, it was used by some illiterate mountaineers in North Carolina, and I have heard that it is used by the same class in Kentucky and Tennessee....

Many of us have also heard, in New York and Boston, the plural *yous*, which seems to be a more recent importation, and which, ... has not spread to the rural districts.
(1927, E.C. Hills, The plural forms of 'you', *American Speech*, II.133)

It is striking that the origins of the plural second person pronoun in these varieties do not appear to be shared, although the similarity in the pattern of formation of the three variants is undoubted: each consists of the base morpheme *you* + a plural marker, whether this is a bound, inflectional morpheme like <-z> or the generalized, bleached lexeme <all> or the bleached and phonetically reduced pronoun <uns> ('ones'). The formal discontinuities, however, are striking in their implications for the reconstruction of the advent of the particular forms of plural second person pronouns. The presence of *youse* in American fiction of New York City is one such example. More telling evidence appears in the early attestations of the plural pronoun in southern hemisphere ETEs.

12.4 Southern hemisphere varieties: Australian, South African, Zimbabwean

The southern native speaker Englishes that I'll consider now all originate in the nonstandard mainland English dialects of the late eighteenth and early nineteenth centuries. By contrast with the language of the first English settlers of North America, the dialects of most of the English settlers of Australia (beginning 1788) and South Africa (1820) could be characterized as less traditional and increasingly urbanised.[8] Turner (1994: 277) remarks, 'most involuntary passengers [to Botany Bay] had already left rural England for cities, accommodating their speech to their new neighbours there', and Branford (1994: 436) reports that the vast majority of the 1820 settlers of the eastern Cape came from London and its immediate environs. It also happens that varying proportions of the settlers of the new colonies were not English English speakers at all, but Irish and Scottish English speakers. Branford notes (436) that significant numbers of settlers in the Cape in 1819–20 were from Ireland and Scotland.

With these things in mind, let's turn first to Australian English, and the plural second person pronoun. The *Australian National Dictionary* entry (660), on the authority of the *English Dialect Dictionary* (*EDD*), suggests that the origins of Australian *youse* lie in Irish English. Its earliest citation is from the Sydney *Bulletin* (May) 1902:

(10)   a. The men persuaded us to try our luck with them, at least for a time. 'Yous can leave us when you like, if it doesn't pay.' (1902, *Bulletin* (Sydney) May 642/2)

The *OED* lists one instance of *yous* and one of *yez* from Miles Franklin's *My Brilliant Career*, published in 1901. The speaker is Mrs M'Swat, 'a great, fat, ignorant, pleasant-looking woman, shockingly dirty and untidy' (170):

(10)   b. 'I don't hold with too much pleasure and disherpation, but you ain't had overmuch of it lately. You've stuck at home

pretty constant, and ye and Lizer can have a little fly round. It'll do yous good.'
(1901, Miles Franklin, *My Brilliant Career*, xxx.187)

Here's another working-class, but not necessarily native, Australian character, the housekeeper Mrs Butler:

(10) c. 'You'd better come in an' 'ave a drop of tay-warter, miss, the kittle's bilin'; and I have the table laid out for both of yez. (*ibid.* xvii.106)

The *OED* citations for both forms include more recent Australian English usages too. Slightly misleading is the *AND*'s choice of illustration for the use of *yous* (actually *yiz*) as a **singular** pronoun. It is misleading because the speech represented can evidently only be Irish English, containing the very clear, almost stereotypical, grammatical marker of *after* + verb, as well as a rounded diphthong in *side* and a markedly aspirated dental [t] in *after* and *street*. The quotation dates from 1885:

(11) a. As he staggered along the footpath, he met a gentleman, whom he thus accosted, 'Plaise, sor, can yiz be afther tellin me which is the other soide ave the sthreet?'
(1885, E. Nevill, *Gleanings with Meanings*, 3)

The other illustration of this usage is considerably later, and strikingly, although the pronoun has singular reference, it has plural concord:

(11) b. 'Listen Harry, if youse were an out of work streaker no one'd lend you a pair of strides.'
(1976, Hurst and Cameron, *In Collaboration*, 39)

In Australian usage, as well as in present-day Belfast, for instance, the pronoun evidently tolerates deployment as a singular. Hudson laments in his disquisition on Modern Australian Usage, that if the 'annoying' lack of distinct singular and plural forms was the original reason for the evolution of *yous* (in Australian English), its 'indiscriminate' use for singular and plural destroys the whole point of the exercise (1993: 438–9).

As almost 30 per cent of the native English-speaking population of Australia was of Irish origin by 1890, it seems that there is a very good chance that the contact of Irish (Scots and other nonstandard English) dialects yields the impetus for the adoption of *yous*. After all, even if the early nineteenth-century speakers of a nascent Australian English felt the absence of Hudson's rather simply put suggestion of the underdifferentiation of form for function, they had a model with which to fill the formal gap. The plural pronoun evidently filled the gap very efficiently, for its variant(s) *yez*, *yiz* become equally established quite early. It is probably important to point out that speakers who are not broad

Australian consider *yous* and its variants 'barbarisms'. In this respect, Australian English *yous* is closer in sociolinguistic meaning to the use in nonstandard Irish English, Scots and in Northern US English of *youse* than to Southern US *y'all*.

The same (Irish) influence might reasonably be assumed to play a significant role in the adoption in South African English (SAE) of *youse*, though here, the possibility of contact with other languages, notably Afrikaans, has to be considered. In Afrikaans, second person is differentiated for number (as well as politeness), *jy/u* being singular and *julle* being plural. I have argued elsewhere that a combination of native form and borrowed semantic function might be held to account for the way in which SAE divides up conceptually and organizes lexically the proximal past and future dimensions of the general present (*now: just now* and *now now*) (Wright 1990). The plural second person pronoun *youse* is particularly vigorous in so-called 'extreme' South African English, the nonstandard variety of English which originated in the 1820 settler community in the Eastern Cape, and spread throughout English-speaking South Africa from the 1870s. The demographics (and consequent sociolinguistics) of South African white society have historically been such that contact between English and Afrikaner is far more consistent among the working classes (labourers and farm workers, then miners). The linguistic consequences of this contact are a lexis that is formally shared (but whose management or pragmatics might contrast), and sound systems which appear to overlap and converge (Lass and Wright 1986). The plural second person pronoun *youse* may thus be the product of a combination of factors. Like other nonstandard Englishes separated from standard antecedents by isolation and the lack of formal structures to allow the encouragement, reinforcement (or imposition) of standard features in the nascent variety, South African English speakers' inclination to enunciate a number contrast in the second person pronoun may be realized without obstacle. The model form was already available in a variety spoken by a sizable settler contingent – Irish English *youse*. In addition, there is further pragmatic reinforcement of the contrast marked in the Afrikaans of fellow-workers and possibly even spouses. In this case, it would seem, there is considerable pressure for the new variety to adopt the number distinction. I should note that the form appears to be wholly colloquial and jocular; it is stigmatized outside the working class, (unfortunately pejoratively) labelled 'extreme' South African English. It is very hard, therefore, to find adequate attestation in existing resources.

The last, and most speculative case I want to consider is that of Zimbabwe L1 English. Since it is even harder to find formally recorded data for this variety, what I have to offer amounts to no more than a suggestion on the topic. I have observed, in the colloquial speech of my peers, but not in the speech of my parents' generation, a plural second pronoun – *you'uns*. *Yous* is an alternative to *you'uns*, but it can function only as a modifier, in a vocative NP, like *youse guys,* in 'Wait for me youse guys/you'uns!' The plural function of these forms is underlined by the overt plural morpheme (/-z/ – attached, and reinforced in the case of *youse guys*). Rather like the Southern US *y'all* in current speech, *you'uns* is primarily a marker of casual or clearly colloquial language, and as such is conditioned by style and situation. I have been aware of the form's presence in L1 (and increasingly evident in L2 speech of young urban speakers) since the early 1970s, and I think it arguably reflects the impact of cultural isolation from Britain during the sanctions imposed during the Smith regime and civil war (1969–80). By contrast, American popular culture and its lifestyles have gained exposure and attractiveness. Along with this trend, has been the gradual acquisition of lexis and phraseology which is typical more of US than British culture. The presence of the plural pronoun appears to me very recent, possibly ruling out historical superstratum effects (which in any case would have been more likely initially to be Scottish than Irish, and since the Second World War, more south-east English than Scottish). The only other contact-oriented factor which might be salient in the spread of the plural second person pronoun might be substratum effects: the principal substratum languages, Shona and Ndebele, are both marked by complex number patterns in pronominal systems, and the resident pidgin language (Fanagalo, transported from the Rand mines by migrant workers since the 1920s) differentiates between singular and plural in the second person pronoun (*wena* vs *yena*).

I came across a curious piece of folk-etymology regarding *you'uns*. A 15-year-old boy used the expression (spelled *you ohns*) in the representation of dialogue in a school essay. When asked where the form came from, he explained that it was first used by RLI troopies (Rhodesian Light Infantry soldiers) and that the expressions *ou's* ('men') and *ou' maat* (old mate) were part of the same thing. (A derivational perspective might allow the contracted form *you'uns* from *you old ones* via the mixed *you ou uns*.) If correct, this innovation would reflect the impact of close and prolonged contact between English speakers and Rhodesian Afrikaners in the armed forces.[9] However attractive the proposition, I'm inclined at this stage to see the form as an innovation based on the forms in circulation at the same time.

12.5 Discussion

The genesis and spread of a pronoun denoting the second person plural in native speaker Englishes outside England do not appear to depend on the insidious influence of a single nonstandard variety. However, Irish English is an obvious candidate for the role of progenitor of *youse* in both northern and southern hemisphere non-English Englishes. More tantalizing than the spread of the particular forms of plural second person pronoun, is the hiatus between the loss of the old system (with a distinctive singular form, such as *thou*) and the emergence of the new one (with a distinctive plural form, such as *yous*). It is tempting to construe the gap as an expressive transition between traditional and new dialects. The new dialects adopt (or retain) exactly the same structural categories but select different forms to fill them. The passing of the traditional dialects, therefore, does not remove an apparent tendency in nonstandard varieties to make use of number distinctions. The formal expression of this tendency might be reinforced by the availability of an appropriate form (*yous*) with which to realize the difference.

Notes

1 The quotation comes, slightly amended, from Caroline Macafee's (1983: 84) transcription of Billy Connolly's story of the Last Supper, performed as part of a stage show in Airdrie. I presented an earlier version of this essay as a paper at the Colloquium on Syntax and Varieties, University of Düsseldorf, 6–8 July 1995. I am grateful for comments and feedback offered by the participants.
2 Tyneside English also makes the number distinction. Beal (1993: 205) indicates that the second person subject singular is *ye*, the plural *yous*, and that some younger speakers generalize *yous* to address one person. Plural *Yous* also occurs in Liverpool dialect.
3 Harris (1993: 147) observes that 'some types of Irish English have plural demonstrative pronoun forms ending in *-un's* (*-ones*): *usun's*, *yousun's*, *themun's*, e.g.: "Yousun's can go now." Henry (1995: 18) comments that though plural in form and reference, these pronouns allow singular concord, as in 'Usuns was late' and 'Themuns has no idea'.
4 The basic typological contrasts between northern and southern hemisphere Englishes are rhoticity and the quality of the vowel in *fast*. Northern ETEs retain postvocalic /r/ and raise and front the vowel in *fast*, whereas southern ETEs do not exhibit postvocalic /r/, and have a back, low realization of the vowel in *fast* (Lass 1987: 274–6).
5 In the absence of specially designed corpora of materials for examining these Englishes in a properly comparative manner, I have relied initially on sources like the *OED*, *English Dialect Dictionary* and supplementary dictionaries.
6 *OED* also records entries for *you-uns* and *you-all*.
7 Thou is realized as /Du/ generally, as /tu/ in the west, and as /du/ in the Northern Isles. This usage continues in Shetland, although young speakers do not consistently observe the *du/ye* distinction. McClure also reports that though *Ye* is now general, *ye* (nominative plural)–*you* (objective plural) distinction survived into the modern period.

8 The dialects then transported to New Zealand from Australia, and to Rhodesia, principally from South Africa, were arguably already budding new Englishes.
9 The etymology here would be quite unlike that of North American *you'uns,* since it would be a phonetic reanalysis of *oud*: deletion of the final voiceless dental stop and replacement with a dental nasal. I think this derivation is unlikely.

References

Beal, Joan 1993. The grammar of Tyneside and Northumbrian English. In: J. Milroy and L. Milroy (eds), pp. 187–213.
Branford, William 1994. English in South Africa. In: R. Burchfield (ed.), pp. 439–95.
Burchfield, Robert (ed.) 1994. *The Cambridge History of the English Language,* vol. V: *English in Britain and Overseas, Origins and Development.* Cambridge: Cambridge University Press.
Dillard, J.L. 1992. *A History of American English.* London: Longman.
Edwards, Jay 1974. African influence in the English of San Andres island. In: DeCamp and Hancock (eds), *Pidgins and Creoles: Current Trends and Prospects.* Washington, DC: Georgetown University Press, pp. 1–26.
Faraclas, Nicholas 1991. The pronoun system in Nigerian Pidgin. In: Jenny Cheshire (ed.), *English Around the World: Sociolinguistic Perspectives.* Cambridge: Cambridge University Press, pp. 509–17.
Franklin, Miles 1901. *My Brilliant Career.* Reprinted 1980, 1981, Virago Modern Classics.
Harris, John 1993. The Grammar of Irish English. In: J. Milroy and L. Milroy (eds), pp. 139–86.
Henry, Alison 1995. *Belfast English and Standard English: Dialect Variation and Parameter Setting.* Oxford: Oxford University Press.
Holm, John 1988. *Pidgins and Creoles,* vol. 1: *Theory and Structure.* Cambridge: Cambridge University Press.
Hudson, Nicholas 1993. *Modern Australian Usage.* Oxford: Oxford University Press.
Hughes, Joan (ed.) 1989. *The Concise Australian National Dictionary.* Oxford: Oxford University Press.
Kallen, Jeffrey J. 1994. English in Ireland. In: R. Burchfield (ed.), pp. 148–96.
Lass, Roger 1987. *The Shape of English.* London: Dent.
Lass, Roger and Wright, Susan 1986. Endogeny vs contact: 'Afrikaans influence' on South African English. *EWW* 7: 201–24.
Macafee, Caroline 1983. *Glasgow* (Varieties of English Around the World). Amsterdam: John Benjamins.

McClure, J. Derrick 1994. English in Scotland. In: R. Burchfield (ed.), pp. 23–93.

McDavid, Raven I. Jr 1979. Social differences in white speech. Reprinted 1980 (from *Language and Society*, W. McCormack and S.A. Wurm (eds), Mouton). In: Anwar S. Dil (ed.), *Varieties of American English: Essays by Raven I. McDavid, Jr.* Stanford University Press.

Mencken, H.L. 1948. *The American Language: An Inquiry into the Development of English in the United States.* London: Routledge & Kegan Paul.

Miller, Jim 1993. The grammar of Scottish English. In: J. Milroy and L. Milroy (eds), pp. 99–138.

Milroy, James and Milroy, Lesley (eds) 1993. *Real English: The Grammar of English Dialects in the British Isles.* London: Longman.

Trudgill, Peter and Chambers, Jack (eds) 1991. *Dialects of English: Studies in Grammatical Variation.* London: Longman.

Turner, George W. 1994. English in Australia. In: R. Burchfield (ed.), pp. 277–327.

Whatley, Elizabeth 1981. Language among Black Americans. In: Charles A. Ferguson and Shirley Brice Heath (eds), *Language in the USA.* Cambridge: Cambridge University Press, pp. 92–107.

Wright, Susan 1990. Present pragmatics and past histories: some temporal expressions in South African English. *Multilingua* 9: 201–30.

CHAPTER 13

Strengthening identity: differentiation and change in contemporary Galician

Johannes Kabatek

13.1 Introduction

The resurgence of minority languages and regional varieties in Europe during the last few decades is a phenomenon that can be observed generally, but the particular historical circumstances in Spain have created social and political conditions that have led to an extraordinary blossoming of the regional languages. The Catalan, Basque and Galician regionalist movement received important impulses as a consequence of the 1978 constitution, where the 'other Spanish languages'[1] became co-official within their respective historical territories. In Galicia, the local language could count on a high percentage of speakers, a relatively low degree of dialect differences, and a certain literary tradition, but there existed neither a generally accepted standard language nor an urban middle class using the autochthonous language, as, for example, in Catalunya. Only a small group of urban intellectuals tried to cultivate Galician as a language for everyday urban purposes; and Galician tended to be spoken only by lower classes and in 'the world of peasants and fishermen' (see Monteagudo and Santamarina 1993: 117 and *passim*).

The new legal situation of Galician created the necessity of quickly elaborating a standard language for official purposes. In 1983, a standard language corpus proposed by Galician linguists was made official by law and implemented by all the possible means of modern language planning such as mass-media, education and administration.[2] This proposed standard plays an important part in the creation of what could be called 'new urban Galician' or 'Galician koiné'. The increasing use of Galician by urban speakers led to a convergence or 'koineization' process that consists not only in the acceptance or rejection of proposals concerning the form of the standard language, but also in a complex social discussion and in a filtering process that separates dialect elements from those regarded as being part of the koiné.[3] This chapter will attempt to show how some of these filtering processes can be observed in present usage and to what kind of effects they lead, describing some differences between the explicit criteria of language planners and the implicit and explicit criteria of the speakers and giving the concrete example of some linguistic changes resulting from the process of a basically spoken, dialectally marked language becoming elaborated and standardized.

13.2 A brief history of Galician

Galician is a Romance language that used to be regarded traditionally as a dialect of Portuguese spoken on Spanish territory. Historically, it was the basis of Portuguese, and Portuguese is the result of the contact between old Galician and the Mozarabic dialects spoken, above all, in Lisbon. While Portuguese became the language of the independent Portugal, Galicia was separated from the south and stayed under Leonese and Castilian influence. During the thirteenth and fourteenth centuries, Galician was used for troubadour poetry and notarial documentation, and some of the important historical chronicles were translated from Castilian into Galician, but from the fifteenth century onwards Galician disappeared from written use and Castilian became the official and written language. During the following centuries, the established diglossic situation between Spanish and Galician became rather stable, but in the nineteenth century, as in the case of several European minority languages, a literary movement, the so-called *Rexurdimento*, reactivated the use of Galician as a written language. A literary tradition with several ups and downs has been maintained up to the present day,[4] but the majority of its representatives were members of the Spanish-speaking middle classes, cultivating only the written language without contributing to the creation of a spoken koiné.

In the 1970s, a discussion about standardization took place with several proposals postulating, on the one hand, direct or step-by-step integration into Portuguese, and, on the other, the creation of an independent standard based on dialect research, on former proposed standards and on the literary tradition. In 1983, this independent standard was made official. The goals of the standard have been defined by the language planners as 'Koiné based on the spoken language, but de-Castilianized, supradialectal, with roots in tradition, coherent and in harmony with the neighbour languages' (*Normas* . . . 1982: 8.). This means that the proposal is against the Castilianized Galician of the dialect tradition and against the hypercorrect separatism frequent in Galician literature. It fixes orthography and unifies morphological forms, but proposes only a frame that has to be filled by the speaker's own activity. A main criterion is 'purification' from Spanish elements: as a result of centuries of contact with Spanish as a prestige language, Galician dialects have adopted much

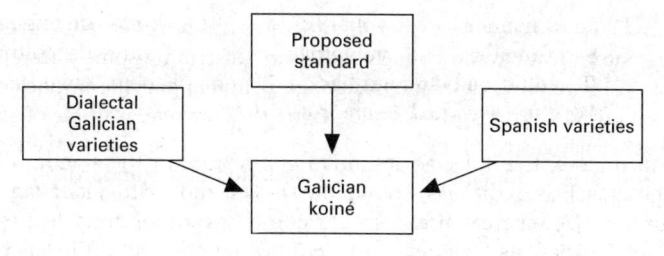

```
        ┌─────────────┐
        │  Proposed   │
        │  standard   │
        └─────────────┘
              │
┌──────────┐  ▼         ┌──────────┐
│ Dialectal│            │ Spanish  │
│ Galician │            │varieties │
│ varieties│            │          │
└──────────┘            └──────────┘
       ╲  ┌──────────┐  ╱
        ╲▶│ Galician │◀╱
          │  koiné   │
          └──────────┘
```

Figure 13.1 The Galician koineization process

from the Spanish lexicon and, in areas with intensive contact, grammar; in the last few years, even the phonetics have been affected by Spanish. This is especially the case since, after the moment when Galician was made the official language, a considerable number of speakers with Spanish as their mother tongue adopted Galician either partially, for professional purposes, or generally, and thereby initiated several interference processes. Another tendency of the standard is not to proscribe features regarded as typical Galician such as, for example, the highly stigmatized *gheada* and *seseo*[5] or certain morphological and syntactic characteristics. Nevertheless, implicit and explicit discussion in the community about the inclusion or exclusion of elements in the koiné had led in many cases to an exclusion of these features and to their attribution to dialectally marked speech.[6]

The Galician koineization process is thus a combination between the acceptance and rejection of elements contained in the standard proposal, the inclusion or exclusion of elements contained in the dialect tradition and of the introduction or rejection of elements of the contact language, the Spanish varieties. This process is represented in Figure 13.1.

13.3 Changes in progress

I will choose three examples to illustrate some of the tendencies observable in contemporary Galician. In all three cases, changes can be observed over the last few years. These can, of course, also be just short-term evolutions without long-term consequences. But this is a general problem of the study of change in progress: only the nature of the present developments can be indicated, but no prediction for the future can be made. We can only conjecture that probably some of the actual tendencies will be consolidated in the future.

13.3.1 Inflected infinitive

Common to Portuguese (P) and Galician (G) is the possibility of inflecting personal endings on the infinitive forms[7]:

(1) P: Seria melhor	voltar*mos*	antes de anoitecer.
    G: Sería mellor	volver*mos*	antes da noitiña.
    'It would be better go back + 1. pers. pl. before nightfall.'
    We'd better go back before it gets dark.

In Portuguese, the inflected infinitive is a feature of the standard language as well as of dialects, both in the spoken and written language (cf. Maurer 1968), whereas it can be considered as a moribund feature in spoken Galician, as Gondar (1978: 155) has pointed out. This has been attributed to the influence of Spanish, where the inflected infinitive does not exist.[8] In contemporary Galician dialects, the inflected infinitive is still an active feature in rural areas with low contact with Spanish and in the speech of the older generation, but it is dying out in younger generations and in areas with higher contact. In spoken urban Galician, the inflected infinitive is almost non-existent. Its disappearance does not cause any real damage to the Galician verbal system, for it can almost always be regarded as a redundant feature that only serves to add precision or to emphasize, and its functions can be easily replaced by other elements. Being a personalizer, its pragmatic functions could be thought of as typical of the spoken language or intimate speech, and this would be a possible explanation for its loss in the filtering processes of standardization, where elements that are considered markers of orality are frequently extinguished. Nevertheless, in contemporary Galician, precisely the contrary is occurring: the inflected infinitive is becoming a marker of elaborated speech and written texts.

In 1978, Francisco Gondar observed that in Galician literature some of the authors never employ inflected infinitives, whereas others use them in abundance or even abuse them.[9] Gondar gives an explanation for the high frequency in some literary publications, suspecting that

> their authors are probably conscious of the peculiarity represented in our language by the existence of this feature and they somehow want to recover it and to avoid its loss, at least in the case of written language. (Gondar 1978: 130–40; my translation)

In the course of time and with the official use of Galician, this tendency has become more and more characteristic of written language. In contemporary scientific texts, a high frequency of inflected forms can be observed, frequently with a large number of redundant repetitions.[10] In 1989, when for the first time a complete Bible translation was published, the translators had the problem of creating a solemn religious text with a certain distance from the spoken language in a language with predominantly oral traditions: one of the frequently observable ways of resolving this problem was the use of inflected infinitive forms.[11] At present, the inflected infinitive can be found in almost all elaborated, written, markedly non-spontaneous discourses that express a certain distance, sometimes with a high frequency: scientific articles, solemn speeches, essays, certain types of literary text, official documents, etc.[12]

Resuming, we could say paradoxically that a feature that is disappearing from spoken Galician as a consequence of Spanish influence reappears in elaborated and written Galician due to the same influence: the absence in Spanish and the desire to save or to recover 'typical Galician' features produces a revival in written language that eventually could also become the basis for its recovery in spoken Galician.

13.3.2 Clitic positions

A similar tendency can be observed in certain cases of clitic positioning, where the Galician system allows more than one possibility. The rules for clitic positions were about the same in Old Spanish and Gallego-Portuguese, but Spanish changed from the thirteenth century onwards (see, for example, Barry 1987, Luna Traill and Parodi 1974), according to a general Romance evolution preferring preverbal positioning in main clauses. Galician, on the other hand, normally retains the postverbal position and only changes the clitic position in subordinate clauses or, under some special circumstances (e.g. focus, negation), in main clauses (cf. Campos 1989).

(2) Span.: Me dijo que se llamaba Pepe.
(3) Gal.: Díxome que se chamaba Pepe.
He told me his name was Pepe.

Strongly Castilianized speakers usually have difficulties with the differences in the use of the clitics, and Spanish interference has damaged the traditional Galician system in the mixed hybrid of so-called *Chapurrao*, a language mixture between Galician and Castilian spoken in small towns and, partly, in the cities (cf. García González 1976). Language planners and prescriptivists have intervened against this tendency and have tried to re-establish the traditional Galician usage still intact in Galician dialects. The correction leads to countless hypercorrect uses by strongly Castilianized speakers, but in general the traditional system is still quite stable and easily re-established even by 'new Galician speakers' with a Spanish mother tongue.

However, language planning does not intervene where the Galician system – according to dialect research and to normative proposals – offers more than one possibility: in this case, the speakers themselves have the choice, as in the following examples:

(4) Gal.: teño que dicilo   (7) Span.: tengo que decirlo
(5) Gal.: teño que o dicir
(6) Gal.: téñoo que dicir

                                  (8) Span.: lo tengo que decir

I must say it.

In this and in similar cases, Galician allows three different positions of the clitic, of which only one coincides with Spanish, whereas in Spanish another position (8) is possible. In spoken rural Galician, (4)–(6) are generally used, probably with different pragmatic functions, but in more Castilianized Galician, the variety tends to be reduced to the use of (4), the only form that coincides with Spanish. For reasons of economy, the 'common core' between the two languages is preferred, a well-known strategy of bilinguals and a general tendency in language contact and language learning (cf. Weinreich 1953: 24). But in the last few years, a revival of (5) can be observed in elaborated, written texts, whereas in urban spoken Galician the form is almost non-existent.[13] Like the inflected infinitive, it has thereby become a sort of marker of a more elevated style. The general tendency is again, as in the first example, the preference for and resurgence of a disappearing dialect feature in written and elaborated texts.

13.3.3 'Solidarity pronoun'

A third case is the so-called 'solidarity pronoun', a feature regarded as 'typical Galician', which consists in a use of dative clitics with a purely dialogic function: the clitic refers to the partner(s) in communication (the examples are extracted from Álvarez *et al.* 1986: 174–5):

(7) Meu pai   vai*che*   a peor,
     'My father goes+dat. pron. (2. p. sing.) to worse,
     que a vellez non *che*   ten cura.
     for the age not dat. pron. (2. p. sing.) has remedy.'
     My father is getting worse, for there's no remedy against age.

(8) Pois o que é a min nunca   *che*   me
     'Well, that what is to me never dat. pron. (2. p. sing.) me
     deu nada.
     gave (he/she) anything.'
     Well, as far as I am concerned he/she never gave me anything.

Galician grammarians distinguish between the 'solidarity pronoun' and the 'dativo de interese' or *dativus ethicus*, using the first for a pronoun referring only to the interlocutor and the second for a contextual reference to a person concerned by the action. Both cases are somehow similar, and in many examples they are not really separable. It might thus be better to subsume both under one deictic function that can refer both to cotextual and to contextual or situational relations. In this way, dative pronouns can also be combined and refer to different persons, as in (9), where the first pronoun (*che*) refers to the interlocutor, the second (*lle*) to a third person concerned by the message (the son whose cow has died) and the third pronoun refers to the sender himself as interlocutor and as someone concerned by the message (the father of the son whose cow has died).

(9) Morréu*chelleme*
'Died dat. pron. (2. p. sing.)/dat. pron. (3. p. sing.)/dat. pron. 1. p. sing./

a vaca do meu fillo.
the cow of my son.'
My son's cow has died.

This clitic use can be genetically related to the Latin ethical dative, but the function can be found in many languages and dialects, being generally considered as a typical element of spoken language or intimate speech.[14] It does not exist in standard Spanish, and so authors like the novelist Miguel Delibes use it as a marker to characterize colloquial, vulgar speech.[15]

Galician, with a continuous oral tradition and lack of standardizing influences almost until the present day, conserves a high number of possible uses and combinations of this feature. The early Galician authors of the 'Pre-rexurdimento' at the beginning of the nineteenth century exaggerated the use of the 'solidarity pronoun'.[16] This can be explained in two ways: on the one hand, the first texts were often dialogues, and they tried to represent the 'typical' elements of popular, spoken Galician; on the other hand, the absence of this element in Spanish made the already Castilianized authors of the nineteenth century consider the 'solidarity pronoun' as a typically Galician element and to use it as a marker of distance between Galician and Spanish,[17] comparable to the case of the current tendencies mentioned in 13.3.1. and 13.3.2.

In the present koineization process, language planners have tried to 'save' the solidarity pronoun in the standardization process by not proscribing it and introducing it, for example, in didactic texts for language learners.[18] But a general tendency seems to be to omit its use in 'formal' texts. There is a simple reason for this: many of the new, standard-oriented texts do not have a direct dialogic function, and the omission of the 'solidarity pronoun' is thus preconditioned by the objective characteristics of these texts. Nevertheless, as a consequence, it is disappearing also from standard-oriented dialogues, and thereby becoming an element generally excluded from the koiné. The non-existence in the contact language might play a further part, for Spanish seems to act here as an example for a standardized koiné.

13.4 Attitudes

Since there are obvious differences between spoken and written usage in the case of the three examples, it seemed interesting to ask speakers involved in the Galician koineization process directly about these features.[19] During a series of interviews about metalinguistic questions, I asked 30 such informants (speakers from the Galician radio and TV, Galician teachers and students of Galician philology) to comment on examples containing inflected infinitive forms, different clitic positions as in 13.3.2 and 'solidarity pronouns'.[20] All three features seemed generally to be highly sterotyped. Asked about an example with the inflected infinitive, the 30 informants generally showed positive attitudes. For all the informants, with only one exception, the feature was well known and metalinguistically stereotyped. Four of them stated that they tried to employ inflected infinitives consciously in order to contribute to their recovery. One informant, a student of Galician philology, said she hardly ever used them in spoken language even though her parents still used them frequently, but she tended to use them more often in written language. The more Castilianized the speaker's background, the more positive were the attitudes towards the inflected infinitive. Only in the case of an extremely Castilianized informant did the feature seem to be unknown. Some of the informants with a clear Galician dialect background showed less positive attitudes and characterized the exaggerated recovery of the feature as artificial, even if they also admitted using it in written language.

In the case of the clitic positions, six of the 30 informants evaluated (5) and (6) as atypical elements of the written language. Several informants stated that they normally used (4) in spoken language. However, in written texts, after reflection, they would consciously introduce (5) from time to time. Three of the informants with a stronger Spanish influence stated that (5) should be preferred, arguing in several cases that one should use a feature distinct from Spanish. Some of the informants, especially five of those with rather clear Galician backgrounds, evaluated the form as 'artificial' and typical of the new texts of highly Castilianized speakers.

The reactions to a sample with 'solidarity pronoun' were also different according to the level of the speaker's degree of Castilianization. Galician mother-tongue speakers and those in close contact with popular Galician tended to evaluate the use of the 'solidarity pronoun' as 'normal', 'simply Galician' or 'typical of dialogues', specifying, in some cases, that it would not be an adequate element for elaborated texts. The more Castilianized the informants were, the more positive was the reaction to the example: it was evaluated as 'nice', 'typical', 'authentic', with reactions frequently accompanied by a smile, especially by those informants with little contact with popular Galician. At the same time, however, the speakers with very positive attitudes didn't use this element themselves in standard-oriented texts: an element associated with originality, intimacy or local colour is automatically excluded in texts where this kind of connotation is to be avoided. It seems, somehow, to

DIFFERENTIATION AND CHANGE IN GALICIAN

correlate with several other 'typical Galician' or almost exotic stereotypes which are evaluated by new speakers as sounding 'nice' or 'authentic', but that are thereby also limited to speech marked as dialect and excluded from the koiné. In this case, the part played by the contact language does not lead to a reinforcement of the divergent elements, but to an acceptance of the contact language as a model for the Galician koiné.

13.5 Conclusions

The three examples show how, in contemporary Galician koineization, a selection or filtering process of elements for different discourse types is taking place. The possibility of conscious reflection and discourse planning seems to play an important part in the creation of the new, elaborated texts, and strategies of conscious intervention are – at least in part – responsible for the general fact that languages change when passing from oracy to literacy (cf. Schlieben-Lange 1983: 83, Kabatek 1994), or when new, elaborated or written texts are created in languages with primarily spoken traditions; and these changes may have a later influence on spoken varieties, too.

In the concrete case of our examples, conscious reflection is influenced or determined by the presence of a closely-related contact language acting in two ways on speakers while they are creating new texts. On the one hand, it acts as a model language in which the new discourse types already exist and where selection and filtering have already long since taken place. On the other hand, however, a desire to stress the particular characteristics of Galician and to differentiate the two contact languages makes the speakers intervene against the pure adoption of the Spanish model for Galician texts. This creates negative differentiation interference and leads to a proliferation in elaborated texts of distinct forms such as those described in 13.3.1 and 13.3.2. The term *negative interference* was introduced by Coseriu in 1977 and refers to an interference type that leads to 'negative realizations' or 'non-realizations' of elements of one language because of the presence of another. There are two types of 'negative interference', one that consists in the preference of common elements between the two languages (overlap) and the non-realization of the distinct elements, and another consisting in the preference for the distinct elements (differentiation) and the non-realization of common elements, for different reasons. Both types can appear combined in one text, affecting different elements or different levels of the language (for an exhaustive study see Kabatek 1996).

The determining influence of interference in the cases described above is evident, even if the contact language does not appear directly in the resulting texts. This phenomenon seems to appear due to rather infrequent, extraordinary historical circumstances. Anyway, in many historical processes of koineization, standardized, written and elaborated contact languages (such as, for example, Latin for the Romance languages) might have acted on the new texts in a similar way.

A third observation can be derived from the above: some elements seem to be excluded from the koiné for objective reasons or because of the communicative characteristics of elaborated texts.[21] This is what happens to the Galician 'solidarity pronoun' or ethical datives, where the exclusion from standard-oriented texts marked by distance between the interlocutors can be explained by the function of the element itself, which because of its dialogical characteristics remains only in the orally-marked nonstandard dialects.[22] This might be an explanation for the obvious historical parallelism in the evolution of this or similar features in different languages. On the way towards literacy, the languages move from the so-called 'pragmatic mode' towards the 'syntactic mode',[23] excluding certain deictic elements as a result of standardization and leaving them behind in their spoken, nonstandard varieties.

Notes

1 Article 3 of the Constitution says: 'Castilian is the official language of the state. All Spaniards have the duty to know it and the right to use it. The other Spanish languages will also be official in the respective Autonomous Communities according to their statutes.'
2 For a description of Galician standardization see Santamarina Fernández (1994), Kabatek (1992) and Albrecht (1992).
3 It might seem surprising to differentiate between 'standardization' and the somehow ambiguous term 'koineization' (see Siegel 1993: 5–6). Different proposals have been made to distinguish between a consciously elaborated standard and the much more complex and – at least partly – implicit processes of linguistic convergence that create a common language or koiné and that separate elements regarded to be 'dialectal' and those accepted in standard oriented texts (see the distinction between different notions of 'standard' in Stein 1994: 1–4). This process includes questions of the acceptance or rejection of the proposed standard (cf. Haugen 1966) as well as 'reduction, levelling and simplification' (Trudgill 1986: 106–7) and also new creations, filtering, differentiation between varieties and fixing of 'normal' usage including 'normal' selection and frequency of elements.
4 The first impulse for a romantic Neo-Galician movement was given by the French invasion at the beginning of the nineteenth century, which provoked Galician resistance, also expressed in popular texts. From the second half of the century onwards, a consolidation of a poetic movement took place with authors such as Pintos, Rosalía de

Castro, Manuel Curros or Eduardo Pondal. Several grammars and dictionaries had been published by the end of the nineteenth century. In 1905, the Galician Academy was founded, and various movements attempted to establish the use of Galician at different levels of society. In 1936, Galician was almost officialized, but the Spanish Civil War and the Nationalists' victory interrupted the potential development of the minority languages in Spain during the Franco era. In the 1950s, editorial activities reactivated the written language and in the 1960s, a chair for Galician was created at the University of Santiago and the language became more and more a symbol for a youth movement and for anti-Francoist opposition.

5 The avoidance of the phonetic features commonly called *gheada* and *seseo* in standard oriented texts by speakers who dialectally show these characteristics is a well-known tendency, even if the language planners do not proscribe them directly. Most speakers' consciousness of these features characterizes them as part of 'intimate' speech not adequate for 'distant' texts. Álvarez *et al.* (1986: 27) consider *gheada* as a possible element of standard pronunciation: '[o fenómeno da <gheada>] foi recollido no galego estándar, como pronuncia alternativa ó sistema de non gheada' ('[The phenomenon of <gheada>] has been included in standard Galician as an alternative pronunciation to the system without gheada.') Later, one of the authors stressed the importance of social acceptance of the standard and, therefore, seemed to consider *gheada* as not conforming with the standard: 'é un feito que a xeneralidade da poboación ten unha mellor consideración da pronunciación con /g/, e parece claro que un modelo exemplar de pronuncia ten que estar asentado no recoñecemento social' ('As a matter of fact, people generally estimate more highly the pronunciation with /g/, and it seems to be evident that a standard model for pronunciation must be based on social acceptance') (Regueira Fernández 1994: 54–5).

6 'Implicit' means by using or not using the proposed elements in discourse, 'explicit' means by metalinguistic reflection or discussion about the elements.

7 Inflected infinitives have been observed in several Romance dialects (see Maurer 1968: 70–6) and in other languages. The genesis in Romance has been investigated by Meier (1950). In the Galician dialect of Rianxo, even the inflection of gerund forms has been observed (see Carballo Calero 1974).

8 See Gondar 1978: 143–4. The occurrences of inflected infinitives in Sephardic Spanish can be explained by Portuguese influence.

9 Gondar 1978: 155. It would have been interesting to specify the grade of Spanish influence in the respective authors and to see if the use of the inflected infinitive correlates with other criteria such as the different text types (dialogues vs narration, etc.).

10 In scientific articles, examples such as the following (extracted from a sociolinguistic study published in 1992) can be found frequently: 'os mozos e as mozas empregarían o castelán nun intento de sobrevalorárense, de facérense superiores, de seren máis desexables', with three repetitions of infinitive inflection.
11 In the official Bible from 1989 (Santiago: SEPT; translated from the original texts by a team under the direction of A. Torres Queiruga and X. Fernández Lago), countless examples can be found. To cite one of them: in Matt. 13, 15, e.g. the translation says: 'e pecharon os seus ollos, para non veren cos ollos, nin oíren cos oídos, nin entenderen co seu corazón nin se converteren', with four inflected infinitives, where former Galician translations only used one inflected infinitive (*convertírense* in the version of Sánchez de Santamaría and Louis Bonaparte 1861; *convertiren* in the version of Gómez Ledo 1974) and Portuguese Bibles, such as the translation of P.A. Pereira de Figueiredo or of P. Matos Soares, do not employ any inflected infinitives.
12 About the categories of *distance* and *intimaty* see Koch and Oesterreicher (1985).
13 Again, as in the case of the inflected infinitive, examples such as the following (extracted from an article about nineteenth-century Galician published in 1994) can be found frequently: *hai que a buscar, sen lle adicar, de se decatar, sen se admitir, teremos que nos enfrontar*, where spoken urban Galician would prefer *buscala, adicarlle, decatarse, admitirse* and *enfrontarnos*.
14 Similar functions exist in Greek, Latin, the other Romance languages, German (see Abraham 1971), Basque and other languages. Some Latin grammarians denounced the ethic dative as an element of vulgar speech and bad style. In the Romance dialects, it is a widely spread feature, but in the standardized literary languages it has a tendency to disappear, as Meyer-Lübke (1899: III.395–400) already observed.
15 See M. Delibes, *Los Santos Inocentes*, Barcelona 1981: 23, 24, 35, 47, 70, 71 etc., with examples such as 'la milana te tiene calentura' or 'también te tienes coraje, Paco'.
16 In some of the early nineteenth-century texts edited by Mariño Paz (1992), a 'solidarity pronoun' appears in almost every sentence, e.g. in the *Conversa entre os compadres Bértolo e Mingote*, first published in 1813, or in the *Proezas de Galicia* and in many other texts. In the Old Galician translation of the *Cronica General* from Castilian, in one case a 'solidarity pronoun' is introduced by the translator in a dialogue (Cast. *ca ellos non an y culpa ninguna* vs Gal. *ca elles nõ che am y culpa nẽ hũa*).
17 This has been observed by Mariño Paz (1992: I.699).
18 See, e.g. the dialogues in the textbook by Colectivo Albariza: *Edigal*, 4 vols, Santiago de Compostela 1985.

19 It is of course problematic to use introspection questions for the evaluation of a speaker's activity (see Seliger 1983). But at the same time, the questions about stereotyped features, where a conscious intervention takes place, are the most reliable, for they do not refer to spontaneous judgements, but to features that are already *themes* of metalinguistic reflection.

20 The questions were part of an exhaustive study about the Galician koineization process (Kabatek 1996), where the linguistic behaviour and some pronunciation features of the 30 informants were correlated with their linguistic biography, their general linguistic attitudes and their metalinguistic evaluations and opinions on concrete linguistic questions.

21 Of course, in concrete historical cases it is sometimes difficult to distinguish between influences from outside and objective, 'inner' communicative needs. In the case of 13.3.3, a combination of both the communicative conditions of the new texts and the non-existence of the element in the contact language seems to determine the exclusion of the element.

22 The 'solidarity pronoun' could also be regarded as a grammaticalized element of 'involvement', see Cheshire (in this volume).

23 See Givón (1979: 98–109) and Bühler (1934: 366–84). For another case of multiple deixis conserved in nonstandard language see Melchers (in this volume); for the relationship between standard and varieties see the general reflections by Wanner (in this volume).

References

Abraham, Werner 1971. Der 'ethische' Dativ. In: Hugo Moser (ed.), *Fragen der strukturellen Syntax und der kontrastiven Grammatik*. Düsseldorf: Schwann, pp. 112–34.

Albrecht, Sabine 1992. *Die Standardnorm des Galicischen*. Bonn: Romanistischer Verlag.

Álvarez Blanco, Rosario, Regueira Fernández, Xosé Luis and Monteagudo Romero, Henrique (1986) *Gramática Galega*. Vigo: Galaxia.

Barry, A.K. 1987. Clitic pronoun position in thirteenth-century Spanish. *Hispanic Review* 55: 213–20.

Bühler, Karl 1934. *Sprachtheorie. Die Darstellungsfunktion der Sprache*. Jena: Gustav Fischer.

Campos, Héctor 1989. Clitic position in modern Gallegan. *Lingua* 77: 13–36.

Carballo Calero, Ricardo 1974. No galego de Rianxo esiste un xerundio flesional. *Grial* 50: 497–9.

Coseriu, Eugenio 1977. Sprachliche Interferenz bei Hochgebildeten. In: H. Kolb and H. Lauffer (eds), *Sprachliche Interferenz: Festschrift für Werner Betz*. Tübingen: Niemeyer, pp. 77–100.

Coseriu, Eugenio 1978. *Sincronía, Diacronía e Historia. El Problema del Cambio Lingüístico*, 3rd edition (first Montevideo 1957). Madrid: Gredos.
García González, Constantino 1976. Interferencias lingüísticas entre gallego y castellano. *Revista Española de Lingüística* 6: 327–43.
Givón, Talmy 1979. From discourse to syntax: grammar as a processing strategy. In: Talmy Givón (ed.), *Discourse and Syntax* (Syntax and Semantics, vol. 12). New York/San Francisco/London: Academic Press, pp. 81–112.
Gondar, Francisco G. 1978. *O Infinitivo Conxugado en Galego* (Verba, Anexo 13). Santiago de Compostela: Universidad de Santiago.
Haugen, Einar 1966. *Language Conflict and Language Planning. The Case of Modern Norwegian*. Cambridge, Mass.: Harvard University Press.
Kabatek, Johannes 1992. Der Normenstreit in Galicien: Versuch einer Erklärung. *Lusorama* 18: 65–83.
Kabatek, Johannes 1994. Wenn Einzelsprachen verschriftet werden, ändern sie sich. Gedanken zum Thema Mündlichkeit und Schriftlichkeit. In: Gabriele Berkenbusch and Christine Bierbach (eds), *Soziolinguistik und Sprachgeschichte: Querverbindungen. Brigitte Schlieben-Lange zum 50. Geburtstag von ihren Schülerinnen und Schülern überreicht.* Tübingen: Narr, pp. 175–87.
Kabatek, Johannes 1996. *Die Sprecher als Linguisten. Interferenz- und Sprachwandelphänomene dargestellt am Galicischen der Gegenwart* (Beihefte zur Zeitschrift für Romanische Philologie, vol. 276). Tübingen: Niemeyer.
Koch, Peter and Oesterreicher, Wulf 1985. Sprache der Nähe – Sprache der Distanz. Mündlichkeit und Schriftlichkeit im Spannungsfeld von Sprachtheorie und Sprachgeschichte. *Romanistisches Jahrbuch* 36: 15–43.
Luna Traill, Elizabeth and Parodi, Claudia 1974. Sintaxis de los pronombres átonos en construcciones de infinitivo durante el siglo XVI. *Anuario de Letras* XII: 197–204.
Mariño Paz, Ramón 1992. *Estudio fonético, ortográfico e morfolóxico de textos do prerrexurdimento galego (1805–1837).* (Diss. on microfilm.) Santiago de Compostela: Universidad de Santiago.
Maurer, Th. H. 1968. *O Infinitivo Flexionado Português. Estudo Histórico-Descritivo.* São Paulo: Editora Nacional.
Meier, Harri 1950. A génese do infinito flexionado português. *Boletim de Filologia* XI: 115–132.
Meyer-Lübke, Wilhelm 1899. *Grammatik der Romanischen Sprachen*, 3 vols. Leipzig: Reisland.
Monteagudo, Henrique and Santamarina, Antón 1993. Galician and Castilian in contact: historical, social and linguistic aspects. In: Rebecca Posner and John N. Green (eds), *Trends in Romance Linguistics and Philology, vol. 5: Bilingualism and Linguistic Conflict in Romance.* Berlin/New York: Mouton de Gruyter, pp. 117–73.

Normas Ortográficas e Morfolóxicas do Idioma Galego 1982. Real Academia Galega/Instituto da Lingua Galega.

Regueira Fernández, Xosé Luís 1994. Modelos fonéticos e autenticidade lingüística. *Cadernos de Lingua* 10: 37–60.

Santamarina Fernández, Antón 1994. Galego: Norma e estándar. In: G. Holtus *et al.* (eds), *Lexikon der Romanistischen Linguistik*, vol. VI/2. Tübingen: Niemeyer, pp. 66–79.

Schlieben-Lange, Brigitte 1983. *Traditionen des Sprechens. Elemente einer pragmatischen Sprachgeschichtsschreibung*. Stuttgart: Kohlhammer.

Seliger, Herbert W. 1983. The language learner as linguist: of metaphors and realities. *Applied Linguistics* 4(3): 179–91.

Siegel, Jeff 1993. Controversies in the study of koinés and koineization. *International Journal of the Sociology of Language* 99: 5–8.

Stein, Dieter 1994. Sorting out the variants: standardization and social factors in the English language 1600–1800. In: Dieter Stein and Ingrid Tieken-Boon van Ostade (eds), *Towards a Standard English*. Berlin/ New York: De Gruyter.

Trudgill, Peter 1986. *Dialects in Contact*. Oxford: Blackwell.

Weinreich, Uriel 1953. *Languages in Contact*. New York: Publ. of the Linguistic Circle of New York.

CHAPTER 14

Left dislocation in French: varieties, norm and usage

Alain Berrendonner and Marie-José Reichler-Béguelin

14.1 Introduction

In this chapter we discuss those syntactic configurations in French which go by the name of 'split constructions' or dislocation, first described by Bally (1965(1994): 60). These are stretches of discourse such as the following (we give all our examples in the original French, together with an indication of their provenance, and a rough gloss in English):

(1) a. Moi, je n'arrive pas à résoudre ce problème.
       Me, I can't manage to solve this problem.
    b. Ce problème, je n'arrive pas à le résoudre.
       This problem, I can't manage to solve it.
    c. Résoudre ce problème, je n'y arrive pas.
       To solve this problem, I can't manage.

These constructions are made up of two parts. The first, which is usually a noun phrase or a predicate phrase, has a characteristic non-final or rising intonation. Its prototypical realization is a melodic medium–high rise followed by a clear pause (Wunderli 1987). We mark this type of intonation '/' in the transcriptions in this chapter, whereas '\' indicates a final assertive intonation contour and '–' the intonation typical of an aside. The second part of the construction is more often (but not necessarily) a clause containing a verb phrase; this occurs with all types of final intonation patterns. Bally labels these two components 'A' and 'Z' respectively, a convenient abbreviation which we shall also use here.

A similar ZA type of construction also exists, with the A segment in second position, with a flat 'final aside' intonation:

(2)   mais ils ont beaucoup évolué\ les signes de ponctuation. (speech, TV)
       but they have developed a lot\ punctuation marks.

LEFT DISLOCATION IN FRENCH

The two types of construction are often assumed to be simple variants, but it is not at all clear that this is the case. For this reason we shall limit our account here to left dislocation of the AZ type. It is important to note that the identification of one part of the construction as either A or Z depends upon its prosodic characteristics (rising intonation for A, falling intonation for Z), rather than on its morpho-syntactic form. Thus despite their syntactic resemblance to (1b) examples such as (3) are considered to be of the ZA type because of their intonational contour:

(3) Le blé d'hiver\ ça s'appelle. (speech < Blanche-Benveniste 1989: 68)
     Winter wheat\ it's called.

We also exclude examples such as (4):

(4) Chacun il a sa chimère. (< Sandfeld 1965)
     Each one they have their dreams.

Occurrences of this type have an unbroken intonation contour with no internal pauses; the initial noun phrase may be indefinite, as in (4), or it may be an indeterminate quantifier. These characteristics, and many others, distinguish them from dislocations (Berrendonner 1993), and suggest that they should be considered as simple elementary verbal clauses. It seems, in fact, that the basic structure of the verbal clause in French contains both an NP subject position and a nominative 'clitic pronoun' position, with the latter marking person inflection in the verb phrase:

[NP] [[CLIT X] $_{INFL}$ V'] VP

In some 'nonstandard' dialects, and perhaps elsewhere, both the NP and CLIT positions can be filled simultaneously, producing occurrences such as (4). In writing, where there is no prosody that can be relied on, examples such as these are often quasi-homonyms with dislocation such as that illustrated in example (1). We will therefore take great care to exclude any doubtful or ambiguous examples.

14.1.1 Left dislocation and the norm

There is a paradox concerning left dislocation: curiously, it evokes contradictory judgements from normativists and prescriptivists. On the one hand, it has a well-established reputation as belonging to a style with low prestige, often termed *le français populaire*, 'the people's French' (Gadet 1992: 76). At times it is even expediently classified as belonging to a pidgin. Queneau compares it to Chinook (see Gadet 1989); others see it as a stereotypical marker of the speech of the 'pied noir' from North Africa.

This negative reputation can sometimes cause purists to deny its occurrence: we once heard a grammarian colleague, undaunted by the paradox, say: *les phrases segmentées, moi, j'en fais jamais*, 'segmented constructions, me, I never use them'.

However, alongside such negative evaluations there are also some more positive judgements:

> *Cet homme, je l'ai vu; ton ami, je lui ai parlé.* (*This man, I have seen him; your friend, I have spoken to him.*) A very vital and expressive turn of phrase, which brings welcome variety to our speech. (Dauzat 1946: 92; our translation)

Furthermore, the last thirty years have seen the majority of school textbooks mentioning left dislocation as an accepted procedure for 'highlighting', on a par with clefting and the stylistically prestigious inversion of noun phrase subjects. Some textbooks, however, advise students that dislocation is 'colloquial' or typical of spoken French. The fact that prescriptivists attribute both positive and negative values to the construction suggests that we can dismiss the possibility of a conflict of norms due to its usage by a particular social group or by a disfavoured minority group in society.

A similar ambivalence is found in the connotations to which the construction gives rise. Left dislocation is used in written texts for contradictory purposes: on the one hand, it serves as a way of creating a spontaneous or colloquial style of language, as in (5); on the other hand, it is used to produce a particularly *recherché* rhetorical effect, as in (6):

(5) Le médecin, il était en uniforme de médecin, tout blanc, c'était lui qui commandait à tout le monde, les infirmières, ça filait doux, fallait voir. (Cavanna)

The doctor, he was wearing a doctor's coat, all white, it was he who ordered everyone around, the nurses, they kept a low profile, you should have seen them.

(6) C'est que vous savez, le monde des choses et le monde des idées que nous devons connaître tous les deux, ils sont immenses, et le temps de notre étude, disons de notre existence, il est si borné, si resserré. (M. Bergmann, Opening lecture of a course on foreign literature, Faculty of Arts, Strasbourg, 1852–3)

It is as you know, the world of things and the world of ideas that we should get to know, both of them, they are immense, and the time we have to study them, that is to say of our existence, it is so limited, so narrow.

In this chapter we have set ourselves the task of finding an explanation for the unusual normative status of this construction. In seeking to understand why left dislocation gives rise to these contradictory value judgements, we shall observe some of the mechanisms whereby a normative doctrine is put together, and we shall note that, in matters of variation, as elsewhere, there is a radical discrepancy between the inherent structure of a language system and the image of the system that is provided by official normative discourse. But first we must analyse the structure of the system.

14.2 Towards a grammar of left dislocation

14.2.1 Micro-syntax vs macro-syntax

Almost all descriptions since Bally's analyse dislocated constructions as sentences, without any further discussion. But to adopt a categorization of this type is to unthinkingly operationalize the everyday idea of 'sentence'; whereas there are good reasons, in fact, for considering the sentence as simply an intuitive and inconsistent orthographic approximation of a functional segmentation of language (Berrendonner and Reichler-Béguelin 1989). We will therefore avoid using this term. In its place we shall introduce a theory of syntagmatic or linear units based upon the hypothesis that discourse consists of two irreducible levels of combinations of elements, superposed on each other, which we shall term 'microsyntax' and 'macrosyntax' respectively. Both the hypothesis and terminology are directly inspired by the work of GARS, the *Groupe aixois de recherche en syntaxe* (Blanche-Benveniste *et al.* 1990).

At a microsyntactic level, that is to say at the lowest level of complexity, the relevant units are meaningful elements such as morphemes or syntactic groups. These elements are related to each other by *concatenation* (sequential constraints) and *government* (which implies a unilateral or bilateral co-occurrence of elements reflecting agreement, binding or selection restrictions). The constraints that apply at this level can be expressed in terms of the distribution of elements in a linear stretch, or chain, of discourse. The largest microsyntactic units of this kind will be called MSUs; an MSU is thus any stretch of discourse that is not governed by a larger unit. MSUs can therefore have a diverse range of internal forms, such as that of a noun phrase, a prepositional phrase, an adjectival phrase, a non-finite verbal phrase or a finite verbal phrase.

Beyond the level of the MSU a threshold is crossed, and the nature of the relationships between units changes. The relevant units are no longer segments of a chain, but heterogeneous entities of information. They are in one sense MSUs, but only in that they express a language act focusing on a certain content. They are also momentary states of *shared knowledge,* and can sometimes be, in fact, *gestures* or *perceptions*. The relations which become established between these elements are of a semantic–pragmatic nature; they are relationships of *presupposition* (where an MSU implies that there is some pre-existing shared knowledge or common ground), or of *production* (where some new shared knowledge can be inferred from the MSU). The units constructed by these relationships are mini-discourse programs which we call *periods*. The macrosyntactic role played by each constituent MSU is indicated mainly by prosodic features – stress, intonation and the like.

Owing to lack of space, we refer you to Berrendonner (1990) and (1992) for an illustration of these concepts. The main point of importance here is the methods of analysis that follow from this framework. We consider as one and the same MSU any linguistic sequence whose elements appear to be connected microsyntactically, in other words which are linked by a formal relationship of government. We then consider as a series of different MSUs, any sequence whose segments can be related only through the intermediary of shared knowledge. Anaphors can provide important indications of this, since they function as referring expressions presupposing some shared knowledge. Furthermore, as forms linked by an antecedent item, they can indicate the presence or the absence of a boundary between MSUs. Thus, in (7), the associating anaphoric relationship *the family . . . them* presupposes that there has been some intermediate inferential reprocessing of shared knowledge (an inference that the class referred to by *family* consists of a collection of individuals). This type of reference implies, therefore, that *the family* and *their* do not belong to the same MSU or, in other words, that (7) is a two-part period:

(7)   Les rares fois où Paul écrit à sa famille, c'est pour leur demander de l'argent. (Student essay)

On the rare occasions Paul writes to his family, it's to ask them for money.

The fact that left dislocations have been studied most often within the framework of a phrasal grammar has led to the relationship between the two components being seen exclusively from a microsyntactic point of view, with A therefore considered either as an element that has been extracted from Z, or as a peripheral addition that is subordinate to Z. This limiting and distorting view has led to several structurally distinct types of dislocation being confused with each other. It is easy to show, however, that there are at least three kinds of AZ sequences, each with a different construction.

14.2.2 *Type I: binary periods*

Here several features show that in most cases there is no microsyntactic connection between segments A and Z. On the one hand, A is quite often an autonomous NP, not governed in any way by Z or by any of its constituents. The AZ connection is therefore purely semantic and implicit, resting on the simple fact that Z asserts something about the referent in A (a relationship of *aboutness*):

(8) Nous allons essayer de faire des pas chassés avec la corde à sauter/ pour ça il faut savoir que *le pas chassé/*[(A)] *on tape le talon l'un contre l'autre*[(Z)] (speech)

We are going to try and do some chassé steps with the skipping rope/ for that you have to know that *the chassé step/*[(A)] *you knock your heels against each other/*[(Z)]

(9) – Je vais acheter le matelas\
– *Le matelas/ je veux aussi venir* (speech)
– I'm going to buy the mattress\
– *The mattress/ I want to come too* (oral)

Newspaper headlines often have a similar structure, except that Z is then a non-propositional clause of an NP type. For example, the following AZ constructions have the same kind of connection, established purely by informational content:

(10) *Italie: Albanais expulsés*
Italy: Albanians deported

Fiscalité: Danger
Taxation: Danger

Furthermore, Z often contains an anaphor of A. Between A and this anaphor it is possible to observe every variety of anaphoric relation that can exist between one MSU and another: so-called 'faithful' nominal anaphors (as in (11)), anaphors that are hyponyms (as in (12)), recategorizing anaphors (13) and associative anaphors of many kinds (14)–(15). These examples show that the anaphor in this configuration is not bound by A, but is a lexically and inflectionally free referring expression. Thus there is an MSU frontier between A and Z:

(11) – Est-ce que tu demandes la transition avec ce qu'on vient de dire ou est-ce que...
– Non non *la transition/* je cherche pas *la transition* (speech, TV)
– Are you asking for change with what has just been said or are...
– No not *change/* I'm not looking for *change*

(12) *La chasse à l'étudiant,* je pense que la police a toujours considéré *cette activité* comme un sport très agréable. (speech < CREDIF)
Hunting students, I think that the police have always considered *this activity* to be a very pleasant sport.

(13) Ah ben *la Seine/* euh *les quais* les quais maintenant sont canalisés/ vous savez. (speech, radio)
Oh well *the Seine/* eh *the embankments* the embankments are channelled now you know.

As might be expected, when the anaphor is a pronoun it does not appear to be subject to strict grammatical agreement with A, which confirms that it is not a bound form with A as its antecedent (Berrendonner and Reichler–Béguelin 1995):

(14) Le collègue avec qui j'ai fait le spectacle ils [iz] ont adopté deux petits Coréens. (speech)

The colleague with whom I did the show, *they* adopted two little Koreans.

Finally, when the anaphor is an argument of a verb marked for case, A retains the form of a noun phrase but without any case marking (for example, in (15) the noun phrase *La première fille*, 'the first girl', is not preceded by the preposition *à*, 'to'. This absence of case marking shows that A is not an extraposed governed item dependent on the verb in Z. Compare in this respect (15) with (18) below:

(15) La première fille qu'il rencontre, il lui raconte tout ça. (speech)

The first girl he meets, he tells her all that.

So far, then, everything suggests that some AZ occurrences are a series of two microsyntactically independent MSUs, forming a period. At a formal level, this type of period is marked above all by its prosodic contour [A/ Z\]; by its recursive structure, the Z component being itself able to take the AZ form (16); and by the fact that a gesture can take the place of Z (17):

(16) Jacqueline/ sa mère/ la bonne/ elle la lui refile/ (oral < Gadet)

Jacqueline/ her mother/ the maid/ her she's palming her off on him.

(17) C'est le seul que je continue. *Le reste*, < *Gesture: hand thrown back over the shoulder*>
(Calbris 1985: 69)

It's the only one I'm carrying on with. *The rest*, < *Gesture: hand thrown back over the shoulder*>

In terms of semantic structure, we shall say that A, the first MSU, has the function of assigning a *field of interpretation* to Z. The notion of field of interpretation comes from the observation that a large number of semantic operations presuppose an awareness of a valid framework or 'mental space' which limits their application. Such is the case for existential constructions, instructions concerning reference, the attribution of truth values, calculations of relevance, implicit inferences and so on. By their nature all these operations only have meaning in relation to a previously defined cognitive field. Our hypothesis is that in an AZ period, the A section explicitly sets out the field of interpretation which holds for all the semantic operations expressed in Z.

It is an established fact that the A position cannot be occupied by a 'specific' indefinite NP (which introduces the object), nor by an indeterminate quantifier (such as *someone* or *no one*), but only by a referential NP (a definite or indefinite generic). This NP therefore indicates a referent already present in the shared knowledge of the speakers. The A segment has the function of marking this referent as the field of interpretation within which Z has its value or, to put it another way, to transform it from the simple object that it was up to that point, into a new 'mental space'. This is why these binary periods act as special tools in the textual routine of changing the *topic*, which involves taking some 'discourse object' (sometimes the one last mentioned by the interlocutor, as in examples (9), (11) and (19)), and transforming it into a field of interpretation for what follows (Sandfeld 1965: 49). This is also why recursive nestings, as in (16), appear to be particularly co-operative procedures, through which the addressee is progressively guided to the correct field of interpretation, by means of the successive closing off of other fields.

In conclusion, in the binary periods of an AZ type, the A section supplies some meta-discourse information with regard to Z which specifies the field within which it should be interpreted. It follows that although A is microsyntactically autonomous, it is not pragmatically autonomous: for obviously any meta-comment presupposes the existence of the clause on which it comments.

14.2.3 *Type II: dislocation*

Sometimes, however, A is a prepositional phrase where the preposition shows that the grammatical case is dependent on the verb in Z. Since a prepositional phrase with the appropriate case marking is missing from the right of the verb, it is probable that A is nothing more than a fronted segment governed by the verb:

(18)   a. *A* Paris, j'allais tous les quinze jours, *à* Londres, une fois par an. (< Grevisse)

   To Paris, I went every fifteen days, *to* London, once a year.

   b. Il vaut mieux donner aux restos du coeur qu'aux impôts, parce qu'*aux restos du coeur on donne ce qu'on veut.*
   (speech, TV < Sabio 1995)

   It's better to give to soup kitchens than to the tax man, because *to the soup kitchens you give what you want.*

With (18), then, we discover a second type of left dislocation, made up of a single MSU. Its dislocated structure suggests the existence in French microsyntax of an operation which, when applied to a constituent, has the effect of moving it to the beginning of the MSU and isolating it prosodically. A characteristic of this fronting operation is that it cannot apply equally to all types of complements. Sabio (1995: 130) demonstrates that it rarely occurs with accusatives and with certain locatives, and that it is preferred with secondary governed items or with circumstantial adverbials.

Semantically, the fronted constituents are marked as contrastive and, in terms of the theme–rheme distinction as non-rhematic. They do not have the usual characteristics of the rheme part of a clause, for they are beyond the reach of negation or interrogation, as well as of restrictive operations; and they are compatible with a cleft Z that already contains an explicit rheme (for example, *A Pierre, c'est un livre qu'on offrira*, 'To Peter it's a book that we shall give'). On the other hand, their fronting has a 'paradigmaticizing' value in the sense of Nølke (1983): it indicates that the referent of A is contrasted with other potential referents within a system which is assumed to be known. The discourse context often makes the contrast explicit, as in (18).

Although in these type II sequences fronting serves essentially as a way of marking rhetorically a referential contrast, in type I periods the A clause does not seem to have an intrinsic contrastive value of this kind. In fact numerous occurrences can be found where it would be difficult to maintain that A contrasts with anything at all, as in (19):

(19) – Comment est venue l'idée d'édifier ici une réserve, puis un jardin zoologique?
 – *Eh bien, cette idée, elle appartient au maire de Villars-les Dombes.*
 (speech < INA corpus (Institut National de l'Audiovisuel))

 – How did the idea come about to build a reserve here, and then a zoological garden?
 – *Well, this idea, it belongs to the mayor of Villars-les Dombes.*

When type I constructions do occasionally take on a contrastive value, this value does not stem from the literal meaning of the MSU, but instead from a sort of inferential over-interpretation of it, based upon implicit reasoning such as: 'If the speaker defines a field A, s/he excludes everything exterior to it.' In this kind of secondary contrast the referent of A (its complement in the universe) remains by its nature a vague entity; whereas in the contrasts expressed by type II, the object-terms are often entirely defined or definable individuals. Nevertheless in spoken discourse such over-interpretations make it difficult to distinguish a semantic difference between types I and II.

The notions of *theme, topic, focus of attention,* and so on, typically used in descriptive grammars with reference to left dislocation, generally confuse the two functions of defining the field of interpretation and identifying a referential contrast. Our data, as we have seen, suggest on the contrary that we are dealing with two distinct and independent semantic operations which, in standard French at least, are expressed by two different types of syntactic construction (type I versus type II). The traditional vague notion of theme indirectly suggests a psychological approach and is not subtle enough *vis-à-vis* the distinctions inherent in language. It needs to be replaced by a detailed paradigm of logico-semantic operations, and to be clearly defined within a model of shared discourse knowledge within which they function.

14.2.4 *Type I/type II: meta-analyses*

Some AZ sequences are ambiguous, in particular those in which A can be interpreted as a noun phrase subject. We can interpret them equally as type I or type II:

(20) Le problème, il était là. (speech < Berthoud 1996)
The problem, it was there.

These stretches of discourse can be analysed in two different ways: either as binary periods, with the subject of the second clause an empty NP (see section 14.1 above), or as single MSUs, with a fronted NP. This can be represented as follows, with the symbol indicating a pause and the subscript 'i' reflecting the microsyntactic binding and agreement of the clitic with the NP subject.

Type I: $[[\textit{the problem}]_{NP}]_{MSU}$ # $[[\emptyset_i]_{NP}[\textit{it}_i \textit{ was there}]_{VP}]_{MSU}$
Type II: $[[\textit{the problem}_i]_{NP}$ # $[\textit{it}_i \textit{ was there}]_{VP}]_{MSU}$

A similar ambiguity exists in utterances where the initial NP can be taken either as an autonomous clause, or as a fronted governed accusative:

(21) Le parfum, j'adore! (advertisement)
Perfume, I adore!

In (21), the absence of a governed accusative item to the right of the verb can, in fact, be analysed in two ways; first, as resulting from the fronting of the titular NP, leaving empty the accusative position after the verb (type II) and, second, as due to the presence, in this position, of a zero accusative item as a non-bound specifier (*I adore ø* substituting for *I adore it, I adore woody odours*, etc. (Berrendonner 1995)), hence a type I structure.

As occurrences of the type shown in (20) and (21) are by far the most numerous, the I/II opposition is in fact neutralized in the majority of cases. It is only unequivocally marked if A, or its anaphora, is an indirect object. We then have distinctive pairs such as (15) and (18), of the type *Pierre, I tell him everything* versus *To Pierre, I tell everything*. Some ambiguous stretches can of course lose their ambiguity in the presence of contextual clues.

Thus, when an AZ sequence acts as a 'subordinate clause' embedded within an MSU, the odds are that it is a type II sequence. Since recursive embedding of clauses is a commonplace microsyntactic phenomenon, it is out of the question that a period, a non-segmental praxeological unit, should be employed as a constituent at a microsyntactic level. Example (22) thus contains a type II structure (since the fronting of the NP subject takes place within an embedded clause after *that*); whereas example (23) is a type I period (the only hypothesis compatible with the fact that the initial NP is outside the clause):

(22) Il pensait que *le rôle d'un enfant jusqu'à dix ans, c'était de pousser et d'être en bonne santé*. (speech < INA)

He thought that *the role of a child up to the age of ten, it was to grow and to be in good health.*

(23) Cette petite femme blonde, c'est extraordinaire l'énergie qu'elle a! (oral < Borel)

This little blonde woman, it's extraordinary the energy she has!

The application of this criterion is, however, complicated by the fact that some apparently 'main' clauses are in reality more or less lexicalized and have the status of simple modal operators, so that they are not really embedded into the clause which follows (this is probably the case with *you have to know that* in example (8)).

If left dislocation has a clearly contrastive function, we are more likely to consider it as fitting into the type II category. However, this is merely a supposition:

(24) a. (...) *moi*, j'écrirai des comédies et *toi tu* écriras tes rêves. (Flaubert, G. *Correspondance I*, Ed. Pléiade)

(...) *me*, I shall write plays and *you you* will write your dreams.

b. *toi t'as eu des problèmes* avec le frigo *moi* avec le robinet je venais dingue je venais dingue. (speech < Berthoud and Mondada 1991)

you you had problems with the fridge, *me* with the tap I was going crazy I was going crazy.

In most cases, AZ sequences remain structurally ambiguous and the resulting almost imperceptible semantic differences can hardly be relied upon to help speakers differentiate between type I and type II constructions. The result is a meta-analysis where both types of construction are perceived as competing and equally possible analyses of a single syntactic entity. They are, in other words, reduced to the status of *variants* (see Sankoff 1994: 28).

14.2.5 Type III: hybrid structures

There is a third type of AZ construction which has some analogies with each of the other two. Its A segment is a prepositional phrase, with the preposition showing that it is a governed item. Its Z segment, as is the case for type I examples, contains an anaphor of A (at first glance, always a clitic pronoun). This third type also, therefore, is only distinct with indirect objects:

(25) a. *Dans* cet extrait de texte de Paul Nizan, on *y* découvre un exposé sur la vie d'un apprenti dans cette société industrielle. (student essay)

   In this extract from a text by Paul Nizan, we *there* discover an account of the life of an apprentice in this industrial society.

   b. *Sur* le sentier pedestre qui conduit les promeneurs du gîte d'Aillères au sommet de la Berra, on *y* découvre à mi-parcours un banc installé à l'ombre des sapins. (newspaper)

   On the pedestrian footpath which takes walkers from the Aillères inn to the top of the Berra, one discovers *there* halfway up a bench under the shade of the pine trees.

   c. Mais *de* ce grand voyage, il n'*en* revint jamais. (student essay)
   But *from* this great journey, he never came back *from it*.

   d. (Il y a ...) un élément passif, et (...) un premier élément actif ou dynamique. *A* cet élément dynamique, Guillaumin *lui* propose un rôle déclencheur ou impulseur. (PhD thesis)

   (There is ...) a passive element, and (...) a primary active or dynamic element. *To* this dynamic element, Guillaumin proposes *for it* a triggering or impetus-providing role.

What is most striking in these examples is that their structure is somewhat contradictory. On the one hand, the preposition marks the A segment as governed by the verb in Z. But on the other hand it cannot be governed by this verb since the relevant position in Z is already filled by an appropriate clitic pronoun. We cannot overcome this difficulty by assuming that the clitic marks an inflected object, as although clitic doubling in French is attested for subjects (see (4) above), it does not generally exist for items that are governed: we rarely find examples such as, **Je le vois quelqu'un*, literally 'I him see someone' or **Je la vois une voiture*, literally 'I it see a car', even in dialects. The pleonasms inherent in the examples in (25) are therefore well and truly structural inconsistencies and need to be explained as such.

We propose that type III cases be seen as hybrid constructions which exist as a result of contamination from types I and II. By this we mean an operation such as:

[ABCE] + [ACDE] → [ABCDE]

That is to say, they result from the joining of two sequences whose surface structures are at the same time both common and differentiated, on the one condition that their word order be compatible, and without regard for their respective syntactic structures. The resulting hybrid thus consists of an amalgam of the morphosyntactic markers belonging to each one of the mixed sequences, without guaranteeing the structural consistency of the whole string. If we assume that type III dislocations are hybrid forms formed in this way, borrowing the preposition of the A part of type II and the clitic of the Z section of type I, we can explain quite satisfactorily the pleonastic and structurally contradictory character of sequences of this type.

Furthermore, the hybridization explanation that we have offered implies that those speakers who produce type III forms are aware of the rules which allow the generation of types I and II, whereas the reverse is not necessarily the case. This explains why the grammaticality of types I and II is not generally called into question, whereas that of type III structures tends to be disputed: some speakers perceive them as ungrammatical pleonasms (Grevisse-Goosse 1986: 508), while others use them without thinking they are doing anything untoward.

Our hypothesis also explains the semantic output of III, which is sometimes that of type I and at other times that of type II. Compare, for example, (26), where A establishes a field of interpretation and (27), where A sets out a contrastive reference:

(26) Bilinguisme à Burmarima.
Au VIIe siècle avant J.-C., *dans la cité mise au jour au nord de la Syrie, on y pratiquait deux langues.* (newspaper)
Bilingualism in Burmarina.
In the VIIth century BC, *in the city to be found in the north of Syria, two languages were spoken there.*

(27) Il parlait très peu de ses souffrances... il les racontait à l'oncle de Charpenay, mais *à nous il nous disait de bien prier pour lui.* (letter, 1915)
He spoke very little of his suffering... he told Charpenay's uncle about it, but *to us he told us to pray for him.*

Finally, the hybridization hypothesis allows us to suggest a pragmatic explanation for the existence of type III constructions, which appear as a consequence of the meta-analysis of I/II. Their main characteristic, in fact, is that in the indirect object examples the remaining visible differences between I and II are neutralized; the meta-analysis generalizes the lack of a distinction between them (or rather between the semantic operations that they express) for all subsequent uses of dislocations. Type III sequences therefore function as analogical regularizers: a meta-analysis may not differentiate between I and II, where the marking has been neutralized, but these sequences create a differentiation by accumulating markers from both. They appear, therefore, to be the key piece of a grammatical variant within which the I/II opposition is totally abandoned.

The hybridization phenomenon observed here is of crucial importance for a theory of variation envisaged as an internal dynamic of linguistic systems. Similar combinations of a meta-analysis and a pleonasm are found in several unstable areas of French syntax. We are therefore tempted to see this as an important regularity in variation, and to propose (28) as a general rule:

(28)   Any partial meta-analysis of two structures X and Y goes hand in hand with the complementary existence of a hybrid which combines markers from X and Y.

That is to say that if, at a given stage of the grammar of a language, a significant X/Y opposition has little phonetic substance and is often neutralized, a competing grammar appears in which the opposition is reduced to a single architerme, partly apparent in meta-analytical forms, and partly in hybrids of X and Y.

14.2.6 Summary

To summarize, we can say that the substructure of left dislocation in French causes two grammatical variants, G1 and G2, to enter into competition with each other. In the G1 variant, the two semantic operations of firstly limiting the field of interpretation (O_I) and of secondly indicating a contrastive reference (O_{II}) constitute a significant opposition, and are distinctively marked: one at a macrosyntactic level by type I periodic structures; the other at a microsyntactic level by fronting (type II dislocated MSUs). However, there is a vast class of occurrences where this distinctive opposition is neutralized. In the competing G2 variant the opposition is reduced to a single syncretic operation (O_{III}), expressed either by neutralized stretches of discourse or by hybrid strings (type III). This can be shown as in Figure 14.1 (overleaf).

14.3   Back to the normative paradox

It is tempting to relate these distinctions to the conflicting norms discussed earlier. A likely hypothesis would be that periodic type I structures, felt to characterize a relatively colloquial usage, are responsible for the negative value judgments, whereas type II dislocations, perceived as an oratory device from a prestigious style of speaking or writing, give rise to positive judgements. This explanation assumes, on the one hand, that there is an objective 'stylistic' correlation at the origin of

TAMING THE VERNACULAR

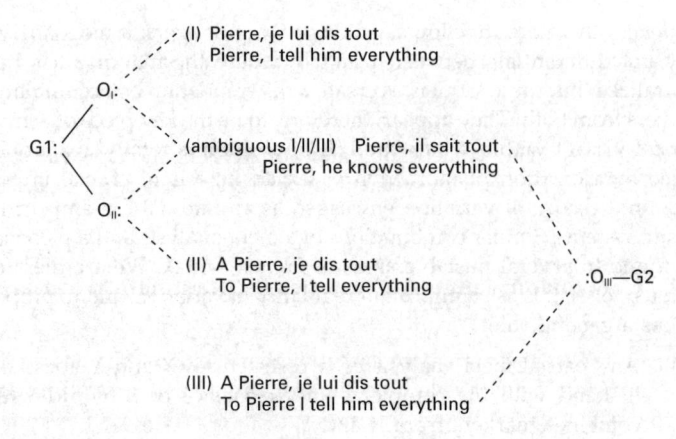

```
              (I) Pierre, je lui dis tout
                  Pierre, I tell him everything
         Oᵢ:
  G1:          (ambiguous I/II/III)   Pierre, il sait tout
                                      Pierre, he knows everything
         Oᵢᵢ:
                                                                  :Oᵢᵢᵢ—G2
              (II) A Pierre, je dis tout
                   To Pierre, I tell everything


              (III) A Pierre, je lui dis tout
                    To Pierre I tell him everything
```

Figure 14.1

normative imagery, which assigns types I and II to two different modes of interaction or to two 'linguistic markets' (Bourdieu 1982) which make unequal demands on speakers. As a result the two types of dislocation acquire different connotations and values. This explanation also implies that the values attached to I and II may accumulate and become mixed together in speakers' conscious awareness. Given that it is often difficult to distinguish the two types formally or semantically, it is not surprising to find mixed feelings of this sort. Nor is it surprising that the structural meta-analysis described in section 14.2.4 is accompanied by a confusion of the styles associated with each structure.

There is some rudimentary quantitative evidence that supports this hypothesis: type I occurrences are relatively abundant in all oral varieties, but almost completely absent in writing (except in the case of the written representation of speech). Type II occurrences, however, are far more rare in general, yet in writing they seem to be relatively well attested. This unequal distribution suggests that behind the confusion of types I and II in speakers' awareness, there lies a separation in their practice, which depends on the nature of the interaction.

Type III constructions, as far as we can tell without having recourse to statistical evidence, appear to be used by lone speakers placed in a discourse situation where they have to keep a strict check on their language: pupils in test situations, journalists, non-literary scientific writers. This leads one to suspect that hypercorrection could be at work in situations of linguistic insecurity such as these. Insecurity in the use of these features can be linked to the fact that contradictory normative judgements are made about the same utterances, making it difficult to be sure about the style to which they belong. Speakers who perceive constructions I and II as variants and who realize that mixed value judgements are made about them, take a great risk when they have to choose between them since they do not know which is the most appropriate, sociolinguistically, in any given situation. The usual response to this type of uncertainty is to use the two competing variants jointly, that is to say to use a *variational syllepsis*. The syntactic operation of hybridization provides the means for this. This is why syntactic hypercorrections so often take the form of a pleonasm.

14.4 Conclusion: language varieties vs grammatical variants

The first lesson to be drawn from these observations is that the categories instituted by the normative *doxa*, whether they are of a descriptive or a normative nature, reflect neither the variational structure of language nor the reality of sociolinguistic practice except in an extremely misrepresentative way.

One of the main causes of this inadequacy are the grammatical notions current in the dominant meta-discourse. Approximative and more or less arbitrary, they impose a way of seeing language on us which does not necessarily allow us to identify the forms which are actually present. This accounts for the fact that all the official doctrine regarding AZ sequences is presented in terms of the sentence, and as a consequence sees only a single and unique syntactic item, usually referred to as a 'split sentence'. We hope that we have demonstrated, however, that if we arm ourselves with the necessary descriptive tools (i.e. the distinction between micro- and macro-syntax) we can distinguish at least three different syntactic constructions here. It goes without saying that if we confuse these three entities we will be unable to grasp the variational structure of the system of which they belong, and we risk not even suspecting that they exist.

Furthermore, the axiological categories or 'varieties of language' which are used by the *doxa* appear to be eminently opportunist and vague. Overlaps and fuzzy margins are tolerated, and this gives rise to situations where left dislocation is simultaneously classed as 'standard' and 'nonstandard' usage (using labels such as 'colloquial', 'familiar' or 'spoken' French). The range that these pseudo-dialects cover thus escapes any precise definition, for they cannot be mapped out in terms of linguistic variables nor in terms of the sociological variables with which they could be correlated. At most the labels reflect an awareness, albeit confused and necessarily contradictory, of some of the connotations with which they are associated. An entity such as 'standard French' thus appears to be something of a myth: the normative categorizations do not help to define it, and it is difficult to see what other criteria could be invoked in order to fix suitable limits *a priori*.

The notion of 'variety of language' itself is perhaps the most inadequate of all, together with the naïvely extensional concept of variation that it implies. Underlying the metaphor is the idea that a language can be divided into several 'treasures' with rival forms, held by different groups or competing with each other for speakers to draw from as they choose. A language would then be no more than a juxtaposition of dialects, and a dialect only a collection of allophones, allomorphs, allo-sentences, and so on. However, in the system that we have been exploring, we find that at the level of syntax the variants that occur are not competing forms or alternative expressions, but rival *grammars* (G1 and G2), i.e. different modes of structuring imposed upon the same area within a given system. What is more, it appears that certain forms can be generated, with a different analysis, from several of these grammars, if not from all of them. It is not possible therefore to consider syntactic variation as a simple collection of dialect drawers, each containing its characteristic forms and put together on the basis of their identical connotations. We should substitute for the notion of *varieties of language*, inherited from a commonsense view of variation, the notion of *grammar variants*. The latter cannot be identified simply by classifying occurrences of different features according to style: instead it is necessary to discover what, in the system of rules and operations that generates them, provides the parameters, i.e. the under-specified, non-fixed and hence not always visible elements (here, this was the process of hybridization, which may or may not be part of the grammar; and the paradigm of semantic operations, which may or may not distinguish O_I from O_{II}).

Finally, if the axiological categories that the normative meta-discourse projects onto the language appear for the most part arbitrary *vis-à-vis* the expression of its internal variation, and if the varieties that it legitimizes are but pseudo-variants, it goes without saying that they cannot be considered as reliable indicators of the structure of language. Any theory of variation which assumes them to be valid *a priori* would not achieve its goal. Through our analysis of left dislocation we hope to have shown that it was not only possible but also advantageous to abandon any division into dialects during the gathering and classification of our data, and instead to deal with the data from a functional perspective only. Doubtless the notion of dialect should be refounded one of these days. But it must be based upon a rational theory, and not upon intuitions that we have unconsciously inherited from the layperson's commonsense ideas about language.

References

Bally, Charles 1994. *Linguistique générale et linguistique française*. Berne: Franke (4th edition 1965).

Berrendonner, Alain. 1990. Pour une macro-syntaxe, *Travaux de Linguistique* 21: 25–36, Gand: Duculot.

Berrendonner, Alain 1992. 'Périodes', *La temporalité du discours*, H. Parret (ed.), Louvain: Louvain University Press, 47–61.
Berrendonner, Alain 1993. Sujets zéro. In S. Karolak and T. Muryn (eds) *Complétude et incomplétude dans les langues romanes et slaves. Actes du VI colloque international, Cracovie, Sept. 1991*, 17–45, WSP, Cracow.
Berrendonner, Alain 1995. Redoublement actantiel et nominalisations, *Scolia* 5: 217–44. Strasbourg: Université des Sciences humaines.
Berrendonner, Alain and Reichler-Béguelin, Marie-José 1989. Décalages: les niveaux de l'analyse linguistique, *Langue française* 81: 99–125.
Berrendonner, Alain and Reichler-Béguelin, Marie-José 1995. Accords associatifs, *Cahiers de praxématique* 24: 1–25.
Berthoud, Anne-Claude 1996. *Paroles à propos: approche énonciative et interactive du topic*, Paris: Ophrys.
Berthoud, Anne-Claude and Mondada, Lorenza 1991. Modes d'introduction et de négociation du *topic* dans l'interaction verbale. In: D. Véronique and R. Vion, *Modèles de l'interaction verbale*, Aix-en-Provence: Université de Provence, 277–303.
Blanche-Benveniste, Claire 1989. Constructions verbales 'en incise' et rection faible des verbes. *Recherches sur le Français Parlé* 9: 53–71.
Blanche-Benveniste, Claire et al, 1990. *Le français parlé, études grammaticales*, Paris: Editions du CNRS.
Blasco, Mylène and Cappeau, Paul 1993. Les relations clitique/lexique. Etude de deux cas particuliers, *Recherches sur le français parlé* 12: 35–58.
Bourdieu, Pierre 1982. *Ce que parler veut dire. L'économie des échanges linguistiques*, Paris: Fayard.
Calbris, Geneviève 1985. Geste et parole, *Langue française* 68: 66–84.
Dauzat, Albert 1946. *Voyage à travers les mots*, Paris: Bourrelier & Cie.
Gadet, Françoise 1989. *Le français ordinaire*. Paris: A. Colin.
Gadet, Françoise 1992. *Le français populaire*, Paris: P.U.F., Que-sais-je No. 1172.
Grevisse-Goosse, André 1986. *Le bon usage*, Louvain: Duculot (12th edition).
Nølke, Henning 1983. *Les adverbes paradigmatisants: fonction et analyse*. Revue romane No. spécial 23. Copenhague: Akademisk Forlag.
Sabio, Frédéric 1995. Micro-syntaxe et macro-syntaxe: l'exemple des 'compléments antéposés' en français, *Recherches sur le français parlé* 13: 111–55.
Sandfeld, Kristian 1965. *Syntaxe du français contemporain, I, Les pronoms*, Paris: Champion.
Sankoff, David 1994. Social interest, Linguistic indifference, *Culture* XIV (2): 27–37.
Wunderli, Peter 1987. *L'intonation des séquences extraposées en français*, Tübingen: G. Narr.

CHAPTER 15

Dialect variation as a consequence of standardization

Dieter Wanner

15.1 Introduction

It is not entirely clear what kinds and what degree of variation syntax admits in (dialectally) related instances.* Morphology and phonology, and especially also lexicology, find themselves in much more secure territory. The following sketch of the Null Subject phenomenon in French and Italian intends to explore this relationship for syntax. While this discussion may sketch the general train of thought followed here, the considerations will not be able to go beyond the surface in addressing the many intriguing questions raised by this topic. This chapter takes the view that dialects may in principle share their syntax, showing strong cohesiveness with the overall grouping into a linguistic area, e.g. French or, more controversially, Italian. On the other hand, other forces and processes tear at the fabric of dialectal cohesion, in particular standardization. Standardization may drive an important wedge between one privileged (or victimized) variety and the other dialects. A postulated syntactic cohesiveness between dialects and a standard language does not yet justify attributing status as a true system to such a configuration, where dialectal variation, stylistic and register differences are all essentially interwoven. Rather, it seems more profitable to stress the open-ended relationship between a dialect as nonstandard language (in the diaphasic and diatopic dimensions; cf. Weinreich 1954) and 'its' standard. The linguistic knowledge of dialect and standard is individually acquired and unpredictably elaborated, with more or less competency, depending on the individual speaker. The attempt to impose rigid patterning on these competing and adjacent linguistic subsystems may misrepresent the reality of the available data. I will therefore try to elaborate the general considerations with a case study to demonstrate a complex and shifting relationship between standard and dialect(s) in the diachronic perspective.

15.2 Variation and change

Variation and change have long been recognized as connected phenomena. The only caveat is the unilaterality of the implicational chain: change implies variation, but the inversion does not hold in any relevant sense; i.e. the existence of variation does not allow the observer to conclude to the emergence of eventual change. The variation permitted within a dialectal domain may be considerable, yet this does not imply emerging linguistic change splitting the closer-knit dialect grouping into a looser bundle of similar languages, at least not as long as the social frame conditions are preserved.

Change, deriving from previous variation, is by necessity socially implemented (cf. Labov 1993). The field of social forces is uneven and shows fault lines which are not connected to formal linguistic dimensions. Thus changes deriving from such an implementation will appear highly unstable in the external view of the observer, the historical linguist. It is one of the main experiences of any practising historical linguist that the famous regularity hypothesis of neogrammarian descent and structural and post-structural reaffirmation leaves much to be desired, at least in the classical fields of phonology and morphology. Syntax, syntactic variation and change take place within the same constellation of forces, but due to the deep cognitive embedding of syntactic principles their manifestations are less variable between core dialects and the peripheral ones. The situation is actually somewhat more complicated, since the unifying forces shaping syntactic expression do not find an even repercussion in the materials available from dialects and standard languages. On the one hand, syntax is at least in part functional, and thus not freely variable. Syntax as the formal aspect of the organization of thought can thus be expected to yield a basic parallelism between dialects and the standard version of a language. On the other hand, the textual and medial dimensions usually separating standard from dialectal manifestations argue for a differential distribution of syntactic procedures between peripheral and central or standard dialects.

15.3 Syntax and dialects

The external perception of salient dialect characteristics is unevenly distributed over the linguistic components. It is usually rather keen for what concerns the lexicon, and may reach oversensitive heights for specific 'accent' and intonation phenomena. However, the sensitivity towards dialectal differentiation is generally low in syntax, except for whole expressions which thereby fall back to the lexical domain. Beyond this, much syntactic awareness concerns linearization as the only observationally prominent aspect of syntax. It is also telling that dialect classification is usually not carried out on the basis of syntactic features.

To flesh out the blunt question on syntactic variation across dialects, the following short panorama will be centred on the formal perspective. Syntax is expected to be differentially variable in its hypothesized components. The Phrase Structure rules (1) are most stable, since they provide the essentially immutable portion of Universal Grammar (Chomsky 1988).

(1) VP → V NP (PP)   Specific verb phrase rule
     X" → Y" X'   general X-Bar rule for maximal projection
     X' → X° Y"   general X-Bar rule for middle level

Such rules and schemata are postulated as invariable, except for the potential controlling aspects of directionality, iteration and similar application parameters. The various principles and modules, e.g. Binding in (2), are also expected to be affected only to a minor degree, since they carry out the role of codifying some general properties of human cognition, e.g. reference.

(2) Binding Theory (loose reformulation)
     A: **Reflexive** (anaphor) bound in smallest clause context (i.e. a reflexive pronoun must find its antecedent in the same simple clause).
     B: **Nonreflexive pronoun** (pronominal) bound outside the smallest clause context (i.e. a non-reflexive pronoun can refer to an antecedent in a preceding clause, or to an entity outside the direct discourse, but relevant for speaker and listener).

Again, the Binding Principles A and B as such are not subject to variation insofar as they embody basic operating conditions of human referential cognition. Yet the steering aspects, i.e. identification and localization of the clause boundary setting off one binding domain from another, may vary across languages and in diachrony (i.e. what it means to be 'within the same clause/outside the smallest clause context' in (2)).

There is potential variability for the so-called parameters, each one with its individual binary value setting (3). Their overarching, holistic reorganization of analytical options makes for an interesting segmentation of otherwise unstructured observations, but the principle organizing the data, the parameter, is considerably abstract. Basically the parameters allow for a principled description of the differences setting languages apart.

(3) a. *Parameters*, e.g. Null Subject, cliticness, Verb Second
     b. presumably constituting a fixed set
     c. variable according to binary value ('+' or '−'), in conjunction with the actual data from a given language.

Still lower in the hierarchy are the morphosyntactic principles such as Agreement (4) which easily permit variations from system to system, with direct surface repercussions. Agreement is analytically true to surface structure; agreement helps the speaker to scan and segment the linear speech chain into a structured, syntactic representation.

(4) a. *Agreement*, e.g. /V-subj/, /V-obj/, /N-Det/, /N-Adj/, etc.
   b. Applicable features are taken from a language specific, but limited set: person, number, gender; time, aspect, mood, voice, etc.
   c. Variable regarding
   - active syntactic configurations of agreement (adjective–noun shows number/gender agreement in Spanish, but not in English)
   - morphosyntactic material
   - specific conditions of realization.

Finally, the grammar component most easily exhibiting variation and thus dialect differentiation is the lexicon. It may be thought of as a partially ordered deposit of 'idiosyncratic' information including item-specific aspects of meaning, morphological and syntactic peculiarities, phonological content, lexico-semantic frames, etc.; cf. (5) for a schematic example. The variability of the lexicon is only constrained by the pragmatic and semantic restrictions imposed on cognitive apprehension (cf. Clark 1993).

(5)   Fr./don/$_{stem}$, 'to give', [Agent V Theme Goal], conj. I, ...

In general, variation and change naturally apply to peripheral, accessible portions of grammar (parameter settings, agreement, lexicon) rather than to the basic structures and their systemic cohesion (phrase structure and basic principles).

15.4 Other dimensions of change: grammaticalization and standardization

Grammaticalization lies outside the structural web and atomistic item-and-principle domain of Universal Grammar plus systematic parametrization; in fact, it cross-cuts these dimensions at an angle. The scales of grammaticalization are independent of their single-language constitution. In contrast to the formal linguistic dimensions, grammaticalization paths seem to derive from broader symbolic tendencies which are not limited to language as such, but which, in contact with linguistic material, are claimed to achieve a certain independence of existence and operationality. According to Bybee *et al.* (1994: 9–26) the recurring patterns of change are determined, among others, by a limited range of potential source materials; they show unidirectionality of change excluding developments going in the opposite direction. Grammaticalization is restricted by universal paths of diachronic development, i.e. not just any development counts. Reduction processes work in parallel on semantic and phonological dimensions.

Grammaticalization amounts to symbolic representational standardization, and thereby is not really specific to language, since it is derived from non-linguistic criteria. The concept of grammaticalization is statistical, extending over the possible scalar values of the specific grammaticalization path and over the totality of the linguistic productions of a linguistic domain and community. The single case of a local development becomes undecidable for the observer as to whether it fits into a broader development of grammaticalization, and it is not decisive from the perspective of individual knowledge by a speaker. Grammaticalization provides an overarching viewpoint of metachronic, *post hoc* recognition, typically useful in a taxonomic classification of change. Grammaticalization belongs to the category of the elusive drift notion, rather clearly perceptible for the external observer, but not directly related to any language internal properties of individualized import.

It might appear that grammaticalization and standardization could complement each other or even share much in accounting for specific forms of variation and change. They both reduce the free expanse of linguistic variation to narrower patterns and less indeterminate results: full grammaticalization leads to renewed regularity, and standardization eliminates non-functionalized variation. There is, however, less commonality than meets the eye. Standardization as an expression of language normativity operates under a specific sociolinguistic cover which sets it apart from grammaticalization. It has variable reach and range for 'dialects' and in this sharply contrasts with grammaticalization as a functional linguistic principle equally applicable to any individuated linguistic system. Standardization as a complex sociolinguistic process of evaluation depends on the dialectal speech communities accepting the efforts of standardization. These become visible and are usually admitted by the speaker in the more accessible domains of language. This also applies to the opposite reaction of decided resistance to interference by standardization.

At the basis of this main effect of standardization stand two principles proposed as cornerstones of First Language Acquisition (Clark 1993), i.e. the Principle of Contrast and the Principle of Conventionality. While these guideposts receive their primary justification from the considerations of the constraints applicable in infant language learning, they are to be understood as fundamental modes of operation of human cognition at any point in life. In particular, the requirements of standardization find an ideal explanation in these two steering principles. The first construct postulates that any two forms differentiated on the surface are to be taken as differing in meaning; i.e. form makes a direct contribution to the functionality of language and its use. The second

DIALECT VARIATION AND STANDARDIZATION

and complementary postulate of complementarity stabilizes the attribution of meaning to form by giving precedence to the already established links between form /F$_i$/ and meaning 'M$_j$'. Together the two principles guarantee the rational and efficient accumulation of a linguistic repertoire for the infant language learner. In an extended perspective, these basic principles assure continued intersubjective comprehension in more advanced language stages. In a more peripheral sense, they also guarantee the functionality of standardization as a linguistic process of relevance. If the two principles of Contrast and Conventionality first apply in child language learning for sorting out rough contrasts, in the more conscious context of adult language standardization they are concerned with the finer shadings of meaning differentiation. In this way Contrast and Conventionality redistribute implications and connotations of a given set of closely related expressions; they are responsible for the extreme rarity of true synonyms, i.e. equivalent and always interchangeable expressions. Try any pair of 'same' words or expressions; they will always fail some substitution test, e.g. *belief/thought, to end/stop* or *to end/finish*. A particularly interesting example is the secondary distribution of the two Modern English modal auxiliaries *shall* and *will* (Arnovick, in this volume). Standardization tried to establish a constant, rational difference between the two variants, using finer meaning distinctions (intention vs simple posteriority) cross-classified with grammatical person, in order to establish some standardized paradigm of the type *I shall* vs *you, (s)he etc. will* for futurity as opposed to *I will* vs *you, (s)he etc. shall* for (futurate) intention. Even though this artificial regulation missed the description of any natural state of English at any time, and failed to entrench itself as a firm standardization overall, it did have its effect on certain registers of Modern English. Its strict attribution of value within context is thus an example of a sophisticated standardization episode, and it illustrates the validity of the principles of Contrast and Conventionality as extending to adult language operation.

Standardization can be subjected to a rough, but sufficient, taxonomy for present purposes. The evident categories are the natural opposites of how the interconnection between two related phenomena can be manipulated: either by increasing the difference between the standard variety and the so-called dialect, or by diminishing the distance. The typical increase in distance seems to imply the existence of two strong linguistic environments, i.e. the nonstandard dialect versus the dialect that has been elevated to norm. Strength probably translates into a relative independence of the two linguistic practices from each other. We will look at such a constellation with the Non-Null Subject syndrome below.

If standardization leads to a decrease of distance between the participating systems, the strength relation requires that the dialect be considerably weaker in social staying power than the standard variety: in fact, the nonstandard dialect acquires standard features not previously grounded in its naturally transmitted form. The nonstandard dialect progressively becomes a derivative of the standard variety in that at least some of its characteristics can only be described in parallel with the standard dialect. Where the information is accessible, a historical discrepancy is then recorded in this respect, since the same property previously obeyed constraints not commensurate with the situation of the eventual standard dialect. The examples are many, given that this is the classical mechanism by which the rich dialectal landscape of a language area is reduced to minor local deviations from a strong standard. This usually affects the phonetic, lexical and phraseological levels, but much less the more deeply embedded linguistic properties of morphology and syntax.

15.5 The Null-Subject phenomenon

At this point, it will be profitable to look at a more elaborate example of syntactic differentiation between dialect and standard language. The Null-Subject phenomenon will be investigated for its cross-dialectal realization in Italian, a case of strong, diverging development. A language such as English is said to be a Non-Null-Subject language, since a normal declarative clause requires one form or another of the subject NP to be expressed (*she/ Beth/ my neighbour next door is looking for another job*, but never **is looking for another job*). Spanish is a typical Null-Subject language, where the overt appearance of a subject expression (other than the verbal ending) implies some degree of emphasis or contrast on the identity of the subject. Consider *Magda cree que (ella) no gana bastante* 'Magda thinks that she does not earn enough', where the optional *ella* 'she' implies some insistence; omitting the pronoun in English would however be totally unacceptable.

The original view of this phenomenon in a formal framework attempted to deal with it in terms of a high-level parametric abstraction, i.e. [±Null Subject], where the unmarked value would need to be 'plus' as in the majority of the world's languages. Later complications in the expanding range of data gradually forced the analysis to split the single parameter into partially independent subparameters (the situation reached by the time of Jaeggli and Safir 1989). At present, only a syndrome remains with a clear core opposition between the expression vs omission of the subject. In the Non-Null-Subject languages (English, German and French) the subject slot is obligatorily occupied by a syntactically active element, whereas Spanish, Italian and Modern Greek with optional occupation of the subject position represent the widely attested Null-Subject languages. Apart from this polar opposition, the borderlines are more complex. The Northern Italian dialects, for example, attain morphological, but not syntactic status as Non-Null-Subject languages (Brandi and Cordin 1989, Renzi 1992, Vanelli *et al.* 1985). The appeal of the original binary differentiation lay in the strong correlation of the central Null-Subject status with otherwise independent properties: (a) 'rich' inflection, (b) free subject–verb inversion, and (c) the *that*-trace effect. The constitution of such an indivisible block of properties makes for a significant hypothesis to the extent that the correlations can be accounted for in an analytical model (see Wanner 1993 for broader discussion).

The first component, rich inflection, was never more than an intuitive, but imprecise, differentiation between the polar models, such as English versus Spanish, regarding the expression of subject congruence in the verb endings. The idea is old: essential morphosyntactic information needs to be kept intact for informational purposes. Thus English depends on expressing the subject through an element of autonomous syntactic status given its morphological insufficiency in the verb. On the other hand, Spanish already takes care of this function through its 'rich' verbal morphology. As clear as this sounds in prototypical cases, it leaves no room for understanding the transition that brought the Null-Subject language of Old French to the intermediate plateau of Middle French (less than obligatory subject expression) and finally to the Early Modern French constitution of a classical Non-Null-Subject syndrome. The difficulty with this transition is the partial conservation of subject inflection on the verb down to present-day French. The specifically transitional stages of the sixteenth and early seventeenth centuries still preserved more of the verbal subject inflection than the modern language, and by any standard significantly more than the corresponding English language forms. Rather than clearing up the Null-Subject status of a language, the 'rich inflection' feature creates difficulties, leading to the recognition that subject clitics (such as the present-day French pronoun *je*) are independent of rich inflection. Modern Florentine has rich inflection intact and has subject clitics, thus denying a direct functional connection as envisaged in the original claim for correlate (a).

Free subject–verb inversion does not fare much better; it is also independent of Null-Subject properties, and requires a finer gradation than a simple toggle switch. The surface impressionistic positioning of a few languages on the upper scale of subject inversion in (6) indicates the difficulty in its correlation with a strict Null-Subject dichotomy as shown in the bottom scale; consider in particular the split nature of German in this context. Free subject inversion is found in the Spanish example (7a), where the postverbal subject NP *Pedro* does not receive any special emphasis and represents old, weakly topical information. In a similar sense the German Verb Second arrangement in (8) is dynamically neutral. In Spanish, the focused subject NP *Pedro* in clause final position in (7b), however, is not in the same sense a case of free subject inversion due to its emphatic content (indicated by capitals in the gloss).

(6)   Free Inversion---No Inversion

Spanish, **German** > Italian > Portuguese > French > English

| Spanish, Italian, Portuguese | **German**, French, English |
| Null Subject | Non-Null Subject |

(7) a. *Me dijo* **Pedro** *todo lo que quería saber.*
    'Pedro told me ALL I wanted to know.'
  b. *Todo lo que quería saber, me lo dijo* **Pedro**.
    'All I wanted to know, I was told by PEDRO.'

(8) *Da fragte* **sie** *sich dann endlich, ob sich das überhaupt lohnen würde.*
    'Then she finally asked herself whether this might be worth the effort.'

The entire complex of 'free subject inversion' has recently shifted out of focus due to the significantly richer structural options available in current Phrase Structure models for subject NPs: VP-internal subject, Verb Second phenomena (as in German), obligatory V movement, special conditions controlling the licensing of subject NPs in specific positions (cf. Fontana 1993).

The third correlate, the *that*-trace effect, does not stand up to closer scrutiny with regard to speaker judgements (Sobin 1987). The ambivalent linguistic argumentation surrounding this rather elusive phenomenon will not be able to clear up the Null-Subject phenomenon in any significant way, so that we can forgo further discussion here.

15.6 Null-Subject divergence between standard and dialect

The historical origin of some Non-Null-Subject situations can be controlled quite closely, and this within the same linguistic subfamily of French and Italian. In principle, the French development is in close parallel to the Northern Italian and Modern Florentine dialects, while at the same time these two groups are frequently seen as instantiating two opposite values on the Null-Subject scale, i.e. Non-Null Subject for French vs standard Null Subject for the Italian dialects. The diachronic mechanism of reaching the modern instantiations in both groups belongs to the morphophonological level of creating unstressed, unemphatic, redundant subject pronouns from full subject pronoun forms. Originally free and referentially dynamically conditioned subject pronouns shift towards cliticization by progressive reduction of their morphophonological substance (visibly shortened forms) and progressive fixation of their place of occurrence next to the verb. This fixed-order juxtaposition is interpreted as a syntactic phenomenon in French, where this proto-subject clitic element continues to occupy the syntactic position of the argument canonically identified with the subject. In Florentine (which may stand for the entire Northern Italian/Florentine group) the same NP derived proto-subject clitic in the same fixed preverbal situation receives an interpretation as morphological marker, no longer occupying the syntactic subject position. The transition and derivation paths in Francien (the medieval dialect of the Île-de-France) and Florentine are identical in their morphosyntax: a progressive increase in environments and incidence of frequent to normal to obligatory subject pronoun exposure (Hirschbühler 1989). The data do not yield any clues as to the point and manner of differentiation between the syntactic and the morphological solutions in the two languages other than that the Florentine and Northern Italian developments are considerably later than the Francien evolution. In Medieval Florentine documents, down to the fifteenth century, the short forms appear frequently (e.g. *i'* for *io*, and *la* for *ella*, *e'*, *gl'*, *gli* for *egli* in different phonological contexts, also confirmed by metrical restrictions), but without any predictability or regularity. From the fifteenth century onward, a strong acceleration takes place with regard to the frequency and regularity of these now clearly clitic elements. They seem to jump from optional 'simple' clitic status and phonological reduction to overwhelming morphological regularity. The general pattern of degradation leads from a free syntactic form to eventual morphological status, as is visible from the developments of the article, object clitics, and compound tense formation in the Romance languages (and elsewhere).

In terms of a grammaticalization analysis, the French and Florentine subject clitic evolutions would represent two different stages on a grammaticalization path for weak referential elements in argument function. The difficulty concerns the connection between the free form and the morphological or syntactic clitic. If they lie on the same pathway, the Florentine type is more developed than the French one along this axis; but this would have happened without Florentine ever passing through the intermediate syntactic stage French represents. If the single grammaticalization pathway is unrealistic, and we need to posit two (or more) diverging spokes toward a differentiated periphery, the appeal of the grammaticalization analysis is lost. What remains are two trajectories for reduction without an *a priori* basis for distinction; grammaticalization will then be not more than a tendency towards making constructions simpler and more rigid.

Could the difference between the Francien to Modern Standard French and the Northern Italian and Florentine evolutions be associated with the degree of standardization, i.e. of functional fixation of their grammars? The relationship between Florentine and Modern Standard Italian is the usual major typological split between local dialect and supraregional language. The intriguing aspect of the question is the fact that Florentine is the genetic base for standard Italian, even though the two are presently considerably removed from each other, standard Italian having acquired a much less regional Florentine or Tuscan aspect than even fifty or one hundred years ago (de Mauro 1970). Yet standard French and the so-called *français avancé* (one commonly spoken version of modern French without any stylistic or social aspirations) are also drifting apart at increasing speed, and exactly in the domain which interests us here: marking of argument roles on the verb. There is a much noted tendency in *français avancé* to construct the proposition as a verbally based core with all argument functions expressed by pronouns, while the lexical content of these arguments may be delivered by the corresponding full NPs somehow arranged around this self-contained core, as in (9). This procedure also affects the subject in the same way (see Ashby 1988, Lambrecht 1981; see also Berrendonner and Reichler-Béguelin, this volume).

(9) a. *Pierre/lui, il la lui a donnée, à Pauline, la bicyclette.*
 Pierre/he he it her has given to Pauline the bike.
 'Pierre gave Pauline the bike.'
 b. *Elle, elle$_{cl}$ viendra demain.*
 She she will come tomorrow.
 'She'll come tomorrow.'
 c. *Elle$_{cl}$ viendra demain, elle.*

(10) a. *Lei, la$_{cl}$ verrà domani.*
 She she will come tomorrow.
 b. *La$_{cl}$ verrà domani, lei.*

The approximation to the Florentine type of morphological concordance in (10) is remarkable if these anecdotal examples are extrapolated to their full extent. The two nonstandard dialects of French and Italian would thereby reach a parallel status of morphological/phonological subject clitic marking. The French result is derived through a categorical syntactic stage, while from all available records it seems that the Florentine one never knew this phase. Again, the grammaticalization paths may not be as important as the conditions of appearance of the two parallel phenomena of morphological Null-Subject expression. The Non-Null-Subject phenomenon in its free development approaches a morphological solution (Florentine and *français avancé*), while a consciously standardized variety with primary written direction tends towards the two opposite syntactic solutions (standard French vs Italian).

The Null-Subject phenomenon makes it possible to pit the standard language against some of its dialects: they may easily lose connection from the point of view of the formal grammar and its topological instantiations. One could almost speak of a bilingual separatism with a shift to typical, but possibly opposed values on each side. This constellation yields some initial indications as to the relationship between the syntax of different dialects. Separate but connected syntax modules, perhaps only specified subregions, for example referring to the subject expression, should thus be able to account for the differences found here. In French, for a speaker practising at the same time the standard version and *français avancé* the connection can be incremental, in that there is a morphological extension to the syntactic subject expression in the *français avancé* component. For an Italian speaker of standard Italian and vernacular Florentine the syntactic machinery will show a major cleavage bridging the gap between the two extreme formations in this question, Null Subject and Non-Null Subject. The schematic representation in (11) is very approximative. For the connected system of (11b) it should in all likelihood recognize more than just the two prototypical vertical levels of the high and the spontaneous register(s). This could easily and realistically be achieved by multiplying the basic pattern to the number and (possibly) hierarchical arrangement of differentiable contexts. The schema aims only to give an idea of the external range of options for connecting related syntactic components relevant to standardization.

(11) a. Separate: syntax D(i) vs syntax D(j)   e.g. std Italian vs Florentine
      b. Connected: syntax L(i) • 'high' style of L(i)   e.g. std French and
                                • spontaneous style   *français avancé*
                                  of L(i)

15.7 Conclusion

In this sense, the concrete situation discussed here supports a view of syntax as showing both cohesion and separateness of syntactic knowledge in the pairing of dialect and standard language for a given speaker. The peculiar process of standardization fits well into this perspective. It can account for the creation of new dialects – the standard variety of a language grouping separate from its genetic base (Florentine/Italian) – and at the same time it allows us to understand the high degree of cohesion between such related dialects (French/*français avancé*). The mechanism of separation and individuation of such dialects is the increasing accentuation of traits which typify the single varieties. The end effect may be a virtual opposition of values regarding certain construction principles, such as the Null-Subject election. If such trends come to full maturation, they will in their final effect yield the mirage of a categorical choice, of the completion of a grammaticalization run. Such interpretations are however *ex post facto* and they do not say anything about the more normal and extended intermediate periods. Here is the point where the internal perspective of the speaker becomes essential to appreciate that the complex first-language learning process by the individual needs to conform to the environmental conditions of the speech community, that it will necessarily mirror the situation found in the real world data, be they spoken, written, reported, or even postulated (as with the English modal auxiliaries; again, see Arnovick, this volume). Relatively minor forces, such as the more stringent organization of thought into an utterance for the Null-Subject question, are ultimately sufficient to provoke lasting syntactic, eventually even formal divergences between grammars. Categoricalness is only an extreme outcome of normal linguistic practice, in the same way that clear syntactic dialect separation in the diatopic and diaphasic dimensions is a rare phenomenon. The natural transition is guaranteed by the inherent variability of linguistic processes in multiple contexts of linguistic adaptation.

Note

* The ideas presented here were elaborated during my tenure of an Alexander-von-Humboldt Research Award (Forschungspreis) for 1994/5 which I spent at the Albert-Ludwigs-Universität Freiburg i.Br. (Germany). My thanks for financial support, inspiration, and constructive criticism go to the organizer and participants of this colloquium, to the vibrant group of linguists in Freiburg led by W. Raible and H.-M. Gauger, and to the Alexander-von-Humboldt Foundation (Bonn). Special thanks to Johannes Kabatek for correcting some errors of linguistic history in an earlier version of the chapter. Responsibility for anything expressed in the text exclusively rests with the author.

References

Ashby, W.J. 1988. The syntax, pragmatics, and sociolinguistics of left- and right-dislocations in French. *Lingua* 75: 203–29.

Borer, H. 1986. *Parametric Syntax. Case Studies in Semitic and Romance Languages*. Dordrecht: Foris.

Brandi, L. and Cordin, P. 1989. Two Italian dialects and the null subject parameter. In: O. Jaeggli and K.J. Safir (eds), pp. 111–42.

Bybee, J., Perkins, R. and Pagliuca, W. 1994. *The Evolution of Grammar. Tense, Aspect, and Modality in the Languages of the World*. Chicago: Univ. of Chicago Press.

Chomsky, N. 1988. *Language and Problems of Knowledge. The Managua Lectures*. Cambridge, MA: MIT Press.

Clark, E.V. 1993. *The Lexicon in Acquisition*. Cambridge: Cambridge Univ. Press.

de Mauro, T. 1970. *Storia linguistica dell'Italia unita*, 2nd edition. Bari: Laterza.

Fontana, J.M. 1993. *Phrase structure and the syntax of clitics in the history of Spanish*. Ph.D. dissertation, Univ. of Pennsylvania.

Hirschbühler, J. 1989. On the existence of null subjects in embedded clauses in Old and Middle French. In: C. Kirschner and J. deCesaris (eds), *Studies in Romance Linguistics*. Amsterdam: Benjamins, pp. 155–76.

Jaeggli, O. and Safir, K.J. (eds) 1989. *The Null Subject Parameter*. Dordrecht: Kluwer.

Kenstowicz, M.J. 1989. The Null Subject parameter in modern Arabic dialects. In: O. Jaeggli and K.J. Safir (eds), pp. 263–75.

Labov, W. 1993. *Principles of Linguistic Change. Vol. 1: Internal Factors.* Oxford: Blackwell.

Lambrecht, K. 1981. *Topic, Antitopic and Verb Agreement in Non-Standard French*. Amsterdam: Benjamins.

Renzi, L. 1992. I pronomi soggetto in due varietà substandard: fiorentino e français avancé. *Zeitschrift für romanische Philologie*.

Sobin, N. 1987. The variable status of COMP–TRACE phenomena. *Natural Language and Linguistic Theory* 5: 33–60.

Vanelli, L., Renzi, L. and Benincà, P. 1985. Typologie des pronoms subjets dans les langues romanes. In: F. Boucher (ed.), *Linguistique descriptive. Actes du XVII CILPR*, vol. 3. Aix-en-Provence: Presses de l'Université, pp. 161–76.

Wanner, D. 1993. L'expression du sujet dans les langues romanes. In: W. Raible and W. Oesterreicher (eds), *Actes du XXe CILPR*, vol. 3(4). Tübingen: Niemeyer, pp. 449–60.

Weinreich, U. 1954. Is a structural dialectology possible? *Word* 10: 388–400.

CHAPTER 16

The patternings of nonstandard syntax in German

Beate Henn-Memmesheimer

16.1 Linguistic varieties in German

16.1.1 Standard and nonstandard

Ammon (1986: 20ff) has shown that categorizations such as *supra-regional, upper class/middle class, invariant, elaborate* and *written* are neither necessary nor sufficient in order to explain the concept of *standard language*. We can briefly touch on the arguments here, using a few examples. Terms for jobs, such as *Tischler* 'carpenter', *Fleischer* 'butcher' or the variants *Schüppe* to *Schippe* 'shovel',[1] are not supra-regional in German; nevertheless they are still regarded as standard. Words such as *Macker* for *Mann* 'man', are supra-regional, but not accepted as standard forms. Syntactic patterns which are regarded as nonstandard and which are described in accounts of dialect syntax can often be demonstrated to be supra-regionally accepted. For instance, the dative *in dem Vater sein Garten* 'in the$_{dat}$ father his garden', dependent on the articles *sein* 'his' and *ihr* 'her' – in the case of a feminine possessor – can be found throughout the entire German-speaking area,[2] *ganz ein anderer Kerl* 'totally a different guy, a totally different guy', *mehr ein anderer Dialekt* 'more another dialect, a more different dialect' can be found throughout the whole of southern Germany.[3] The criterion of *strata-specific usage* is not practicable in linguistic terms. No varieties of German can be demarcated as correlating with *strata*, no matter how this is defined sociologically. *Homogeneity* cannot be regarded as a criterion either, as even German orthography, which is its most strictly formalized area, allows for variant forms. For standard German, it is possible to identify a greater degree of *elaborateness*; that is, a broader degree of applicability to different text-types is observable for the standard. But this does not produce criteria by which we can designate individual patterns as standard or nonstandard. In view of the fact that we make a distinction between spoken and written standard and that nonstandard languages are also written, *written usage* cannot be employed as a criterion either. *Codified* is all that remains, then, as a defining characteristic for the standard. Codifications are associated with description, institutional regulation and recognition.

The differentiation between standard and nonstandard is generally accepted today in Germany in spite of differences in the way linguistic competence is distributed and in spite of the way the domains of the nonstandard are spread in social and geographical terms. This is the result of training in school, which sanctions many linguistic forms as 'correct' and others as 'incorrect' and attempts to make pupils clearly aware of norms. The distinction is generally accepted, although in individual cases it produces uncertainty. This can be seen from the success of dictionaries and reference books (e.g. *Duden-Wörterbuch für Zweifelsfragen* (Duden Dictionary of Dubious Cases)).

The recognition of particular selections from all collectively and repeatedly encountered patterns as being standard is linked to particular academic institutions. These can be characterized in sociological terms and they vary from one historical period to the next: grammarians, academies, universities and schools in which German is taught as a major subject define particular patterns as standard patterns, while describing others pejoratively as 'jargon', 'unclear', 'rural' and so on.

In order to decide whether a particular pattern is standard or not we refer to particular dictionaries or grammars, although they occasionally contradict each other. For anyone wishing to speak the standard, these books have acquired institutional status. They are thought by their authors to be reproductions of a traditional canon of institutions teaching language, even if they claim to be only descriptive. In addition, all linguistic forms which German speakers have learned somewhere, which are labelled as German and considered as being German, and which can be located in corpora[4] (without being codified), can be regarded as German, but nonstandard.

16.1.2 Sociology and pragmatics of varieties in Germany: empirical arguments for a standard–nonstandard continuum

For many years linguistic variation in Germany was merely described dialectologically as regional. Dialects were traditionally considered to be systems of communication in a geographically restricted section of the population which had intensive internal contacts and was free from external contacts. Colloquial forms, or deviations from standard German in texts which were otherwise considered standard were then explained in terms of interference between standard systems and different dialectal systems. Today this view is unacceptable as far as both sociology and pragmatics are concerned. There are no longer any self-contained vernaculars ('Mundartsysteme') whose speakers are involved in intensive internal contacts, but not in external contacts, as laid down by the original dialectological definitions. Neither are there any sociologically homogeneous groups in Germany which can be assigned to closed linguistic systems.

Macha (1991) discusses the fundamental flexibility of Rhenish speakers (the speakers in this study were master craftsmen). On the basis of people's individual linguistic biography, he differentiates between genuine dialect speakers who encounter only standard German in school, genuine non-dialect speakers, and speakers who have acquired both a dialect and non-dialect competence from the start (Macha 1991: 56). All the speakers surveyed employ standard patterns and near-dialectal forms; they code-switch, and they are conscious of this when they are asked. Those speakers who are familiar with dialect and standard forms from the very beginning regard themselves as being at an advantage with respect to those speakers who use mainly 'standard' forms, but who attempt to use a few dialect signals (Macha 1991: 52f). In 1983 Bellmann already registers 'loss of diglossia' in terms of dialect and standard; he points clearly to the context-dependent and situative function of nonstandard patterns:

> The variants selected by the participant are motivated in different ways [...] A certain proportion of the choices in variation can perhaps be accounted for, if we have recourse to an improved speech-act theory. For the frequently cited role concept fails to account for variations even in short utterances which are completely homogeneous in terms of role. Instead, the more differentiated notion of situational definition is likely to have considerably more explanatory power. (Bellmann 1983: 129, my translation)

So far, such analyses of nonstandard usage which touch on their function as metacommunicative and situation-defining elements are limited in number and are only embryonic in form.[5] There is still a marked absence of analyses based on speech-act theory. Thus, there has so far been no investigation linking speech-act oriented linguistic variance to a macro-sociological distribution of standard and nonstandard – for instance, studies of the fact that, in southern Germany rather than in northern Germany, nonstandard forms are accepted by speakers for more topics and, indeed, are even required in many situations. References to the dichotomy between 'correct' and 'incorrect' produced by schooling, or the prescriptive evaluation of 'better' or 'worse' has little explanatory power in this context. Similarly inadequate are explanations provided by descriptions operating with models of social stratification in a society such as ours, in which group-formation is increasingly 'individualized', 'unstable' and is apparently 'arbitrarily' based on interactions within many-layered interrelated networks (Bohn 1991: 136).

If speakers move along a continuum of standard and nonstandard patterns, then the patterns recognized as standard in the competence of these speakers are merely a subset of habitualized patterns. What this means on a macro-level is this: the patterns codified as standard are only a subset of all the patterns used as German in the German-speaking area. This view is implicit in linguistic histories which emphasize that what is described as literary language or high language does not represent 'the complete state of a language at any given time' and is not 'solely decisive for general linguistic change' (Polenz 1978: 7, my translation).

In view of this, we postulate the following for syntactic descriptions: neither syntaxes based on speaker competence nor syntaxes which are based as far as possible on available corpora should describe the change between standard and nonstandard forms in terms of a switch between different systems ('code-switching'). What is required are descriptive models which account for movements as 'shifting' within **one** system with both a standard and nonstandard domain.

16.1.3 Consequences for a systematic description

Theoretically, the term *subsystemic description* (Goossens 1980: 445, my translation) is usually employed in studies of German to characterize nonstandard patterns as variants within a system. Goossens exemplifies this in the case of areal linguistic descriptions of variants:

> Subsystemic areal linguistics is concerned with differentiating discrepancies and correspondences between the geographical variants (subsystems of a language). [. . .] Subsystemic areal linguistics can clearly be viewed as the study of variability within one linguistic system. Strictly speaking, diasystemic areal linguistics (on the other hand) is to be seen in contrastive terms as the investigation of variation, because it proceeds from the assumption that the entities to be compared are different linguistic systems.
> (Goosens 1980: 445, my translation)

Up to the present time this latter, diasystemic, view has determined almost all syntactic description of nonstandard patterns, including those based on generative or universal grammar.[6] Syntactic patterns which are regarded as nonstandard are then duly assigned to regional or dialectal systems (cf. Henn 1983), or as interferences between standard systems and one of the dialect systems. This leads to counterfactual assertions to the effect that nonstandard patterns are regionally exclusive and that they can be isolated as 'anomalies' (cf. the example given above of the dative *dem Vater sein Garten, der Annette ihr Fahrrad*, dependent on *sein* and *ihr!*). A subsystemic description, using the terminology of the Goossens quote is capable of incorporating the whole range of linguistic forms. Thus, dialectal and standardized patterns can be seen to be parts of the system.[7]

Thus using broad rule formulations, a 'German system' can be reconstructed, within which more precise formulations of these rule formulations differentiate patterns regarded as standard or nonstandard.[8]

16.2 Syntactic examples

Descriptions of nonstandard patterns will now be assessed from a universal grammar and a typological perspective, so as to advocate a broader, all inclusive description. To exemplify this, I shall choose a relatively neglected syntactic fracture of a particularly illustrative character.

I shall leave out the discussion of descriptive terms and rule formats and shall use a surface-structure-oriented description which postulates dependency relationships.[9]

16.2.1 Verb phrases: realization of dependencies

The following sentences are recorded for the Palatinate area:[10]

(1) vɛːʃ du, ob Ø kumn?
Weißt du, ob kommen?
Know you, whether Ø come?
Do you know, whether some of them will come?

(2) iç hab soː kɛ gɛld, un jets kumʃ du un vid ax nox Ø!
Ich habe sowieso kein Geld und jetzt kommst du und willst auch noch!
I have in any case no money, and now come you and want also Ø!
I don't have any money in any case and now – to make things even worse – you come and want some, too!

(3) iç glaːb nit, das æ Ø kaːfd hod.
Ich glaube nicht, daß er gekauft hat.
I believe not that he Ø bought has.
I don't believe that he bought any of that.

(4) de peːdæ isd Ø.
Der Peter ißt.
The Peter eats Ø.
Peter is eating some (of it).

Comments on context and interpretation will be helpful in order to understand the examples. In (1) the preceding context contains a discussion about students; someone asks if any of them are coming. (2) should be understood as: ... *und du willst auch noch welches.* (... and you want some, too.) In (3) someone has been discussing mushrooms and/or salt; doubt has been expressed as to whether someone has bought mushrooms or salt. Example (4) can be read in two ways. If the preceding context mentions vegetable or meat, the sentence can be read as: *Peter ißt etwas davon* (Peter eats some of it). The other reading is based on the contrast: *Peter arbeitet nicht, Peter ißt* (Peter is not working, he is eating). The first reading is taken here. Elvira Glaser argues convincingly that what she calls 'zero realization' of verb valency in Palatinate, has the same range of application as the pronoun *welch-* in standard German, which 'has anaphoric reference to an indeterminate part of a quantity explicitly named before in the rule, or to an indeterminate quantity of a previously mentioned entity, of a mass noun' (Glaser 1993: 100, my translation). Such a zero-realization is not possible in the case of anaphoric use of definite expressions.

(5)   in de ʃchublaːd liçds dox.
       In der Schublade liegt es [liegt's] doch.
       In the drawer lies it of course.
       (Of course) There it is, in the drawer.

Here pronouns are needed, just as in the case of anaphors. Glaser presents all this with care, drawing the conclusion that the 'indefinite-partitive anaphoric reference' (Glaser 1993: 104, my translation) in standard German has a different grammatical realization than in the selected dialect areas, and 'that it is a question of different types in the language variants described. The standard linguistic system has its own pronoun, which is only used with mass nouns and plural terms, south-west dialects use a syntactic Ø position' (Glaser 1993: 113).[11] It must now be shown whether it is legitimate to postulate systematic differences on the basis of standard grammars.

In her dissertation about verb valency (1992), Angelika Storrer deals exclusively with the standard.[12] She gives the example:

(6)   *Auf dem Fest gab es viele Kuchen. Diesmal aß auch Jan.* (Storrer 1992: 112)
       At the party gives it many cakes. This time ate too Jan Ø.
       At the party there were many cakes. This time Jan ate too some.

In systematic terms, we are dealing here with the same case as in (2), (3), and the first reading of (4). Like Glaser, Storrer distinguishes this from cases like:

(7)   *Das Streifenhörnchen scheint sich von seiner Krankheit zu erholen. Jetzt ißt es wieder.* (Storrer 1992: 112)
       The chipmunk seems itself from its illness to recover. Now eats it again.
       The chipmunk seems to recover from its illness. Now it's eating again.

(8)   *Sie bat nicht, sie befahl.* (Storrer 1992: 112)
       She asked not: she ordered.
       She didn't ask; she ordered.

Here, similarly, argument positions are unoccupied but there has been no preceding thematicization of possible filings: she observes that the realization 'is not relevant for the given utterance context and may remain unknown for the speaker and the listener' (Storrer 1992: 111, my translation). The description of example (6) resembles that of Glaser in the sense that the relevance of the realization is pointed out, as is the fact that the empty position can be replaced 'by a corresponding anaphoric expression' (Storrer 1992: 111, my translation).[13] Storrer does not take into account the issue of partitivity, because she merely focuses on the speech and situational context in her comments. I tend to agree with Glaser, who assumes that the zero realization which is under discussion is not contingent on pragmatic or situational decisions, but on specific systematic possibilities.

Unlike Glaser, I work on the assumption that the same systematic regularity should be established for standard and nonstandard forms. This rule must allow for the zero realization of indefinite-partitive anaphoric verb complements. At the level of the differentiation of varieties, we may then be able to formulate whether and in what way Palatinate makes broader use of this regularity than does standard German. More precisely, different restrictions would need to be formulated for the standard than for Palatinate. Such variant-specific restrictions, however, are not yet evident on the basis of the material available nor by appealing to native-speaker competence.

16.2.2 Noun phrases: mass nouns with ein-article

The regional differences in the use of particular nouns with the *ein*-article can also be described as different realizations of the same systematic rules. Grammars which describe the standard subclassify the nominal part of speech according to grammatical criteria (according to morphology and distribution) into count-nouns, mass nouns and proper names.[14] According to the rule formulation of most grammars, from Duden to Weinrich, mass nouns are used without an article and are not used in the plural, and 'when mass nouns occur with the individualizing article, or in the plural, they are count nouns' (*Duden-Grammatik* 1995: §343).[15] In order to avoid such a circular classification, I follow Eisenberg, who regards mass nouns as a class of nouns whose grammatical characteristics are shown, above all, in the use of the article, in plural formation, or in the plural meaning (Eisenberg 1994: 177). Eisenberg gives the following examples:

(9) *Stahl wird immer teurer.*
     Steel is getting more and more expensive.

(10) **Auto wird immer teurer.*
     *Automobile is getting more and more expensive.

(11) *Japan versorgt Europa mit Stahl.*
     Japan provides Europe with steel.

(12) *Japan versorgt Europa mit Auto.
*Japan provides Europe with automobile.

and formulates the regularity which describes standard patterns as follows: 'mass nouns, unlike count nouns, can also occur in the singular without the article or another determining element. The difference in the syntactic behaviour of *Stahl* [...] and *Auto* [...] would be sufficient to ascribe these nouns to different grammatical categories' (Eisenberg 1994: 177, my translation).[16] The examples given can easily be supplemented by examples with the *ein*-article:

(13) *Japan beliefert Europa mit einem billigen Stahl.*
Japan delivers a cheap steel to Europe.

(14) **Japan beliefert Europa mit einem billigen Auto.*
*Japan delivers a cheap automobile to Europe.

Eisenberg links noun phrases like *ein billiger Stahl* with the plural form, with what is called the plural-of-sorts:

(15) *Werkzeug- und Edelstähle, Öle und Fette, Biere und Säfte.* (Eisenberg 1994: 179)
Tool and stainless steels, oils and lards, beers and juices.

Thus plural formations and singulars with *ein* are systematic possibilities for mass nouns in German. Eisenberg's further comment can be read as a reference to the systematic nature and to the use, that is, the application of this rule:

> The plural-of-sorts is relatively recent and is spreading rapidly. It is applied to an increasing number of mass nouns, because there is a need to make increasingly fine distinctions for more and more substances and to name these. [...] There is no reason to regard the plural-of-sorts as in any sense unsystematic or marginal. It is so well established that singular forms already exist for them. *Ein Öl*, for instance, can be read in the sense of 'a sort of oil'.
> (Eisenberg 1994: 179, my translation)

In addition to this function as a plural-of-sorts, a further function of mass nouns can be identified in German: the designation of 'amounts of quantities' (Eisenberg 1994: 179).[17]

(16) *Wir bestellen fünf Biere und drei Schnäpse.* (Eisenberg 1994: 179)
We order five beers and three schnappses.

Examples like

(17) *ein Kaffee, einen Kaffee*
a_{nom} coffee, a_{acc} coffee

are to be read as singulars of example (13) or (14), according to context. Even in cases where a plural does not seem to be possible a singular-of-sorts occurs in the standard:

(18) Es war ein dunkles Gold, ein rotes Gold. (invented example)
      It was a dark gold, a red gold.

(19) Sie hatte eine bewundernswerte Geduld. Sie hatte eine Geduld, die von allen bewundert wurde. (Helbig and Buscha 1979: 338)
      She had an admirable patience. She had a patience which by everybody admired was.
      She was admirably patient. She exhibited a kind of patience which was admired by everybody.

The requisite condition for the use of *ein* here is (according to Helbig and Buscha 1979) that the noun is 'clarified' (Helbig and Buscha 1979: 338) by an adjective or subsidiary clause. For the area of his grammar, that is, for the standard, Eisenberg comments, 'Altogether, more and more of the grammatical forms typical of count nouns can be used for mass nouns' (Eisenberg 1994: 179, my translation).

A typical awareness of standard correctness, however, seems to stand in the way of grammatical forms characteristic of count-nouns being used too widely as mass nouns. The author comments on:

(20) Nur ein Geld braucht man in der Welt draußen. (Zehetner 1970: 125)
      Only a money needs one in the world outside.
      One only needs money in the outside world.

which can be found in edited transcripts of Bavarian speech, that the *ein*-article is 'the N(ormal form) with mass nouns and collective nouns' (Zehetner 1970: 125, my translation); he puts the *ein*-article in brackets (indicating deletability) (Zehetner 1970: 125)[18] for standard interlinear versions. Authors of Bavarian grammars, or grammars for the Lake Constance area, grammars for the Egerland and Nuremberg give as the standard version of the following syntagmatic structures each time a structure without an article, and regard the version with *ein* as a regionally specific form:[19]

(21) ich habe einen Durst, die hat einen Zorn, der hat einen Ernst bei der Sache, der macht bloß einen Spaß,
      I have a thirst, she has a rage ...

(22) es kommt ein Regen, heute kommt noch ein Schnee, die Wäsche war wie ein Schnee,

(23) gib mir einen Zucker, ein Mehl, eine Kreide, ich möchte ein Gemüse, ich will für dreißig Pfennig eine Wurst, und in einem kleinen Säckchen ein Grieß und ein Mehl, in einem Schälchen eine Butter, ich kaufe ein Brot, einen Tabak, sie war wie ein Wachs [so bleich, so gelblich],

(24) ich kaufe eine Tinte, ein Rahm ist schon drinnen gewesen, gibt es heute eine Suppe?,

(25) *ich habe ein Geld gefunden, hast ein kleines Geld?, haben Sie ein Feuer?, mach ein Licht,*

(26) *gib eine Ruhe, du hast ein Glück gehabt,*

(27) *wir machen eine Musik.*

Even examples such as

(28) *ein Wasser, ein Bier, ein Wein,*

glossed as *ein Glas Wasser, Bier, eine Flasche, ein Glas Wein,* are quoted by older authors as regionalisms. Glaser (1992: 108) gives the examples:

(29) *ich möchte eine Suppe, ein Fleisch, ein Kraut,*
 I would like a (some) soup, a (some) meat, a (some) cabbage

and comments on Bavarian in line with the literature: 'indefinite reference with mass nouns always occurs in the individualizing form with the indefinite article' (Glaser 1993: 108, my translation). This could well be a contrast to the standard. Although mass nouns are possible with an *ein*-article in both standard and nonstandard, this only represents a countable entity in the standard, whereas, according to Glaser, 'in Bavarian no distinction is made between countable and noncountable entities' (Glaser 1993: 108, my translation).[20] But this contrast disappears when we see that Bavarian authors not only recognize 'individualising forms', as Glaser does, but also individualizing (or 'singularizing') meaning. At an early date Schiepek writes: 'The indefinite article, as it is called, links the singularizing meaning with the indefinite meaning, the context determining whether one (and which) of the two meanings is predominant' (Schiepek 1908: 358, my translation).[21] In line with a generalizing meaning of the article *ein*, Eroms writes: 'Even in this case, the use of the indefinite article can be explained in terms of the general specificatory function of all articles. Nouns are signalled with the features individual and specific' (Eroms 1989: 326, my translation).[22] 'For standard German and for most non-Bavarian nonstandard, we can assume that mass nouns are not signalled with the features individual and specific and that these are not implied either' (Eroms 1989: 326, my translation), but that it is possible in principle to use them in an individual and specific manner (and to 'think' them) by adding an *ein*-article. It is just as inappropriate to diagnose from this that Bavarian speakers are 'insensitive to the distinction between countable and uncountable' (Glaser 1993: 109)[23] as it is to infer differing systems.

16.2.3 *Adverbial phrases: adverbs with noun phrases*

I will choose a third example from adverbial syntax, which is particularly clear. In

(30) *Er stieg den Berg hinauf.*
      He climbed the mountain up.
      He climbed up the mountain.

I will treat *den Berg hinauf* as a configuration whose syntactic position can be occupied by the pro-form *hinauf* alone, or by other adverbs like *dorthin, weiter*. If we eliminate or replace the adverb *hinauf* with an adverb such as *dorthin*, etc., the accusative noun phrase no longer exists. This is the basis of the analysis according to which *den Berg* is dependent on *hinauf*. Although *herunter, hinunter, hinauf*, etc., are sometimes written as elements of word formation with the verb, I shall treat these deictic/anaphoric entities, which commute with prepositional phrases, as adverbs.[24]

In addition to example (30), the following are recognized as standard:

(31) (...*jagte*) *die Steigung hinauf*,
      (...ran) the slope up,
      (...ran) up the slope,

(32) (...*fuhr*) *den Berg herauf*, (*kam*) *die Treppe herauf*,
      (...drove) the mountain up, (came) the stairs up,
      drove up the mountain, (came) upstairs,

(33) *den Fluß hinunter*, (etc.)
      the river down,
      down the river, etc.,

(34) *den Winter hindurch, das (ganze) Jahr hindurch*,
      the winter through, the (whole) year through,
      throughout the winter, the year,

(35) *eine Minute darauf, eine Minute danach*,
      a minute there-upon, a minute there-after,
      a minute later,

(36) *ein paar Wochen zuvor*,
      a couple of weeks before,

(37) *drei Tage vorher.*[25]
      three days before.

In addition to this, further configurations can be found in regional corpora and grammars:

(38) *da rennen sie den Hof raus* (i.e. *heraus*),
      there run they the courtyard out,
      they ran out of the courtyard,

(39) *er kommt die Tür herein*,
      he comes the door in,
      he enters the door,

(40) *er geht den Gang ehinner (i.e. nach hinten), den Gang evor (i.e. nach vorn),*
he walks the hallway to-back/to-front,
he walks down the hallway,

(41) *wir gehen hinauf die Stiege, hinauf die Festung,*
we go up the stairs, up the fortress,

(42) *1906 bin ich hinein die Schule gekommen,*
1906 am I into the school came,
I entered school in 1906,

(43) *wir wollen hinaus die Welt,*
we want out into the world,

(44) *(sie waren) oben die Straße (i.e. oben auf der Straße),*
(they were) up the street,
(they were) up on the street,

(45) *(sie waren) droben den Boden (i.e. dort oben auf dem Boden),*
(they were) there-up the attic,
(they were) up in the attic,

(46) *der Treppe hinauf gefallen,*
the$_{dat}$ stairs up fallen,
fallen up the stairs,

(47) *dem Abhang hinunter gekollert, der Brücke hinunter in den Rhein geguckt,*
the$_{dat}$ slope down rolled, the$_{dat}$ bridge down into the Rhine looked,
rolled down the slope, looked down from the bridge into the Rhine,

(48) *seinem Fenster heraus-gucken, er zieht ihm die Würmer der Nase raus,*
his$_{dat}$ window out-look, he pulls him the worms the$_{dat}$ nose out (idiomatic),
look out of one's window, he's dragging the information out of someone (pulling teeth),

(49) *dem Fenster hinaus geschmissen, dem Tor hinaus gehen,*
the$_{dat}$ window out thrown,
to throw out of the window,

(50) *der Tür herein, dem Fenster herein,*
the$_{dat}$ door into, the$_{dat}$ window into,
into the door, into the window,

(51) *dem Haus draußen,*
the$_{dat}$ house outside,
outside the house,

(52) *er geht hinein der Kirche, hinein der Stadt, hinein den wärmeren Ländern,*
he walks into the$_{dat}$ church, into the$_{dat}$ town, into the$_{dat}$ warmer countries,

(53) *hinaus der Rosenau.*
out the$_{dat}$ Rosenau.
out towards the Rosenau.

A further systematic descriptive rule with reference to parts of speech can be formulated as follows: adverbs can have a noun phrase depending on them.

This rule must generally be limited to a group of deictic and anaphoric adverbs. For a description of the standard, the list must be limited further than a generalizing syntax going beyond standard and nonstandard. The noun phrase is in the accusative, either immediately or non-immediately placed in front of the adverb. The following applies with reference to nonstandard patterns: the noun phrase is in the accusative or in the dative; it is immediately or non-immediately placed before or after the adverb.

I shall formulate the rule in this form, without any further elaboration of co-occurrence rules and without reference to regional and diaphasic distribution.

Table 6.1

Noun phrase	*hinauf hinab*	*hinein herein*	*draußen*	*ehinner evor*	*oben droben*
Accus. prep.	std.	nstd.	......	nstd.	......
Accus. postp.	nstd.	nstd.	......	......	nstd.
Dative prep.	nstd.	nstd.	nstd.	......	......
Dative postp.	......	nstd.	......	......	......

Table 16.1 illustrates how small and fortuitous a part of the total possible system is used by the standard. Only future analyses of corpora will reveal whether the places marked by a dotted line (......) can be filled by nonstandard patterns.

16.3 Theoretical status of a generalized syntax of standard and nonstandard

The three examples from different areas of syntax have shown that it is possible to describe syntactic nonstandard patterns as realizations of a system generalizing standard and nonstandard. The construction of such a macrosystem is necessary so that neither standard nor nonstandard patterns are regarded as isolated particularities. The distinction between the patterns as standard or nonstandard is made below the level of a description of systems. Typological comparisons are subordinate to a description in connection with the standard. Random selections from the syntax of historical languages cannot be taken as a basis for typological claims.

Notes

1 *Duden-Das große Wörterbuch der deutschen Sprache*, q.v. *Schüppe* also: Duden-Rechtschreibung.
2 Cf. Ammon 1986: 21ff; the expression can be paraphrased: *der Garten, der dem Vater gehört* 'the garden which belongs to the father', or *der Garten des Vaters* 'the garden of the father'.
3 According to Henn-Memmesheimer (1986: 169), the expression can be paraphrased as: *ein ganz anderer Kerl, ein Dialekt, der in mehr Merkmalen anders ist.*
4 In this order! On the use of corpora and the criticism of corpora, cf. Henn-Memmesheimer 1986: 59ff.
5 Exceptions are the work of Auer (1986), Bausch (1994), Keim (1994–1995), Schwittala (1994–1995).
6 Cf. Benincà (1989: 2). In the context of research on universal grammar Benincà, proceeding from Richard Kayne's paper (in Benincà 1989) addresses the relevance of the interdependence of dialects: '... the more the dialects are similar to one another, the more possible it becomes to find, for a specific grammatical area, the ideal case of some dialects differing only in respect to phenomena that can be traced back unambiguously to a single parameter' (p. 3). But this cannot be interpreted as an interest in constructing a descriptive system which generalizes with regard to the standard and dialects.
7 Goossens applies his discussion of models only to the description of dialects.
8 I show this in the case of noun phrases, pronoun phrases and some adverbial phrases (cf. Henn-Memmesheimer 1986, 1989). The distinction made is largely based on Coseriu's differentiation between a (broad) description of systems and a (more narrow) description of realization norms (cf. Coseriu 1975: 11–101, partic. pp. 72ff dealing with the 'difference [...] between norm and system in the area of syntax'). Coseriu, however, never describes the relationship between dialects, or between the dialects and standard variants of an historical language.
9 For more details see Henn-Memmesheimer (1986: 26–55).
10 Cf. Glaser (1993: 100ff). Glaser refers to the south-east Palatinate and her 'own linguistic competence and field surveys' and for other areas to 'overheard instances'. I use the transcription of Elvira Glaser and her interlinear version.

11 Furthermore, according to Glaser, the Palatinate zero realization cannot be compared to Italian zero realizations, but to the Spanish 'indefinite object drop' (cf. 1993: 103).
12 The author is concerned with the theoretical and methodical bias of a lexicographic description of verb valence (cf. *op. cit.*: 323), containing relevant information for German learners (cf. *op. cit.*: 199ff).
13 When Storrer speaks of 'indefinite optionality' (1992: 11), she uses the term 'indefinite' drawing on literature on verb valence differently from Glaser. Storrer uses 'indefinite' to mean 'unknown to the speaker/listener' and 'can be replaced by an indefinite pronoun' (*ibid.*) and 'not unequivocally implicit' (1992: 255, my translation). Storrer uses the term 'definite' in such a way that it can be applied to the examples quoted by Glaser and the example (6) she quotes herself; that is, 'definite' is used for all cases when the 'occupancy of the position [. . .] can be inferred from the speaker and the situative context' (1992: 111, my translation, cf. also p. 297!).
14 Cf. e.g. Eisenberg (1994: 177ff): 'Gattungsnamen, Stoffnamen, Eigennamen'!
15 Cf. also §539 and §368. Weinrich too sees a transition from one category to the other: 'Stoffnamen [. . .] werden im Plural zu konturenschärferen, relativ konkreten Gattungsnamen umgebildet.' 'Der gleiche Wechsel zwischen Abstrakt und Konkret ist nun auch im Singular möglich und zwar bei kataphorischem [d.h. *ein*-]Artikel' (Weinrich 1993: 427).
16 Eisenberg also lists morphological peculiarities: *der Preis japanischen Stahls*, but **der Preis Stahls*.
17 Cf. also Henn-Memmesheimer (1986: 111f).
18 On the edited corpora and the examples quoted there, cf. details in Henn-Memmesheimer (1986: 109f).
19 Cf. Henn-Memmesheimer (1986: 109–16).
20 Glaser treats noun phrases like *ein Wasser*, *ein Saft*, *ein Geld* in the context of an incompletely substantiated plural form of the article *ein* and the pronoun *einer*, which stand with count nouns or make anaphoric reference to count nouns. She refers 'in particular to overheard evidence' (p. 106, my translation). Furthermore, the relation between *õa* and *õi* (mentioned by Glaser) and standard *einige*, and quantifiers in general (in contrast to articles; cf. Eroms 1989: 326) is not elaborated.
21 Cf. also the examples and classifications in Schiepek (1908: 358–61).
22 Eroms, like Schiepek, then also mentions generic interpretations: 'Here, generic interpretation is *one* way of interpreting in a suitable, that is, pragmatically clearly signalled context' (1989: 326, my translation).
23 Glaser qualifies her diagnosis herself with the remark: 'Allerdings wird die Opposition zählbar/nichtzählbar bei der unterschiedlichen

Fähigkeit [der Individuativa und Kontinuativa] zur Pluralbildung durchaus berücksichtigt' (1993: 109).
24 For detail see: Henn-Memmesheimer (1989: 171–6). For the parts of speech see also: *Duden-Grammatik* (1984: §§585–6) and (1995, §606), Eisenberg (1994: 210).
25 For the collection of evidence, cf. *Duden-Das große Wörterbuch*, q.v. *herunter, hinauf, hindurch* (Clément and Thümmel 1975: 181).

References

Abraham, Werner and Bayer, Josef (eds) 1993. *Dialektsyntax*. Opladen: Westdeutscher Verlag.
Ammon, Ulrich 1986. Explikation der Begriffe 'Standardvarietät', 'Standardsprache' auf normtheoretischer Grundlage. In: Günter Holtus and Edgar Radtke (eds), *Sprachlicher Substandard*. Tübingen: Niemeyer, pp. 1–65.
Auer, Peter 1986. Konversationelle Standard/Dialekt-Kontinua ('code-shifting'). *Deutsche Sprache* 14(2): 97–124.
Bausch, Karl-Heinz 1994–1995. Regeln des Sprechens, Erzählstile, soziale Typisierungen, Sprachvariation und Symbolisierungsverfahren unter Jugendlichen der Kerngesellschaft von Neckarau. In: Werner Kallmeyer (ed.), pp. 387–466.
Bellmann, Günter 1983. Probleme des Substandards. In: Klaus J. Mattheier (ed.), *Aspekte der Dialekttheorie*. Tübingen: Niemeyer, pp. 105–30.
Bellmann, Günter 1985. Substandard als Regionalsprache. In: *Germanistik – Forschungsstand und Perspektiven*, 1. Teil. Berlin/New York: de Gruyter.
Benincà, Paola (ed.) 1989. *Dialect Variation and the Theory of Grammar*. Dordrecht: Foris.
Bohn, Cornelia 1991. *Habitus und Kontext*. Opladen: Westdeutscher Verlag.
Clément, Danièle and Thümmel, Wolf 1975. *Grundzüge einer Syntax der deutschen Standardsprache*. Wiesbaden: Athenaion.
Coseriu, Eugenio 1975. *Sprachtheorie und Allgemeine Sprachwissenschaft*. München: Fink.
Duden-Grammatik der deutschen Gegenwartssprache 1984, 4th edition. Mannheim: Duden-Verlag.
Duden-Grammatik der deutschen Gegenwartssprache 1995, 5th edition. Mannheim: Duden-Verlag.
Eisenberg, Peter 1994. *Grundriß der deutschen Grammatik*, 3rd edition. Stuttgart/Weimar: Metzler.
Eroms, Hans-Werner 1989. Artikelparadigmen und Artikelfunktionen im Dialekt und in der Standardsprache. In: Erwin Koller *et al.* (eds), *Bayerisch-österreichische Dialektforschung. Würzburger Arbeitstagung 1986*. Würzburg: Königshausen and Neumann, pp. 305–28.

Glaser, Elvira 1993. Syntaktische Strategien zum Ausdruck von Indefinitheit und Partitivität im Deutschen (Standardsprache und Dialekt). In: Werner Abraham and Josef Bayer, *Dialektsyntax*. Opladen: Westdeutscher Verlag, pp. 99–116.
Goebl, Hans 1986. Mundart, Maß und Meinung. In: Jean-Denis Gendrom and Peter H. Nelde (eds), *Mehrsprachigkeit in Europa und Kanada*. Bonn (Plurilingua VI): Dümmler.
Goossens, Jan 1980. Areallinguistik. In: Hans Peter Althaus *et al.* (eds), *Lexikon der Germanistischen Linguistik*, 2nd edition Tübingen: Niemeyer, pp. 445–52.
Gumperz, John 1994. Sprachliche Variabilität in interaktionsanalytischer Perspektive. In: Werner Kallmeyer (ed.), pp. 611–39.
Helbig, Gerhard and Joachim Buscha 1979. *Deutsche Grammatik: Ein Handbuch für den Ausländerunterricht*. Leipzig: Verlag Enzyclopädie.
Henn, Beate 1983. Syntaktische Eigenschaften deutscher Dialekte. Überblick und Forschungsbericht. In: Werner Besch *et al.* (eds), *Dialektologie. Ein Handbuch zur deutschen und allgemeinen Dialektforschung*, Artikel 78. Berlin/New York: de Gruyter.
Henn-Memmesheimer, Beate 1986. *Nonstandardmuster*. Tübingen: Niemeyer.
Henn-Memmesheimer, Beate 1989. Über Standard und Nonstandardmustern generalisierende Syntaxregeln. Das Beispiel der Adverbphrasen mit deiktischen Adverbien. In: Günter Holtus and Edgar Radtke (eds), *Sprachlicher Substandard II*. Tübingen: Niemeyer, pp. 169–228.
Hinrichs, Uwe 1991. Beitrag zu: Lehfeldt, Werner/Jachnow, H./Freidhof, G./Koester-Thoma, S./Hinrichs, U./Wiesner, G./Zemskaja, E.A. (Russisch). Das Verhältnis von Literatursprache (Standardsprache) und nichtstandardsprachlichen Varietäten in der russischen Gegenwartssprache. *Welt der Slaven* 36: 1–72.
Kallmeyer, Werner (ed.) 1994–1995. *Kommunikation in der Stadt*, Teil 1–4. Berlin/New York: de Gruyter.
Keim, Inken 1994–1995. Kommunikative Stilistik einer sozialen Welt 'kleiner Leute' in der Mannheimer Innenstadt. In: Werner Kallmeyer (ed.), *Kommunikation in der Stadt*, Teil 3. Mannheim.
Macha, Jürgen 1991. *Der flexible Sprecher. Untersuchungen zu Sprache und Sprachbewußtsein rheinischer Handwerksmeister*. Köln/Weimar/Wien: Böhlau.
Mattheier, Klaus J. 1995. Sprachwandel in Erp? In: Ivar Werlen (ed.), *Verbale Kommunikation in der Stadt*. Tübingen: Narr, pp. 263–76.
Polenz, Peter von 1978. *Geschichte der deutschen Sprache*, 9th edition, Berlin/New York: de Gruyter.
Schiepek, Josef 1908. Der Satzbau der Engländer Mundart, Prag Verlag des Vereins für Geschichte der Deutschen in Böhmen.
Schwitalla, Johannes 1994–1995. Kommunikative Stilistik zweier sozialer

Welten in Mannheim-Vogelstang. In Werner Kallmeyer (ed.), *Kommunikation in der Stadt*, Teil 4. Berlin/New York: de Gruyter.

Storrer, Angelika 1992. *Verbvalenz. Theoretische und methodische Grundlagen ihrer Beschreibung in Grammatikographie und Lexikographie.* Tübingen (RGL 126).

Weinrich, Harald 1993. *Textgrammatik der deutschen Sprache.* Mannheim/Leipzig/Wien/Zürich: Duden-Verlag.

Zehetner, Ludwig G. 1970. *Freising.* Tübingen. (*Lautbibliothek der europäischen Sprachen und Mundarten. Deutsche Reihe*, Bd 7. Monographien 2.)

Index

a-prefixing, 177
abstract nouns, *see* nouns
Academy, 135, 138, 195, 233
accent, 164, 219
accessibility hierarchy, 159
actualization, 130–3
adaptation, 27
address*ee*, 63, 74–5, 77–8, 115, 117, 207
adjectives, 22, 100–4
adverbs, 44, 104–6, 244
adverbials, 54, 65, 241–4
affective, 6, 78, 91, 116–17, *see also* emotive/emotional
African American Vernacular English (AAVE), *see* Englishes
African languages, 126
Afrikaans, 25–6, 180
after + verb, 179
agentivity hierarchy, 119
agreement, 40, 111, 126, 173, 179, 206, 220–1, 225
alternatives, *see* choices
ambiguity, 99, 104, 161, 209–10
American English, *see* Englishes
American South English, *see* Englishes, American English
analogy, 1, 25, 28, 39, 120, 159–60, 163, 165, 213
analytic(al), 5, 41
anaphora, 204–6, 209, 220, 237–8, 242, 244, 246
Anglo-Irish, *see* Englishes, Irish English
animacy/animateness, 8, 112, 116–17, 122

Arabic, 22
archaic, 14, 16, 90, 177, *see also* dialect
argument structure, 61
articles, ch. 9
   definite, 18, 130–2
   ein, 238–41
   indefinite, 100, 129–30
as', *see* genitives, of relative pronouns
aspect, 37, 41, 43, 221, *see also* do
at's, *see* genitives, of relative pronouns
Australian English, *see* Englishes
Australian National Dictionary (AND), 178–9
authorities, 55–6, 58, 138
autonomous, 43, 207, 225, *see also* non-autonomous
auxiliaries, 25–6, 58, *see also* inversion; modal
avoidance strategies, 31–2, 159

'barbarisms', 180
Basque, 185, 196
Bavarian, *see* German
be, invariant, 47, 177
Belfast English, *see* Englishes, Irish English
Berkshire English, *see* Englishes, British English
bi-lectal, 16, 18
bilingual, 164, 190, 228
Binding Theory, 203, 220
Black Vernacular English, *see* African American Vernacular English (AAVE)

INDEX

borrowing, 22
brace construction, 41
British English, *see* Englishes
Brooklynese, *see* Englishes, American English

case, 6, 22, 94, 106–7, 159, 164, 206–7, ch. 8, *see also* inflections
Castilian, *see* Spanish
Castilianization, *see* Galician
Catalan, 126, 131, 185
change, linguistic, 24–7, 30, 47, 69, 89, 93, 102, 135, 145, 152–3, 158–64, 219, 221–4, 235, ch. 13
  from above, 37
  in progess, 187–91
  natural, 7, 21, 24–7, 29
  semantic change, 146
  unidirectionality of, 222
Chapurrao, *see* Galician
Chinook, *see* pidgin
choices, 9, 24, 38, 95, 112, 116–17, 122, 133, 139, 149, 155, 159, 189, 229, 234
class, 137
  lower, 9, 113, 185
  middle, 153, 163, 185–6, 232
  upper, 9, 113, 232
  working, 174–5, 179–80
class nouns, *see* nouns
clause
  boundary marking, 58, 60
  combining, 5, 52, 53–4, 56, 63
  extraposition, 59
clefting, 202, 208
clitics, 189–90, 192, 201, 210, 220, 225–7
Cobuild Corpus, 154, 162
code-switching, 234–5
codification, 7, 11, 68–9, 73, 76, 79, 126, 135, 148, 220, 232–4
cohesiveness, 218
Collins Dictionary of the English Language, 71
colloquial, 1, 2, 5, 10, 35, 38, 40, 42, 44, 46, 69, 71–2, 155, 160, 163, 180, 202, 215, 233, *see also* single languages
colloquial style, *see* style

'colloquialisms', 27
common nouns, *see* nouns
competence, 233–5, 238
concord, *see* agreement
concrete nouns, *see* nouns
concreteness, 127, 129
conditionals, 55, 57
congruence, *see* agreement
contact, 41, 54, 172, 180–1, 186–8, 190, 193–4, 197
continuation, 43, 53–4, 65
continuum of varieties, *see* varieties
Contrast, Principle of, 222–3
contrastive, 208, 210, 212–13
Conventionality, Principle of, 222–3
convergence, 47, 185, 194
conversational
  implicatures, 75
  inferences, 77, 80
  language, 43
corpora, 3, 54, 95, 110, 233, 235, 245–6 *see also* Cobuild corpus; Helsinki corpora
correctness, 3, 47, 138–9, 142, 146, 148, 160, 233–4, 240, *see also* cultivated; grammarians; norms; prescription, prescriptivists; 'incorrect'
  doctrine of, 138, 72
count nouns, *see* nouns
Cree, 83
Creole languages, 126
cultivated, 14, 20, 23, 30
Czech, 83

dative, 40, 120, 190, 232, 235
  ethical, 40, 190, 194, 196
definite article, *see* article
'de-grammaticalization', 91
deixis, 6, 8, 15, 18, 42, 142, 159, 190, 194, 197, 242, 244, ch. 6
demonstratives, 42, 47, 84–91
  adjectives, 84, 89–90
  pronouns, 83–4, 86–9, 130, 182
  that, *see that*
deontic, 111, 115–16, 119, 142, 144, 146–7, *see also* modal; modality
Derbyshire, *see* Englishes
derivational, 26, 31, 103

251

INDEX

descriptive, 113, 147, 215, 233, 235
  grammars, *see* grammar(s) (books/descriptions of)
detachment, *see* dislocation
determination, 130, 132
determiners, 83, 100
diachronic, 135, 145–6, 158–9, 218, 220, 222, 226
dialect, 1–5, 7, 9–10, 14, 71, 90, 137, 158–60, 163–4, 170, 173–4, 190, 219, 235, ch. 2, ch. 3
  archaic dialect features of, 13, 20–1, 31
  function of, 13, 20
  grammar, *see* grammar
  morphology, 164
  syntax, 93, 164, 232, ch. 1, ch. 3, *see also* syntax
  variation/variability, 7, ch. 15
  vocabulary, 164
'dialectal', 46, 90, 137
  inflection, *see* inflection
dialectology, 3, 24
dialects, 3–5, 7, 83, 90, 99, 219, *see also* single languages
diaphasic, 218, 230
diasystemic, 9, 235
diatopic, 218, 230
dictionaries, 68, 85, 90–1, 121, 136, 138, 195, 233
Dictionary of English Normative Grammar 1700–1800, 44, 136
diglossia, 186, 234
discontinuous constituents, 41, 44
discourse, 88–90
  grounding management, 37
  meaning, 41–3
  spontaneous, 61, 63, 65, 202, 229
dislocation, 41, 43, 53, 60, 62, ch. 14
  left dislocation, 9, 42, 44, 59–60
distal, 83, 90
distance, 189, 196
divergence, 48
do, 36–7, 39, 41, 45, 47
do-support, 93
doctrine of correctness, *see* correctness
doen-periphrasis, 32–3
donor language, 22–3

doon-support, 93–4
double
  binds, 64
  marking, 39
  modals, 39
  negation, 29, 36, 39
  relatives, 39, 43
doubling, 38–40, 43, 53–4, 59–60, 210
drift, 222
Duden, 233, 238, 245, 247
Dutch, 7, ch. 2
  dialects, 93
    central Holland, 31
    eastern dialects, 20, 31–2
    southern dialects, 20, 25, 31
    urban dialects, 14
    western dialects, 31
  grammarians, *see* grammarians
  informal, 104
  Latin influence on, 14, 22, 27, 31
  standard, 99

Early Modern English, *see* English
Early Modern French, *see* French
educated, 68, 70, 72–3, 75–7, 79–80, 110, 113, 153, 177
ein-article, *see* article
elaboration, 5, 24, 28, 185–6, 194, 232
ellipsis, 40–1, 55
emotive/emotional, 6, 37, 40, 42, 45, *see also* affective; subjective
empirical, 2, 35, 236–8
English, 4–5, 54, 94–5, 105, 107, 221, 224–6, ch. 3, ch. 5, ch. 6, ch. 10, ch. 11
  colloquial, 8, 77–8, 155, 162
  dialect, 6, 71, 78, 170
  Early Modern English, 145–6, 93, 156, 160, 172
  formal, 160, 164–5
  Literary, 35
  Middle, 6, 85, 90–1, 105, 146, 160
  Old English, 69, 85, 90, 146, 160
  nonstandard, 8, 83–4, 178, ch. 5
  regional, 5, 156, 163–5, *see also* dialect(s); Englishes
  spoken, 8, 68–9, 72, 78

INDEX

standard, 8, 69, 83–4, 88, 89–91, 106, 152, 154, 156, 159, 164–5, 173, ch. 5
standardization of English, 6
urban English, 90, 137, 156
varieties of English, 9, *see also* Englishes
English Dialect Dictionary (EDD), 85, 152, 155–6, 159, 178, 182
English Dialect Grammar (EDG), 85, 152, 159
Englishes, ch. 12
  American English, 153–4, 162, 166, 174
    African American Vernacular English (AAVE), 47, 177
    Brooklynese, 175
    Irish American, 175
    Louisiana, white plantation English of, 175
    North American, 146, 170–1, 175, 180
    southern US, 170–8
  Australian English, 79, 170–1, 178–81
    Irish influence on, 180
  British English, 154, 166
    dialects, 85, 146, 182
    English English, 170, 178
      Derbyshire, 156
      Essex, 156
      Leicestershire, 157
      Liverpool dialect, 182
      North England, 77, 83–4, 87, 90, 155–6, 158
      Northumberland, 83
      Reading, 69
      Somerset, 156
      South England, 87, 137, 153
      South England, influence on Zimbabwe English, 181
      South Zeal, Devonshire, 84, 89
      Tyneside, 182
      West Country, 83
      Yorkshire, 77, 88
    Irish English, 83, 138, 153, 170, 171, 172–8, 179, 182
      Belfast, 172, 173, 174, 179
      influence on Australian English, 180
      influence on Zimbabwe English, 181
      nonstandard, 180
    Scottish English, 83–4, 138, 153, 155–6, 161, 163, 170–80
      Broad Scots, urban varieties, 174
      Glasgow, 84–5, 174
      influence on Zimbabwe English, 181
      Shetland dialect, 84, 86, 88, 90–1, 182
    Wales, 156
  New Zealand English, 183
  northern hemisphere Englishes, 171–8, 181–2
  Rhodesian, 181, 183
  South African English, 171, 178–81
  southern hemisphere Englishes, 171, 178–82
  Zimbabwe English, 171, 178–81
    Irish influence on, 181
    Scottish influence on, 181
    South English influence on, 181
epistemic, 45–6, 111, 116–17, 142, 144–6, 147, *see also* modal; modality
ergative, 115
Eskimo, 83
essayist literacy, 6, 35, 37, 40
Essex, *see* Englishes, British English
ethical datives, *see* dative, ethical
exaptation, 107
existential constructions, 112–13, 206
experiments, 88
expressive-subjective, *see* subjective
expressivity, 75, 77
external factors, 8–9, 38, 48
Extra Territorial English (ETE), 170, 171, 172, 182, *see also* Englishes
extraposition, 59

face-to-face communication, 6, 10, 78, 79, 80, 154
filtering process, *see* standardization
Finland Swedish, *see* Swedish

253

INDEX

Finnish, 5, 10, ch. 4, ch. 8
  colloquial, ch. 8
  dialects, ch. 8
    Eastern dialects, 54
    Helsinki, 54
  grammars, *see* grammar(s) (books/ descriptions of)
  grammatical tradition, 111
  nonstandard, 8
  spoken, 5, 52, 61, 65
  standard, 6, 9
  Swedish influence on, 54, 56
First Language Acquisition, 27, 222–3, 229
Florentine, *see* Italian
focus
  of attention, 208
  cognitive, 47
folk-etymology, 181
folklore ideas about language, 39, 48, 177
formal
  grammar, 54, 221, 224, 228, *see also* generative grammar
  styles, *see* style
  written prose, *see* written language
français avancé, *see* French
Francien, *see* French
French, 9, 130–1, 133, 218, 225–9, ch. 14
  Early Modern French, 225
  français avancé, 228–9
  Francien, 227
  Middle French, 225
  Old French, 225
  spoken French, 202
fronting, 209, 213
future/futurity, 136, 138, 142, 144–6

Galician, 5, 8, ch. 13
  Academy, 195
  Castilianized, 186, 190, 192
  dialects, 186–9, 195
    Chapurrao, 189
  elaborated, 189
  grammarians, *see* grammarians
  koiné/koineization, 185–7, 190–4, 197
  Portuguese influence on, 195
  Spanish influence on, 188–9
  spoken, 188–9, 190, 196
  standard, 8
  standardization, 194, 9
  urban Galician, 185, 190
Gallego-Portuguese, *see* Portuguese
gap in system, 152, 155, 163, 174, 179, 182
gender, 18, 20, 126, 221, *see also* variation
generative grammar, 4, 54, 164, 235
generic, 132, 207, 246
genitive, 8
  group genitive, 160–1
  his-genitive, 160, 163, 165, 232
  subject, 111–12, 114–15, 117–19, 121–2
genitives, of relative pronouns, ch. 11
  as', 156–9, 161
  at's, 155–6, 158–9, 161, 166
  that's, 153–5, 158–9, 161, 166
  what'/what's, 156, 158–9, 161, 166
German, 5, 10, 41, 53, 116, 127, 196, 225–6, ch. 7, ch. 16
  influence on Dutch, 14, 22, 24, 27
  nonstandard, 9, 104
  standard, 94–5, 99–100, 102–3, 106–7, 125, 131, 232
    colloquial standard German, 96
  varieties of German, 9, 99
    Bavarian, 42, 96, 125, 130, 132, 240–1, *see also* grammars
    Low German, 94, 103
      Middle Low German, 105
      Northern Low German, ch. 7
    Northern German dialects, 6, 234
    Palatinate, 236–7, 245–6
    Rhenish, 83, 234
    Southern German, 131–2, 234, 237, 242
Germanic languages, 25, 42, 53–4, 57, 61, 93
gerund, *see* infinitive, inflected
Glasgow English, *see* Englishes, British English
glottal stop, 71
government, 204, 207–8

INDEX

grammar(s) (as system), 17, 22–4, 35, 45, 58, 113, 146, 187, 213, 216, 221, 230, *see also* system
  dialect, 35, 94, 171
  standard, 35
grammar(s) (books/descriptions of), 42, 55–6, 68, 84, 113–14, 138–40, 146–8, 195, 233, 238, 242
  Bavarian, 240
  descriptive, 6, 11, 91, 208
  on dialect syntax, 56
  for the Egerland, 240
  English, 90, 135
  Finnish, 53, 55, 113, 122
  for the Lake Constance area, 240
  for Nuremberg, 240
  pedagogic, 4, 11
  phrasal, 204
  prescriptive, 53, 138
  reference, 4, 233
grammarians, 6–8, 10–11, 29, 44, 68–9, 79, 84, 90, 113, 125–6, 136, 138, 144, 146–7, 201, 233, *see also* norm(s); prescription, prescriptivists
  Dutch, 24, 93
  Galician, 190
  Latin, 196
  Lowth, Bishop Robert, 136, 138, 141, 143–4
  prescriptive, 3, 7, 11
  structuralist, 135
  Swedish, 53
  Ward, William, 136, 141–4, 149
grammaticalization, 41, 43, 52, 65, 94–5, 119–22, 145, 147, 197, 221–4, 227–9, *see also* 'de-grammaticalization'
Greek, 196, 224

h-dropping, 70
heavy phrases, 59–62, 64–5, *see also* nominal phrases (NPs)
Helsinki dialect corpus, 88
Helsinki Spoken Language Corpus, 65
Hiberno-English, *see* Englishes, Irish English
his-genitive, *see* genitive

historical linguistics, 4–5, 219
hybrid structures, 211–13, 215–16
hypercorrection, 189, 214–15

Icelandic, 53
iconic, 40, 108
ideology, of standard, *see* standard
illocutionary, 144, 146–7, 149
  illocutionary act, 142, *see also* speech act
imperative, 22, 55
'incorrect', 71–2, 75, 79, 233–4
indefinite
  article, *see* articles
  pronouns, *see* pronouns
indexicality, 89, 110, 116–19, 122
  continuum of, 123
individualization, 128–9
inferences, 74–5, 78, 116, 204, 206
infinitives, 95–7, 106–7, 113, *see also* split infinitives
  inflected, 8, 20, 106–8, 187–9, 192, 195–6
  prefixed, 98–9
  split, 40, 47
inflection, 5, 10, 14, 22, 24, 26, 100–6, 159, 165, 178, 201, 225, *see also* case; infinitives
  of adverbs, 104–6
  of conjunctions, 7, 28
  dialectal, 159
  innovations, 107
  loss of, 160
  passive, 111, 121
  verbal, 10, 32, 225
informal styles, *see* styles
innovation, 24, 107, 159, 165, 171, 174, 181
intensifier, 78, 104
intensity, 37, 40–2
interactive, 63, 65
interference, 131, 187, 193, 233, 235
internal factors, 30, 36–8, 41, 171
interrogation, 55, 208
intonation, 15, 200–1, 204, 219
inversion, 41–3, 47, 54, 56, 202, 225–6, *see also* Verb Second (V2)
involvement, 6, 8, 84, 89, 107, 197, ch. 5

255

INDEX

Irish, 126, 172
Irish American, *see* Englishes, American English
Irish English, *see* Englishes, British English
irregular verbs, 25, 32, 36
Italian, 42, 130, 131–2, 218, 224, 226–7, 229, 246
   Florentine, 225–9
   informal Italian, 131
   Northern Italian, 224, 226–7
   Tuscan, 228

Japanese, 83
Johnson's *Dictionary*, 90, 138

koiné/koineization, *see* Galician

language
   change, *see* change
   contact, *see* contact
   engineering, *see* language planning
   learning, 4, 25, 31, 181, 190, 246, *see also* First Language Acquisition
   planning, 14, 21–4, 185–6, 189, 191, 195
   system, *see* system
   teaching, 4, 56, 84, 114
Latin, 14, 22, 83, 190, 194, 196
   grammarians, *see* grammarians
   influence on Dutch, 14, 22, 27, 31
   models, 38, 41, *see also* standard, logic factor of
left dislocation, *see* dislocation
Leicestershire English, *see* Englishes, British English
lexicalization, 55, 210
lexicology, 218
lexicon, 17, 24, 26, 120, 180–1, 219, 221, 223
Linguistic Atlas of England, 87
linguistic
   geography, 84
   historiography, 46
   insecurity, 214
Linguistic Survey of Scotland (*LSS*), 84, 86–8
literacy, 35, 45–6, 68, 193
literary language, 35, 90, 235

Liverpool dialect, *see* Englishes, British English
loan words, 26–7, 155
locatives, 42
logic factor, *see* standard
Lowth, Bishop Robert, *see* grammarians

macrosyntax, 203, 213, 215
Manual of Modern Scots, 85
marked forms/structures, 26–7, 41, 43, 45, 55, 98, 126, *see also* unmarked
marker, 177
   of casual language, 181
   of colloquial language, 181, 190
   of distance, 190
   of early American white speech, 176
   of elaborated speech, 188
   of elevated style, 190
   of identity, 89, 177
   of Irish English, 175
   of orality, 188
   of 'pied noir' from North Africa, 201
   of social groups, 75, 79–80
   of solidarity, 177
   of written texts, 188
mass
   continuum, 130
   nouns, *see* nouns
meaning-form relation, 39, 69, 71, 79–80, 140, 223
methods, 3, 4, 77, 204, 246, *see also* corpora; questionnaires
microsyntactic unit (MSU), 204–5, 207–8, 210, 213
microsyntax, 203–13, 215
Middle English, *see* English
Middle French, *see* French
minority languages, 185–6, 195
modal, 110, 112, 114–18, 120, 122, 210
   auxiliaries, 44, 138, 223, 230, ch. 10, *see also* deontic; epistemic; shall; will; necessity
modality, 111, 115–16, 118, 141–2, 143, 145–6, *see also* deontic; epistemic

INDEX

Modern Finnish Dictionary, 56
mood, 149, 221
morphology, 1, 25–7, 31, 69, 108, 152, 186, 218–19, 224, 226–7, *see also* inflection
morphophonology, 226
morphosyntax, 113, 120, 159–60, 212, 220
Mozarabic dialects, *see* Portuguese

narration, 46, 62–3
natural, 27, 43, 159, 161, 163
  change, *see* change
  morphology, 108
necessity, verbs of, ch. 8
negation, 69–76, 93, 208
Neo-grammarians, 126, 219
never, 69–76, 79–80
New Zealand English, *see* Englishes
nominal phrases (NPs), 59–61
  heavy NP, 60, 62
non-autonomous, 40–3, 46
nonstandard, 1–3, 5–6, 9–10, 73, 83, 135, 170, 215, 234, *see also* single languages; varieties
  functions of, 10
  regional forms, 152
  syntax, 2, 5–9, 11–78, ch. 16
  urban speech, 156
norm(s), 2, 4, 7–8, 11, 15, 24, 26–7, 44, 56–7, 65, 68, 76, 163, 189, 201, 214, 222–3, 245, ch. 8, ch. 14, *see also* correctness; grammar(s) (books/descriptions of); prescription, prescriptivists
  awareness, 25–7, 29, 233
Northumberland, *see* Englishes, British English
nouns
  abstract, 18, 125, 127–9, 131–2
  class, 125, 127, 129–31
  collective, 128
  common, 7, 18
  concrete, 125, 127–32
  count, 7, 238–40
  mass, 7, 125, 128–30, 238–41
  proper, 7, 26, 125, 127–32, 238
  quantifying, 130

Null Subjects, 218, 220, 224–9
number, 111, 120, 125–9, 221, ch. 9, ch. 12

Occitan languages, 126
Old English, *see* English
Old French, *see* French
Old Norse, 155
Old Spanish, *see* Spanish
'one meaning-one word', *see* meaning-form relation
oral language, *see* spoken language
orality, 35, 37–8, 42, 188, 193, *see also* re-oralization
orthography, 70, 175, 186, 203, 232
The Oxford Dictionary and Usage Guide to the English Language, 147
Oxford English Dictionary (OED), 90, 160, 172–5, 178, 182

Palatinate, *see* German
paradigm, 208
  defective, 152
parameters, 9, 220–1, 224
participant observation, 88
particles, 6, 43, 45, ch. 4
partitive, 237–8
passive, 111, 121
past
  participle, 36, 95, 99–100
  tense, 26, 32, 36, 69
pedagogic grammars, *see* grammar(s) (books/descriptions of)
performance, 27, 58
periods, 204–7, 209–10, 213
Persian, 22
person, 111, 113, 116–19, 120, 122–3, 201, 221, 223
  hierarchy, 110, 112
phonetics, 70, 131, 173, 187, 224
phonology, 3–4, 6, 10, 28–9, 218–19, 222
  influence on syntax, ch. 7
  phonological reduction/weakening, 160, 227
phrasal grammar, *see* grammar(s) (books/description of)
Phrase Structure models, *see* generative grammar

257

INDEX

pidgin, 181, 201
  Chinook, 201
pleonasm, 39, 211–12, 215
plural, 127–30, 179, 182, 238–9, *see also* pronouns, second person plural
Portuguese, 128, 131–2, 186–7, 226
  Gallego-Portuguese, 189
  influence on Galician, 195
  Mozarabic dialects, 186
possession/possessive, 24, 100, 121, 130, 163, *see also* genitive
postvocalic /r/, *see* rhoticity
'pragmatic mode', 42, 194
pragmatics, 5–6, 42, 45, 48, 112, 140, 144, 188, 190, 194, 207, 212, 233
prefixation, 98–100, 107
preposings, 41–5, 64
prepositions
  copied, 97–8
  preposition stranding, 41, 97–8
prescription, 3, 7, 11, 37, 40, 46–7, 53, 65, 70–1, 113, 135–6, 138, 144–8, 234, *see also* correctness; grammar(s) (books/descriptions of); norm
prescriptivists, 56–8, 71–2, 76, 80, 135, 189, 201–2, *see also* grammarians
prestige, 27, 201–2, *see also* style
  covert, 89
  languages, 7, 21–2, 27, 186
presupposition, 203–4
preterites, *see* past tense
processing, 58–9, *see also* speech production
production, *see* speech production
pronominal
  copies, 39, 53
  deixis, 15, 18
pronouns, 7, 25, 155, 170, *see also* relatives/relativizers; demonstratives
  indefinite, 130
  personal, 24–5, 117, 122
  possessive, 24, 100, 130
  reflexive/nonreflexive, 24, 220
  second person plural, 8, ch. 12
    y'all/you all, 170–1, 175–7, 180–1
    ye/you, 172
    yez, 172–4, 178–9
    yiz, 179
    you 'uns, 170–1, 176, 180–1, 183
    yous/youse, 170–5, 178, 180–1
  'solidarity pronoun', 13, 190–4, 196–7
  speech act, 117–19
pronunciation, 70–1, 195
proper nouns, *see* nouns
prosody, 29, 201, 204, 206, 208, ch. 7
proximal, 83, 180
punctuation, 37

quantifier, 69, 74
questionnaires, 72, 86–7, 90, 154, 158

Reading, *see* Englishes, British English
reanalysis, 160–1, 163, 165
reference, 118, 206, 220
reflexives, 24, 40, 113, 220, *see also* pronouns
regional
  English, *see* English
  forms/language, 1, 9, 69, 77, 83, 155, 157–61, 163–4, 185, 235, 242
  varieties, *see* varieties
regionalisms, 241
registers, 17, 23, 30
relatives/relativizers, 8, 42, 47, ch. 11, *see also wh*-relativizers; zero-relativizers
relativization, 9, 153, 164–5
relevance, 206
re-oralization, 47
resumptive structures, 39, *see also* pronominal copies
Rhenish, *see* German
Rhodesian, *see* Englishes
rhoticity, 182
role semantics, 114–17
Romance
  dialects, 195–6
  languages, 9, 127, 196, 227
root, *see* deontic
rural, 71, 163, 173–4, 233

INDEX

Sanskrit, 22
Scandinavian languages, 53
schools, 70, 114, 202, 233
Scotticism, 153
Scottish English, *see* Englishes, British English
Scottish National Dictionary (SND), 85, 153, 155, 161–3
second person plural pronouns, *see* pronouns
selection process, *see* standardization, filtering processes of
semantics, 105, 112, 125–32, 140, 206, 209, 213, 216, 222, *see also* role semantics
 semantic changes, *see* change
 semantic weakening, 69, 71, 75
sentence
 concept of, 215
 embedding, 15
Sephardic Spain, *see* Spanish
shall, 7, 29, 47, 223, ch. 10
shared knowledge, 80, 203–4, 206, 209
Shetland dialect, *see* Englishes, British English
social
 factors, 1, 9, 13, 27, 46, 171–2, 215, 219
 marker, *see* marker
 norms, *see* norm(s)
 stratification, 234
 varieties, *see* varieties
sociolinguistics, 4, 84
'solidarity pronoun', *see* pronouns
Somerset, *see* Englishes, British English
South African English, *see* Englishes
South England, *see* Englishes, British English
southern hemisphere Englishes, *see* Englishes
Spanish, 8, 83, 131, 186–7, 189, 190, 221, 224–6, 246
 Castilian, 186, 194
 influence on Galician, 189
 languages, 185, 187, 194
 Old Spanish, 189
 Sephardic, 195
 spoken by Catalans, 131

The Spectator, 76, 137
speech, 3, 68
 production, 21, 27–31, 43, 45, 63–5, 203
 speech act, 118, 141, 152, *see also* illocutionary act
 adverbials, 54
 participant, 117, 119, 122
 pronouns, *see* pronouns
 role, 118
 theory, 234
spellings, *see* orthography
split constructions, 40, 47, 200
spoken
 language, 2, 14–15, 39–40, 42–3, 45–6, 51, 54–6, 58–9, 64–5, 91, 188, 194, ch. 1, ch. 2, *see also* single languages
 standard, *see* standard
 syntax, *see* syntax
standard, 2, 4–11, 51, 68, 84, 106, 135, 138, 144–5, 163–4, 185, 219, 232, ch. 2, *see also* single languages
 grammar, *see* grammar
 functions, 10–11, 13, 17, 20
 ideology, 7, 10–11, 35, 37–8, 42
 logic factor of, 4, 7–8, 10, 29, 38–40, 45, 71, 126, 132, 160
 norms, *see* norms
 spoken, 2, 7, 14–20
 syntax, *see* syntax
 usage, *see* usage
 varieties, 1–5, 7–9, 132, 147, 153, 170, 194
 pre-standard varieties, 51
 written, 3–7, 9, 14–20, 51, ch. 3
standardization, 2–3, 5, 6–7, 9, 36, 68–70, 76, 79, 110, 112–13, 122–3, 131, 186, 190, 194, ch. 15
 filtering processes of, 5–6, 8–10, 185–6, 188, 193
stigmatization, 38, 41, 51, 70, 79, 84, 174, 180, 187
stress clashes, ch. 7
structural linguistics, 3, 77, 135, 219
style(s), 9, 23, 58, 132, 181, 196, 197, 201, 214

259

INDEX

colloquial, 9, 73, 154, 202
elevated, 56, 190
formal, 17–20, 30, 35
high, 37, 56, 132, 229
informal, 1, 17–19, 20, 24, 77, 91
prestigious, 213
spontaneous, 202, 229
theories of, 45
vernacular, 35
written, 37, 46
subjective, 7, 37, 145, *see also* emotive/emotional; epistemic
subordination, 62–5
substratum, 172, 181
superstratum, 171, 181
supraregional, 227, 232
Survey of British Dialect Grammar, 72, 84, 90
Survey of English Dialects (SED), 84, 86–8, 153, 156–8, 162–4, 166
Swedish, 53–6, 58, 113, 116–17
   colloquial varieties, 53
   dialects, 83
   Finland Swedish, 61
   grammarians, *see* grammarians
   influence on Finnish, 54, 56
Swift, Jonathan, 138–40, 147–8
synchronic, 28, 135
syncretism, 25
synonyms, 223
syntactic
   change, *see* change
   'syntactic mode', 42, 194
   weight, *see* heavy phrases
syntagmatic, 91, 203
syntax, 3, 24, 61, 69, 113, 213, 218–20, 224, 228–9, ch. 1, ch. 15, ch. 3
   spoken, 2–6, 11
   standard, 2–3, 5–7, 9–10
   vernacular, 2–4, 8
system, 4, 6, 9, 13, 25, 89, 133, 160, 203, 213, 218, 220, 222, 235, 237, 241, 244–5, *see also* grammar (as system)

tags, 43
   set-marking, 78–9
target forms/variety, 4, 172, *see also* standard

teaching, *see* language teaching
tense, 37, 221, *see also* past tense
textual
   satellites, 61–3
   variants, 138–9
that, 80, ch. 6
   complementizer, 164
   deictic, 159, ch. 6
   demonstrative, 76–7, ch. 6
   relativizer, 76–9, 152, 166
   trace, 225–6
that's, see genitives, of relative pronouns
theoretical linguistics, 3–5, 42
this, 159, ch. 6
thou/thee, 5, 170, 172, 174, 182
topic, 206, 208, 225
topicalization, 42–3, 112, *see also* dislocation; inversion; preposings
tun, 36, *see also* do
Turkish, 23
Tuscan, *see* Italian
Tyneside English, *see* Englishes, British English
typological, 236, 245

unidirectionality of change, *see* change
Universal Grammar, 220–1, 235–6, 245
Universals, 126, 171
unmarked, 19, 26, 112, 120, 126
upper class, *see* class
urban, 14, 90, 137, 173–4, 185, 190, *see also* single languages
usage, 71, 77, 138–40, 144–7, 152, 157, 159, 186, 202, 213, 232, ch. 14
   actual, 135, 144, 148, 176
   common, 55, 135, 138, 140, 145
   guides, 7, 56, 71, 73, 76
   nonstandard, 73, 135, 215, 234
   polite, 138
   spoken, 155, 191
   standard, 73, 163, 215
   written, 145, 191, 232

value judgements, 202, 213, *see also* prescription

INDEX

variables, 112, 215, *see also* choices
variants, 2, 7, 9, 11, 41, 44, 83, 95, 98, 106, 138–9, 146, 164, 171–5, 177–80, 201, 210, 213–16, 223, 232, 234–5
variation, 4, 68, 122, 202, 213, 215, 233–4
  gender, 103
  morphological, 69
  phonological, 4, 10
  syntactic, 2, 9–10, 59, 216, ch. 7
  stylistic, 107
  theory of, 213, 216
varieties, 4, 8, 11, 37, 215–16, ch. 3, *see also* single languages; standard
  continuum, 1, 2, 35, 41, 46, 233–5
  non-prestigious, 21, 27
  nonstandard, 3–4, 7, 41, 126, 128, 130, 135, 146, 153, 163, 171, 174, 194
  oral/spoken, 1, 3, 13–14, 35, 84, 193, 214, ch. 9
  regional, 4–5, 9, 96, 107, 163, 185
  social, 4, 9
  sociology of, 233–5
  standard, *see* standard
  stylistic, 9, 132
  written, 2, 14, 69, 84
verb
  inflection, *see* inflection
  valency, 237, 246
  verb-last order, 22, 31
  verb-particle constructions, 173
Verb Second (V2), 54, 56, 220, 225–6, *see also* inversion
vernacular, 1–4, 8, 22–3, 35, 43, 144, 233
'vulgar', 35, 42, 45–6, 137, 196

Wallis Rules, 135–6, 138, 140–6, 148
Ward, William, *see* grammarians
Webster's *Dictionary*, 136, 138
wh-relativizers, 76, 164
what'/what's, *see* genitives, of relative pronouns
will, 7, 29, 47, 223, ch. 10
word order, 19, 45, 54, 57–8, 212, *see also* grammaticalization
working-class, *see* class
written
  language, 1–4, 14, 19, 28, 37, 46, 51, 53–4, 58–9, 61, 64, 65, 68–80, 186, 188–9, ch. 2, *see also* essayist literacy
  standard, *see* standard
  usage, *see* usage
  variety, *see* varieties

y'all/you all, *see* pronouns, second person plural
ye/you, *see* pronouns, second person plural
yez, *see* pronouns, second person plural
Yiddish, 41
yiz, *see* pronouns, second person plural
yon, ch. 6
Yorkshire, *see* Englishes, British English
you 'uns, *see* pronouns, second person plural
yous/youse, *see* pronouns, second person plural

zero-relativizer, 39–40, 47
Zimbabwe English, *see* Englishes